OUTRAGE

BERTIL LINTNER

OUTRAGE

Burma's Struggle for
Democracy

WHITE LOTUS
London and Bangkok
1990

© Bertil Lintner, 1989, 1990

1st edition published in Hong Kong by
Review Publishing in 1989

2nd edition published inthe UK in 1990 by
White Lotus UK
12 Slaidburn Street
London SW110 OPJ

ISBN 0 9515814 1 4

and in Thailand by
White Lotus
16, Soi 47, Sukhumvit
PO Box 1141
Bangkok

ISBN 9748495 36 1

Printed in Hong Kong

CONTENTS

ACKNOWLEDGEMENTS

ALTHOUGH my name appears on the cover of this book, it should be regarded as a collective product, compiled by me, but based on the experiences of numerous young and old Burmese people. After the military takeover in Rangoon on 18th September 1988, thousands of students and others fled to the Thai-Burmese border areas. During several trips to the border camps, I interviewed more than a hundred refugees from Rangoon, Mandalay, Meiktila, Chauk, Bassein, Prome, Toungoo, Pyinmana and other towns in central Burma as well as Moulmein, Mudon and Kamawek in Mon State, Myitkyina in Kachin State and Taunggyi in Shan State.

In order to cross-check and supplement their accounts of the turbulent year of 1988 in Burma, I sent in questionnaires and cassette tapes to Rangoon and other towns and asked people there to relate what they had seen with their own eyes. My intention has been to base this book only on first hand sources and eye-witness accounts. At great risk to themselves, many people readily answered my questions. In this way, I was able to collect more than 20 hours of taped interviews. Other sources wrote long letters telling me of their experiences. To protect my sources — arrests and summary executions are still continuing in Rangoon and elsewhere — most of them have been given aliases.

When I was researching this book I was frequently told by Burmese people that I should "tell it as we saw it." Since the present military government in Rangoon is in the process of re-writing history, I have followed this advice as much as possible. Any inaccuracies in this book are entirely my own for which these sources should not be blamed.

Last but not least, I would like to thank my patient wife Hseng Noung for helping me translate numerous tapes, letters, newspapers, documents and statements from the original Burmese into English. Without her assistance, this book would not have been possible.

Bertil Lintner
BANGKOK, 1990

People are chusing to live among the Wild Beasts, than be at the Mercy of the cruel and tyrannical Government, which at present has a King, without any experience, and intirely ruled by Ministers, without any other knowledge but a bare private Interest, which makes the Country in general wish for a change, because every petty Governour of Towns and Cities, if he can but satisfy the Minister at Court, can at his pleasure oppress the people under him, without any fear of punishment, which has caused the Revolt of the richest and largest Provinces of this Kingdom.

*An account written about 1750 by an anonymous Englishman
commenting on an uprising in the province of Pegu
against the Court of Ava.*

One. # SEVEN DAYS
THAT SHOOK
RANGOON

DURING THE SECOND week of March 1988, nothing exceptional seemed to be happening in Burma's sleepy capital, Rangoon. On the surface, everything appeared normal with decrepit old passenger buses, crammed with *longyi*-clad commuters, grinding their way down the tree-shaded avenues of the city. Trade was brisk in all the markets which, as usual, offered a wide selection of contraband goods, smuggled in from most of Burma's neighbours: Thailand, China, India and even Bangladesh.

The central committee of the country's only legally permitted political organisation, the Burma Socialist Programme Party (BSPP), had convened to prepare for the yearly budget session of the *Pyithu Hluttaw*, or the parliament. Burma's dreary, tabloid-sized newspapers were filled with stories which contained the obligatory lists of names of the participants, who had acted as master of ceremonies, and in what order the various delegates had "discussed in support of the proposals" — which everybody knew in any case had already been decided upon by the man who had been the undisputed master of the country for exactly 26 years, general Ne Win.

As always, the newspapers offered nothing in the way of actual news. The state-run *Working People's Daily* on 11th March carried an editorial which reminded the country's students of their health. Students, who are anxious about the "fast approaching annual tests", should not study late into the night. A regular and well-balanced timetable is required, the paper pointed out.

Three young men who heeded that advice were Win Myint, his name-sake Win Myint and Kyaw San Win — all three students at the prestigious Rangoon Institute of Technology (RIT) in the northern suburb of West Gyogon. In the evening of the 12th, a Saturday, they strolled down to a small teashop opposite their campus on Insein Road. It was a simple, country-style bamboo structure with an earthen floor. The walls were decorated with Burmese calendars and posters of Thai filmstars, purchased on the ubiquitous black market in the capital. The teashop, though not fancy, was still popular with the locals as well as the RIT students. It was cheap and it had a tape recorder with a collection of the latest cassettes of popular

OUTRAGE

Burmese music.

As the three students entered the bamboo hut, a love song by the famous Burmese crooner Kaizar filled the sparse premises. A group of local people, drunk judging from their loud voices, were seated at a crude wooden table. The students ordered a cup of tea each and had some cakes. They had brought with them a tape of their favourite, Sai Hti Hseng, a singer from the Shan national minority whose songs slightly resemble Bob Dylan's, but set in a Burmese context.

Kaizar's romantic gush never seemed to end, however, and the students became increasingly impatient. They called the owner of the teashop over and asked him to play their tape. One of the drunkards protested loudly.

"Sai Hti Hseng? That intellectual bullshit!"

The students ignored his remark and insisted that they wanted to listen to their tape. One of the drunkards grabbed a chair and struck Win Myint on his head. A fight broke out and the students soon beat a retreat. Fearing Win Myint's head was severely fractured, his friends took him to a nearby clinic. They also reported the incident to the nearest police station, which was at Insein. After recording the details, police went to the teashop and arrested the culprits. The case seemed to be in hand. Win Myint, suffering from his injuries, returned to his hostel with a bandaged head.

On the following day, the accused were released. As it happened, the young man who had struck Win Myint on his head was the son of the chairman of the local People's Council, one of the hand-picked administrative units which formed the local power base of Ne Win's authoritarian one-party state.

When this news reached the RIT students, they were infuriated. About thirty students went down to the People's Council office to protest. The council chairman refused to listen to their grievances. The students picked up whatever rocks and stones they could find and hurled them at the office. Window panes shattered and the more daring protesters went inside the office and smashed chairs and tables.

There was still no response from the officials. But the students, feeling exposed, returned to their campus to gather more friends. In most university towns, there is a traditional tension between students and local youths — and Gyogon West Ward was no exception. A crowd of students, including the three who had visited the teashop the night before, went down to provoke the local people. They clashed, a knife was drawn and the second Win Myint was stabbed.

The students pelted back to their campus to get reinforcements. This time, from 200 to 300 students marched down to the intersection close to the teashop. When they arrived an unexpected sight awaited them. There were

2

firemen with waterhoses ready — and about 500 men of the dreaded *Lon Htein*, or riot police, armed with clubs and G-3 automatic rifles.

Anger blossomed into reckless fury. A few stones were thrown in the direction of the riot police. Suddenly, the sound of riflefire rang out and bullets shredded the air. Several students fell to the ground, bleeding profusely. One of them was Maung Phone Maw, a 23-year old RIT student. His friends carried him back to their hostel where he died shortly afterwards, in the arms of one of his teachers. Two or three dozen others received bullet wounds.

"Two of them were my friends Soe Naing and Myint Oo," recalls Min Naing, a 24-year old RIT student who participated in the demonstration but escaped unhurt. "We were devastated when we visited them at Rangoon General Hospital — and discovered that they were shackled to their beds, despite their wounds. There were policemen posted at the entrance of the separate ward where our friends were kept."

Six wounded students were also hand-cuffed and taken away to Hlaing police station. Four of them were already unconscious, according to their friends. Their fate is unknown — but Soe Naing and Myint Oo died in hospital after a few days. Soe Naing had a G-3 bullet in his liver, Myint Oo one in his abdomen and another in his bladder. They would most probably have survived — had higher authorities not forbidden the doctors to operate on them.

The brutality in itself was bad enough. But the students were especially affected by the fact that Maung Phone Maw, the first casualty, had been a leading member of the *Lanzin* Youth, the BSPP's youth organisation, and one of the leaders of the RIT Red Cross team. He had also been at the top of his course, chemical engineering, for several years.

In what at first appeared to be a related incident, a nearby 'People's Store', or government-run cooperative, was burnt down. The police claimed that the students were responsible, while others asserted that the owner himself had torched the store, taking advantage of the mayhem, to destroy his own fiddled account books and depleted stocks of goods. The Burmese fiscal year ends in March — and this is when government enterprises have to submit their annual accounts, which means that fires are usual at that time of the year.

That night, the enraged RIT students held a meeting in their hostels. A seven point proposal was drafted. The students demanded that a full report of the killings should be released by the media "as it actually happened". They also wanted compensation for the families of the students who had been killed and wounded and that the real culprits should be punished. There was also a vague reference to officially establishing "a body that could take responsibility in executing the rights of the students". The more radical ones demanded a state funeral for Maung Phone Maw. Thirteen young firebrands formed a tightly knit brotherhood, saying that they were prepared to sacrifice their lives for the sake of revealing the truth.

The deputy minister of education, Dr Maung Di, came to the campus that night. All the proposals were dismissed. Just before midnight, a group of students went out to put flowers on the spot where Maung Phone Maw had fallen. Some knelt on the road in front of the flowers, touched their foreheads to the ground, weeping and condemning what they perceived as gross injustice.

On Monday 14th March, the students returned to class after the stormy weekend. That morning, the usually tranquil atmosphere at the RIT had changed.

"There was a sullenness in the air," Min Naing remembers. "But the grief turned to anger when we suddenly spotted rows of *Lon Htein* with clubs and cane shields around the campus. It was a clear provocation and we shouted abuse at them. But nobody moved."

Meetings were held in the afternoon, however, and the students produced hand-written leaflets and posters inside the rooms of their hostels. They were determined not to let the matter pass. Activists from the RIT went to other university campuses in Rangoon, distributed the leaflets and told their fellow students elsewhere what had happened. The first steps towards organised dissent had been taken.

On the following day, more than 600 *Lon Htein*-men and soldiers stormed the RIT. At 3.15 pm, army lorries roared through the gates of the campus and disgorged club-wielding *Lon Htein*-men who charged the crowds.

"We fled in panic," recalls Tun Oo, another RIT student. "The ones who were not quick enough were apprehended and hauled into the lorries. At least 300-400 of us must have been arrested. No shots were fired but several students were beaten severely. Together with eight friends, I slipped into a sewer. We put the manhole cover back on and crawled through the tunnel. It was only about four foot high and it was very dark. But we were lucky. We weren't even wounded".

That night, the state-run Burma Broadcasting Service (BBS) carried a report about the events at RIT. All of it was the fault of the students. Therefore, police and army units had "entered the RIT campus this afternoon and brought the situation under control after discussions with the students, explaining their action," the announcer solemnly declaimed, adding: "The authorities concerned will take necessary action against the students who rioted, disturbing local peace and the law and order situation."

The news about the killings, beatings and arrests had soon electrified other campuses all over Rangoon. By Wednesday, the protests had taken a very definite anti-government stance, especially after the grossly distorted version that the BBS had broadcast the night before. That day's issue of the *Working People's Daily* also ran a story, according to which Maung Phone Maw had succumbed to knife injuries inflicted in a clash with "local civilians".

In the shady compound of Rangoon University (Main Campus), on the southern flank of Inya Lake, thousands of young students gathered to demonstrate their solidarity with their RIT comrades. Speeches were made and leaflets distributed outside the Convocation Hall, a solid, white-washed building from the British colonial era.

At 1 pm, Dr Chit Swe, the rector of the university, gave a speech in an attempt to sooth the crowd. But when an official diplomatically asked the students what their demands were, the reply was a massive chant: "We want to overthrow the fascist regime!" Taken aback, Chit Swe assured the students that nothing would happen to them, if they stayed within the limits of the campus.

"We marched around the campus to the various hostels, Amara, Toungoo and Mandalay, and shouted slogans. 'We want democracy!' 'Down with the one-party system!' The slogans echoed across the entire campus. More and more students emerged from their hostels to join the demonstration. Soon, there were about four to five thousand of us," says Ko Lin, a 22-year old student in the medical field who participated in the first movements in March. Like Maung Phone Maw, Ko Lin had also been a Lanzin Youth organiser until the unrest broke out.

"Let's march to the RIT!" a young speaker called out and was cheered by thousands of fist-waving students.

"We marched off at 3 pm, actually heading for the Hlaing Campus on Prome Road," recalls Tun Oo. "It was a fantastic feeling. Thousands of students marched down Prome Road, chanting anti-government slogans in unison. I had never seen anything like it in my whole life!"

At the front of the massive column that streamed out of the main gate in front of RU (Main), strode a young man, holding high an improvised red flag with a superimposed yellow fighting peacock, the traditional symbol of Burmese nationalism. Along the way, teenage high-school pupils in their characteristic green longyis joined in. The crowd swelled to a sea of people who moved slowly like waves along the road, slogans reverberating in harmony. The mood was joyful; nearly all the demonstrators were young, too young even to have a clear memory of the last anti-government demonstrations that had taken place in Rangoon more than a decade before.

"When we had passed a culvert, which we call 'the White Bridge', on

5

Prome Road, near the bank of Inya Lake, we suddenly halted. A barbed wire fence had been strung across the road in front of us. Beyond it, to our horror, we saw soldiers armed with automatic rifles — which they were aiming at us. An armoured car with a Bren machine-gun was parked in the middle of the road, behind the troops," Tun Oo relates.

"Spontaneously, we struck up our national anthem as well as the army song. Some shouted 'Pyithu Tatmadaw (the People's Army) is our army!' Then, we looked behind us. We were petrified. There were hundreds of Lon Htein in steel helmets and armed with clubs, rifles and cane shields. To the left of us were the high walls of the houses in Kamayut township, and to the right, a flight of steps leading up to the promenade along Inya Lake. We realised we were trapped."

An order rang out and the Lon Htein charged the students. Clubs swished and bones cracked. There were groans and shrieks as students fell to the ground bleeding. Panic-stricken students, trying to escape up the flight of steps towards the lake, were felled in droves. Some Lon Htein concentrated on the girls in the crowd; their jewelry and watches were snatched. Other policemen chased fleeing students into the dark waters of the Inya Lake, overpassed them, forced their heads under water and held them there until they drowned. The more fortunate demonstrators, among them Tun Oo, managed to scale the walls of the houses on the left where outraged civilians, who had witnessed the carnage, hid them in their houses.

After about an hour, the orgy in violence was over. Sprawling corpses lay oozing in pools of blood all over the street. Even the so-called 'White Bridge' was now red; estimates of slaughtered students and school children varied between 20 and more than 100. Empty lorries came forward from behind the line of Lon Htein-men and the dead and wounded were dumped aboard. As loaded lorries pulled out, these were succeeded in their turn by waiting fire engines. Without delay, the street, the small bridge and the flight of steps to the Inya Lake promenade were hosed clean. They were left to gleam, pristine, in the sun.

Evidently, the action had been meticulously planned to teach the students a harsh lesson. It had been directed from the BBS building on Prome Road—and the man in charge was reported to be no less a person than Ne Win's right-hand man, the BSPP's joint secretary general and chief of the Lon Htein, Sein Lwin.

Eye-witness reports of the bloody events at 'the White Bridge' sped throughout Rangoon. Some people refused to believe them — especially the few foreigners in the capital to whom Burma was a gentle land of smiling people and golden pagodas. But the vast majority of Rangoonians, who had lived under the military regime for 26 years and remembered government barbarities during student riots in 1962 and the mid-1970s, had little diffi-culty in crediting the news. But they were aghast because the government now was clearly prepared to be even more repressive than ever.

Late at night on the 16th, Ko Lin had retreated to a small teashop on Prome Road to recover from their traumatic experiences:

— Just before midnight, we saw a red Datsun pickup coming with *Lon Htein* men on the back. They stopped by the bank of Inya Lake and we saw them drag three young girls up to the promenade. We didn't dare to go out, but when the Datsun had left, without the girls, we went up to the bank of the lake. There, we found the three girls. They were bleeding from their lower abdomen and were almost unconscious. We carried them back to the teashop. They were groaning all night and I thought they would bleed to death. We were afraid to go out in the dark, but at 5 am on Thursday morning, we took the girls to Rangoon General Hospital. A nurse told us that they had received several such cases. One girl had even died; her uterus had been ruptured after a gang-rape.

Possibly sensing the increasing anger among the public at large, the government on 17th March announced that an Enquiry Commission had been formed to investigate the matter — but only the death of the first casualty, Maung Phone Maw. Unexpectedly, the government now admit-ted that he had not been stabbed, but had died from gunshot wounds. Not a word, however, was said about the massacre at 'the White Bridge'.

The three-man commission was headed by Ba Maw, a member of the Council of People's Justices, Hla Tint from the Council of People's Attor-neys and Dr Maung Shein of the Council of People's Inspectors. In other countries, these institutions would be called the offices of the chief justice, attorney general and auditor general. But adding 'people' in front of everything and anything was one of the fixations of Ne Win's regime, aimed at giving the basically military dictatorship an aura of 'socialist democracy'.

Nonetheless, the appointment of the commission was unprecedented. To many students, it was a partial victory. But instead of calming them down, the decision encouraged the students to press on. More than two thousand gathered once again outside RU (Main)'s old Convocation Hall and announced that they had set up an independent students' union. At the University's Recreation Centre, one speaker after another mounted the stage to denounce the government.

Maung Maung Kyaw, a 3rd year mathematics student, was one of the first to do so. He was followed by a charismatic youth called Min Zeya and Yu Yu Maw, a fiery young woman. Taik Maung, an older ex-student who had participated in the last large-scale demonstrations in 1974, related his experiences from that time, when troops had stormed Rangoon University campus to recover the body of UN secretary general U Thant, a Burmese for whom the students had wanted to perform their own funeral rites. Scores of demonstrators were believed killed at that time as well. Other speakers highlighted the fact that Burma had sought and been granted the UN-afforded status of Least Developed Country (LDC), thus recognising the potentially rich country as one of the 'poorest' nations in the Asian-Pacific region - which some claimed was an outcome of 26 years of military misrule under the guise of Ne Win's 'Burmese Way to Socialism'.

An incident earlier that morning had also caused the tempers of the students to rise considerably.

"I had heard that Maung Phone Maw was going to be cremated at Kyandaw that morning," recalls Yan Naung, a 25-year old post-graduate chemistry student from RU. "Thousands of us gathered outside the crematorium to pay our last respect to the first student who had been killed by the *Lon Htein*. We waited for hours. But at 1 pm, we learnt that Maung Phone Maw's body had been taken in an unmarked coffin, carried by a vehicle which was closely guarded by the police, to Tamwe crematorium at the other end of Rangoon and cremated there. We were outraged."

When Yan Naung returned to his hostel, he spotted commandos posted all around the RU's main campus. They were wearing red scarves which indicated that they were elite units from the army. The campus had been surrounded by more than 1,000 soldiers, plus 1,000 *Lon Htein*. Bren-carriers were positioned outside along with fire engines. At noon, Dr Chit Swe gave another speech, assuring the students that they would be safe inside the campus.

"But don't go out," he added.

But the promises of an academic meant little by this time. At 2 pm, the army and the *Lon Htein* charged through the gates of RU (Main) with their clubs raised. Tear gas cannisters were fired into the crowds. According to Yan Naung:

— I was in the Inya hostel when the troops came. Covered prison vans followed the troops and the police into the campus. Thein Aung, the chief of the police, was there and urged us to come out. "You won't be arrested," he said. But when we came down, 150 students from my hostel alone, including 40 girls, were hauled into covered prison vans and driven away.

Hostel after hostel was searched and an estimated 1,000 students were arrested. Among them was Maung Maung Thwin, a third year history student at the RU(Main):

—— I guess the van we were locked into was meant to carry twenty people. But there were nearly 100 in the one I was driven away in. It was terribly hot

Above: Confrontation in Rangoon, 8.8.88

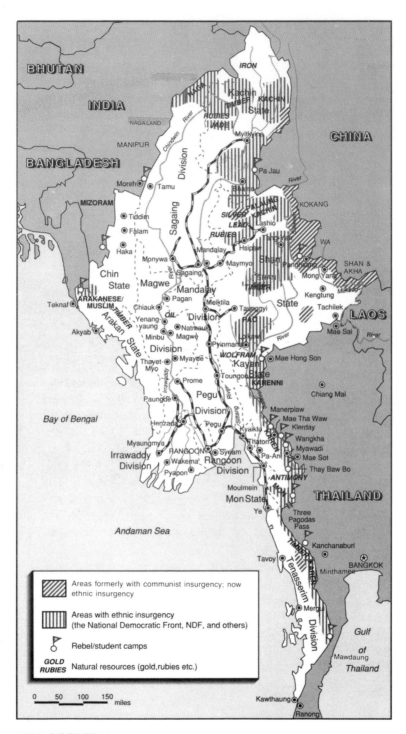

MAP OF BURMA

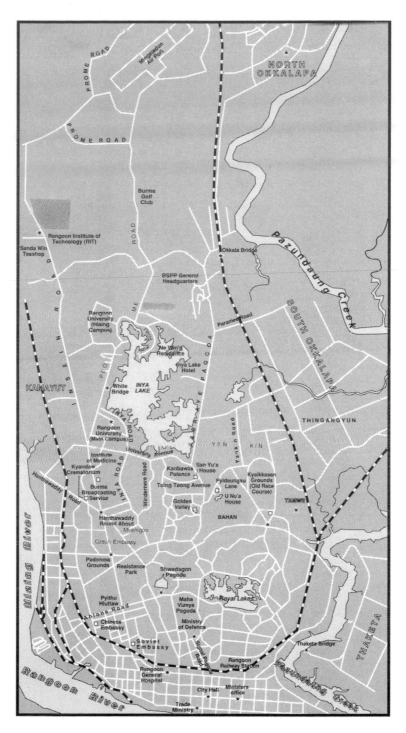

MAP OF RANGOON

Previous: "*Tatmadaw* man takes refuge in the bosom of the people",
photo and caption from the *Guardian* (Rangoon), 11th Sept. 1988
Upper: Women workers from North Okkalapa demonstrate
Lower: Hunger strikers outside the central market, Mandalay

Upper: "Ne Win the Thief", posters in Kawthaung (Conard-Swan)
Lower: Air Force men join demonstrations (*Guardian*, Rangoon)

Left: students of the Rangoon Institute of Technology demonstrate
Right: pupils of the Dagon State High School No.1 strike

Upper: "A political talk held at the junction of Barr Street and Mahabandoola Road…",
Photo and caption from the *Guardian* (Rangoon) 9th Sept 1988.

Lower left: housewives in Mandalay
Lower right: hunger strikers confront the Rangoon City Hall shortly before the Sept. 1988 takeover

Previous: Air Force men strike at Mingaladon Air Base. Many have since been executed or fled to the Thai border (*Guardian*, Rangoon)
Upper: truck supplied by Japanese aid converted into armoured vehicle (P. Conard)
Lower: barricade in central Rangoon (P. Conard)

Upper: barricade in central Rangoon (P. Conard)
Lower: 22nd Light Infantry in Rangoon, Aug. 1988 (P. Conard)
Next: students appeal to soldiers during the General Strike in Rangoon, 8.8.88 (Ryo Takeda)

and we were all dizzy because of lack of oxygen. Several of us were still suffering from the after-effects of tear gas attacks and baton charges. There were a few girls in our van and we let them stand at the front of the van, where there was a small opening, so they could breathe. I saw nothing, but judging from the twists and turns along the way, and the time it took to get to the jail, I assume that the van must have taken a round-about way to avoid attracting the attention of the public.

Some students inside the vans died from suffocation. A 12-year old boy was trampled to death inside an over-packed van. But the arrests continued. About 1,000 students were taken away to the infamous jail at Insein, just north of Rangoon. The government had decided to strike with an iron-fist to cow the unruly students into submission.

"By now, we realised that we had to organise ourselves," says Aung Win, a student of international relations at RU (Main). "Too many lives had been sacrificed to give up and somehow we felt that we had the upper hand. The public was sympathetic and sent food, money and cheroots to the campus when we held rallies there. Everybody was fed up with the government's misrule and encouraged us to continue our protests. Instead of becoming afraid, more and more people joined the movement."

Aung Win and others took the first steps towards building up an intricate network of contacts throughout the four campuses of Rangoon University (the Main Campus, Hlaing, Botathaung and Kemmendine) the two Institutes of Medicine, the Institute of Dental Medicine and even some high schools. "When we first took to the streets, we lacked experience," says he. "So we contacted older ex-students who had participated in the anti-government demonstrations in the mid-1970s for their advice. We learnt from their experiences."

Ironically, the first structure borrowed heavily from the military and the BSPP — the only two institutions the young students were familiar with. An information department became responsible for producing leaflets and posters and conveying the student demands to the public. A social welfare department collected money, food and water and distributed these among the students at rallies on the campuses. Students who had gained experience with Burma's Red Cross gave first aid and collected medicine.

An intelligence unit, called the protection department, collected information on the movements of the security forces and, most important, tried to identify government informers within their own ranks. From the very beginning, the students were well aware of the threat posed by Burma's hated but highly efficient military intelligence apparatus. "We even set up our own 'prison' in a student hostel where we interrogated suspected informers," Aung Win says. "Three students were found guilty and killed."

The organisation that was slowly beginning to take shape was put to the test on Friday 18th March. The newly formed students' union had given the government a deadline, the 17th, to announce the truth about the teashop incident and subsequent events. The authorities had ignored the demand and ordered its own Enquiry Commission to produce within a month an official report into "the death of a student...to prevent similar occurrences in future."

"That was when we decided to leave our campuses and the university area near Inya Lake to stage a large-scale demonstration in downtown Rangoon," Tun Oo recalls. "Small groups of students left separately from their institutions and hostels. By word of mouth, the message had been spread around. I and five others arrived by car on Sule Pagoda Road at the appointed time, 12 noon. Other groups of students were waiting here and there. Then, we gathered into one solid column."

As startled townspeople looked on, about 300 fist-waving and slogan-chanting students marched around the Sule Pagoda right in the heart of the city. Most taken aback, perhaps, were a group of young foreign travellers who were inside the Tourist Burma office, opposite the pagoda. They looked up from their guidebooks and maps in bewilderment. Wasn't this the peaceful, Golden Country of Burma?

The girls from the reception desk hurriedly shut the iron grille across the door. A young traveller snapped a few shots with his instamatic camera through the interstices of the closed grille; these were the only pictures of the March demonstrations that later appeared in the international press, apart from some shots taken by another tourist from a nearby guest house.

"What's going on?" a worried tourist asked.

"It's the students. They're demonstrating against the government," one of the young, female information clerks replied calmly.

"Do you support them?"

"Of course we do. Everybody's fed up with this government. But what can we do? They've got the guns. We have nothing."

"Within an hour, 12,000-15,000 people had joined the students. Others were standing in their windows applauding every anti-government slogan and cheering when the students destroyed government property and set fire to state-owned vehicles," says Thomas, a West German student from Berlin who was inside the Tourist Burma office that day. "The people were very selective. They smashed traffic lights, burned government cars and targeted other state property. I did not see any destruction of private property, or widespread looting."

About 50 policemen from the civil People's Police Force (PPF) who had gathered outside Bandoola Park near Sule Pagoda fled in panic when they saw the massive, angry crowds. But within minutes, heavily armed *Lon Htein* arrived at the scene, unleashing baton charges and firing warning shots in the air — after all, they were much more exposed here in central Rangoon, within sight of several foreign embassies, than they had been two days before at 'the White Bridge'. Black prison vans and army lorries shrieked to a halt nearby. Hundreds of demonstrators were rounded up, headed for Insein Jail.

"I was on my way to a mosque in the area when I heard the shouting and the firing in the air," says Zaw Zaw, a 23-year old Muslim student in Rangoon. "It was about 2.30 pm and a large crowd had gathered outside the People's Department Store on Shwe Dagon Pagoda Road, opposite Theingyizay Market. They set fire to the ground floor as on-lookers clapped their hands and shouted anti-government slogans."

Local 'uprisings' broke out spontaneously all over Rangoon and the *Lon Htein* hurried from place to place in a vain attempt to disperse the crowds; the situation was already out of hand. When three fire engines came speeding down Bogyoke Aung San Street, towards the burning department store, scores of enraged people blocked their way. One fire engine was set ablaze. The other two drove quickly away from the angry crowds. More traffic lights were smashed and telephone cables cut. Soon, black smoke billowed from scattered locations all over the capital.

Truckloads of troops from the 22nd Light Infantry Division (LID) arrived in convoys from their base in the Karen State capital of Pa-an that afternoon. These were followed by more elite troops from the Thaton-based 44th LID and the 77th from Hmawbi Air Base just north of Rangoon. Armoured cars were positioned outside the Presidential Palace and Ne Win's Ady Road residence on a narrow peninsula in Inya Lake. Bren-carriers rumbled down Shwe Dagon Pagoda Road to prevent more students from reaching the city centre.

Thomas, the West German tourist, copied down in his notebook a sign he spotted, in English, pinned up outside the Shwe Dagon Pagoda:

S.O.S.
To Editor Time c/o UN
Help us!
Burma University Students

That afternoon, an order to arrest anybody in sight appears to have been given by the authorities. Since it was a Friday, thousands of Muslims had attended their Jumma prayers in the mosques located in the merchant quarters west of Sule Pagoda. They were hustled onto lorries and into vans as well; truckload after truckload was seen heading towards Insein Jail. Several thousand people were arrested and when Insein was full, the lorries and vans, loaded with people, carried on to Tharrawaddy, 100 kms north of the capital. Some suspected leaders of the uprising ended up near Mingaladon Airport in the infamous *Yay Kyi Aing*, or 'Clearwater Pond', top security prison, the domain of the dreaded Directorate of the Defence Services Intelligence (DDSI).

A Rangoon-based diplomat from a Muslim country reported back to his foreign ministry, commenting on the order to arrest everybody: "The term 'public' became synonymous with people of South Asian origin, most of whom hold the discriminatory identity of Foreigners Registration Certificates. Most of these people are dispossessed associate Burmese citizens with very few economic and political rights under the citizenship act of 1982. The majority of these people live around downtown vending foodstuff and wares or working for a day-to-day living. The downtown agitations added another dimension as Muslims converged on the waysides after Friday prayers and hence were unwarily caught in the heart of the unfolding events of demonstrations and anti-government sloganeering."

Slightly more fortunate were groups of students from upcountry campuses who had boarded trains and buses for Rangoon to participate in the demonstrations. Seventy students from Mandalay University and twenty from Ye Zin Agricultural College in Pyinmana were turned back at Hlegu railway station near Rangoon before they could reach the capital.

By nightfall that Friday, an eerie quiet returned to Rangoon after seven days of turmoil. Smoke billowed incessantly from the chimney at Kyandaw crematorium, behind the BBS building, as the victims of the carnage were being burnt. The streets were empty; thousands had been arrested. No curfew was officially announced, but government vehicles mounted with loud-speakers toured the streets, ordering the people to stay at home. So they did, but the first outburst of public unrest and outrage had shaken Rangoon — and the target of the public's anger was the commander of the *Lon Htein*, Ne Win's crony Sein Lwin. And by sheer coincidence, the teashop in Gyogon West Ward where the unrest had begun was called 'Sanda Win'. That also happens to be the name of Ne Win's favourite daughter.

Two THE GOLDEN LAND

ON 1ST MARCH, 1962, a visiting Chinese ballet troupe staged a performance in Rangoon. It attracted a large audience, among whom could be seen General Ne Win, then Commander-in-Chief of Burma's Armed Forces. The show went on until late in the evening. When it was over, Ne Win shook hands with the leading Chinese ballerina, and then quietly left. The audience thought that also he was going home to sleep after watching the show.

Meanwhile, Burma's prime minister, U Nu, had been meeting Shan and Karenni (Kayah) leaders at his official Windermere residence. Secessionist elements within the Karen minority and smaller groups of Karenni, Pa-Os and Mons, plus communist insurgents, had been up in arms since about a year after Burma's independence from Britain in 1948. They had been followed by some Shans in 1958 and Kachins in 1961 — and now there were rumours of an impending, large-scale rebellion all over the frontier areas.

U Nu had convened a seminar in Rangoon, where the minority leaders had submitted a proposal to amend the limited federalism the then constitution provided for in order to placate the increasingly restless non-Burman nationalities of the Union, who comprised some 40% of the total population. These concessions were suggested to prevent the Shans and the Kayahs from exercising their constitutional, but highly controversial, right to secede from the Union as well as to appease other minorities, who did not have that right, but who demanded it.

The armed forces had other plans, however, and in the early hours of 2nd March, troops moved in to take over strategic positions in the capital. About two o'clock in the morning, U Nu was arrested in his home in Pyidaungsu Lane. Five other ministers, the Chief Justice and over thirty Shan and Kayah leaders also were taken into custody. There was no bloodshed in Rangoon, apart from a shoot-out at the house on Kokine Road of Sao Shwe Thaike, a Shan leader who had served as Burma's first president 1948-52. His 17-year old son Sai Myee was gunned down by the raiding soldiers on the night of the coup when Sao Shwe Thaike "resisted arrest", as the official report said. Sai Myee's elder brother, Sai Tzang, later recalled:

—When I examined my brother, I found two wounds. A rifle bullet had ripped into his ankle and there was another hole, from a small calibre round, in the back of his head. It was evidently cold-blooded killing. He was, it can be said, the first of the many thousands of unarmed young citizens of Burma killed with calculated coldness by the military regime.

At 8.50 am, General Ne Win went on the air and announced: "I have to inform you, citizens of the Union, that the armed forces have taken over responsibility and the task of keeping the country's safety, owing to greatly deteriorating conditions of the Union". In a special message to the country's traditionally militant students, Ne Win said: "I urge the Education authorities and the students who are in the midst of their examinations to carry on their work".

On the following day, the federal '1947 Constitution' was suspended and the bicameral parliament dissolved. At a press conference on 5th March, a Revolutionary Council, chaired by Ne Win, declared that the army believed in democracy, socialism and 'healthy politics'. In principle, that meant a strong, central government controlled by the military. U Nu's fourteen-year long experiment with federalism and parliamentary democracy was over.

The military takeover was at first not entirely unwelcome. Burma's democratic period, from 1948 to 1962, has been described by many historians as a politically chaotic time. A common joke among expatriates there was that the country had at least a dozen different political parties — all of them Marxist. There was rampant corruption within government circles and the civil service. The military takeover, some people argued, would usher in a new era of stability, and it was worth it, even if the price the people had to pay was to sacrifice the freedom they had earlier enjoyed.

Burma, they argued was indeed a land of gentle and creative people — but they needed a firm leadership to stay in line, enabling them to develop their actually enormously rich country. Since time immemorial, Burma has been known to travellers as *Shwe Pyi Daw*, the Royal or Golden Country and it has almost always been described in glowing terms. A comparatively low population density combined with fertile agricultural land, vasts forests with different kinds of hardwood, and a soil abounding in gems and minerals placed Burma's development potential way ahead of those of other countries in the region.

But the whole question of stability in Burma reflects an extremely complicated historical dichotomy which has always been the country's dilemma. On the one hand, Burma has a strong authoritarian tradition which, in the past, was represented by the monarchy. A Burmese king was "shielded from the eyes of his subjects, wrapped in ritual, and responsible for the [Buddhist] faith; his authority was viewed as semidivine and unbridled," to quote US Burma scholar Josef Silverstein. By the ancient tradition of divine kingship, the monarch wielded unquestioned power over life and death of his subjects. The values and beliefs of the people provided no basis for a doctrine of popular sovereignty.

Consequently, the people were never consulted and any kind of elections was unheard of. "Authority from above has been accepted by the majority of people, and the leader who holds the palace or seat of government and controls the symbols of authority has the right to rule," Silverstein continues his analysis. "As a result of this pattern, the people were little concerned with the affairs of the state. The average peasant did not expect the state to do anything to improve his life." In short, the belief in the god-king meant that it was *lese majeste* to suggest or even to imagine any possible limits to his omnipotence.

Therefore, the state never served as a vehicle for social and economic change. If the state became too oppressive, for example, if it took an excessive amount of taxes or forced men to fight in needless wars, there was no reason for the individual to rise up against the tyranny. "The political culture of the Burman early was characterised by the people's stoic acceptance of misfortune and the government's excessive demands and victimisation through theft, war and plunder," Silverstein concludes.

The other side of Burma's heritage is represented by a solid intellectual and creative tradition. The yearly cycle in any Burmese village includes a number of *pwes*, which is usually translated as fairs, but they are actually much more than that. Every *pwe* worth mentioning includes a theatrical performance and there are few people in the world who are so fond of culture and drama as the Burmese. Sir J.G. Scott, a Scotsman who wrote about Burma under the pseudonym Shway Yoe in the last century, aptly said that "probably there is no man, otherwise than a cripple, in the country who has not at some period of his life been himself an actor, either in the drama or in a marionette show; if not in either of these, certainly in a chorus dance".

Burma has always had a high literacy rate and education has been a source of national pride since pre-colonial days. At the age of seven or eight, every Burmese boy was sent to the local monastery to learn to read, write and to memorise Buddhist chants and Pali formulas used in pagoda worship. For girls, education was less universal but even so, the census for British Burma in 1872 stated that "female education was a fact in Burma before Oxford was founded".

The long and strong tradition of widespread literacy was further enhanced with the introduction of British-style education during the colonial era. Needless to say, the colonial authorities were mainly interested in procuring a stratum of English-speaking civil servants and skilled clerks for foreign companies — but the inevitable results also included an abundance of newspapers and bookshops with foreign literature. Along with them came strong Western intellectual influences. The removal of the monarchy in 1885 had cleared fertile ground for the new ideas. The highly creative Burmese psyche flourished and became increasingly politicised. A powerful, intellectual and anti-authoritarian tendency began taking shape which, in many ways, was as deeply rooted in Burmese tradition as the monarchic system.

The origin of all political organisations in modern Burmese history was the Young Men's Buddhist Association (YMBA), obviously modelled after the British YMCA but with its own, indigenous tone, which was set up in 1906. At a meeting in Prome in 1920, the YMBA was transformed into a much broader nationalist movement, the General Council of Burmese Associations (GCBA). It drew its supporters mainly from the educated urban middle class; for instance, one of its most prominent leaders in the earlier days was Chit Hlaing, the son of an England-returned barrister.

Dr Maung Maung, once a renowned Burmese historian, commented on the emergence of the nationalist movement in his classic *Burma's Constitution*: "The press lent support to the GCBA movement. The *Sun*, of course, shone bright, joined by the *New Light of Burma*, the *Liberty*, the *Modern Burma*, the *Bandoola Journal*, and a few others in Burmese; the *Observer*, the *New Burma* , the *Free Burma*, and the *Rangoon Mail* In the English language. In the early years, the press was one for the common cause, and journalists, like barristers, stood in the vanguard of the movement. Newspapers were numerous and poor, and editors had to be a little of everything on their papers, but they were inspired and dedicated. Only when politics became a profession with political jobs to grab and spoils to distribute did some newspapers sink to the level of personal or party organs."

Another group of urbanites who became involved in the nationalist movement at an early stage were, of course, the students. At that time, the centres of higher schooling were Rangoon College, established in 1884 as an affiliate to Calcutta University, and Judson College, a small Baptist institution founded ten years later. In December 1920, a large body of students launched a strike to protest a new university act which would transform Rangoon University into an élite institution designed to produce a narrow stratum of qualified Burmese who could take over the jobs done by foreigners. This proposal, the students claimed, had been made without consulting the Burmese public. The students camped at the foot of the gold-covered stupa of the Shwedagon Pagoda — Burma's holiest shrine that still dominates the city's skyline.

The townspeople were enthusiastic over this first 'student strike' in

Burmese history and contributed food and money to support the students. The authorities eventually gave in to some of their demands and they returned to their classrooms. It should be noted here that 'strike' in a Burmese context does not necessarily mean the same as in the West; the closest equivalent would be the famous Indian *bandh*, i.e. everything closes down and everybody goes out in the streets to press specific demands.

The popular support base of the movement was, however, broadened even further when U Ottama, a Buddhist monk returned from India in 1921. In the Gandhian way, he transformed a basically political issue, national-ism and independence for Burma, into a religious one in a manner which appealed even to those who had not received a British education. A fiery speaker and agitator, U Ottama attracted a large following of mainly Buddhist monks, who organised demonstrations and meetings.

The movement took a much more violent turn in 1930 when a revolt broke out in Yetaik village in Tharrawaddy district from where it spread throughout southern Burma. Its leader was Saya San, who himself personi-fied much of Burma's intellectual dilemma. His followers, known as *galons*, after a powerful bird in Hindu mythology, believed that their tattoos and amulets would make them invulnerable to British bullets.

The rebellion was eventually crushed, though its impact was tremen-dous. Saya San was the traditional *minlaung* (pretender) to the throne — a figure often produced in times of crisis. He wanted a return to the old Buddhist kingdom of pre-British days, but the young, militant nationalists did not miss the point that most of his followers were young monks and im-poverished farmers, and the rebellion had clearly demonstrated their political potential in a much more violent way that as followers of U Ottama.

Leftist ideas had entered Burma from India and Britain and the royalties from a book written by Saya San provided the funds to establish a library of the first Marxist literature to reach Burma. The young nationalists were avid readers and the authors whose works they studied included Karl Marx, Lenin, Nehru, Sun Yat Sen, Mazzini, Garibaldi, Voltaire, Rousseau, Upton Sinclair, John Strachey, John Reed and various writers from Ireland's Sinn Fein movement. The nationalists were sufficiently educated to realise that there was no way back to the Burmese monarchy, so the utopia of a socialist state became the alternative for the country's young Buddhists: "Marx," wrote Ba Yin, a former minister of education, "must directly or indirectly have been influenced by the Buddha".

From then onwards, leftist thinking influenced nearly every political party in Burma, although most of them advocated a democratic version of socialism rather than a totalitarian one. Since almost all Burmese are devout Buddhists, religion on balance served as a moderating factor in the political field. The most militant nationalists during the pre-World War Two period were organised in the *Dohbama Asiayone*, or 'Our Burma Association' — and some of its members later emerged as the most important statesmen in postwar Burma. They called themselves *thakins* which actually means 'master' and was a title set aside for the British. By adding this to their names, they wanted to show who the real masters of the country were.

The *thakins* propagated the belief that socialism would free people from poverty and enable them to perform acts of charity and build monasteries. A leading figure of this movement was Thakin Kodaw Hmaing, a former monk turned socialist. He steered Burma's leftist movement in a uniquely Burmese direction. As a 10-year old monastery pupil, he had been in the mourning crowd that saw Burma's last king, Thibaw, being led away under British captivity in 1885. In the 1930s, he announced that independence for Burma under socialist rule meant "nirvana-within-this-world". To achieve this goal, monks participated in violent demonstrations against British rule. Whenever a monk was killed or hurt, it caused an outcry among Burma's civilian population, intellectuals, farmers and workers alike, stirring up nationalist emotions.

A number of other political parties also emerged at the same time, but they often overlapped and activists were sometimes members of more than one organisation simultaneously. Dr Ba Maw's *Sinyetha*, or Poor Man's Party, a breakaway group from the GCBA, was once described by an historian as "a salad mixture which offered to the villagers everything they were supposed to be demanding, topped with a touch of reddish Marxist dressing" — not unusual for Burmese political parties at that time.

The centre of much of this activity was the leafy campus of Rangoon University. Among the more prominent student leaders in the mid 1930s were the young quintet Thakin Nu, Thakin Aung San, Thakin Kyaw Nyein, Thakin Thein Pe and M.A. Raschid, a moslem of Indian origin. In 1935, Thakin Nu was elected president of the powerful and prestigious Rangoon University Students' Union (RUSU), and the other four became members of its executive committee. According to Dr Maung Maung, "they promoted art and culture, exhibitions, and social events, and encouraged sports and competition".

But they also took an active part in Burmese politics, and a second students' strike shook Rangoon in 1936. Thakin Nu had been expelled from the campus after making a speech criticising the university authorities. Shortly afterwards, Thakin Aung San, then the editor of the students' annual *Oway* magazine, was also expelled for refusing to reveal the name of the author of an article that ridiculed the university authorities. Their comrades demonstrated outside the principal's office and marched around their campus, shouting slogans.

In front of the procession, a standard-bearer held high the RUSU flag: a yellow fighting peacock on a scarlet ground. The Burmese peacock was actually a traditional heraldic device of the ancient royalty — like the eagle in Germany — but the young nationalists had claimed it for their symbol as an oblique challenge to the colonial authorities. Even the title of their magazine was the onomatopoeic rendering of the peacock's cry: Oway! Oway!

On 25th February 1936, over 700 students set up a strike centre at the Shwe Dagon pagoda — and again, the people of Rangoon contributed food and money. Although the main demand was the re-admission of those who had been expelled from the university, the movement also had a much clearer nationalistic perspective now than the case had been in 1920. The colonial authorities were attacked and some demanded home rule for Burma. The strike spread all over the country, Thakins Nu and Aung San were re-instated — and the students had scored another victory.

The strong, popular anti-colonial movement that was spreading through Burma in the 1930s was not, however, confined to the activities of groups of militant students in Rangoon. The peasants, hard-hit by the collapse of the international rice market in 1930, and burdened by heavy taxes, were rapidly loosing their land. Rural discontent had triggered the Saya San rebellion, which failed. After that, the situation continued to deteriorate in the rice-growing areas in the central plains and the Irrawaddy delta. By the eve of World War Two, Burma's peasants had lost three-fourths of their land, chiefly to British banks but also to Indian money-lenders, most of whom belonged to the *chettiar*-caste. "Even the professionals, the lawyers and the doctors, were foreigners, and a continuous flow of Burmese university graduates found themselves without adequate careers," wrote Kyaw Nyein, a deputy prime minister later in the 1950s. "The country presented a picture of a social pyramid which had the millions of poor, ignorant, exploited Burmese at its base, and a few outsiders, British, Indians and Chinese , at its apex."

Intermingled with the Indian community were the Muslims. The first Muslims were actually Moorish, Arab and Persian traders who arrived by sea in the 9th century. Most of them married local women and their offsprings became the forefathers of the Muslim communities which exist in almost every Burmese town even today. During the British time, thousands of Indians were brought in to work on the railways, in the postal services and the civil administration. Many were also soldiers in the colonial army— and a large portion of them were Muslims.

Before World War Two, 45% of Rangoon's population was of South Asian origin — Hindu, Muslim or Sikh. The early nationalist movement campaigned not only against the British, but also against the South Asians who worked for the colonial administration and, most detested of all, the *chettiars*. Generally speaking, any person of South Asian origin was — and still is — looked down upon and referred to as *kala*, a pejorative meaning 'foreigner' or Indian'. Interestingly, Caucasians are called *kala pyu*— 'White Indians'. Therefore, the nationalist movement often had undertones of communal tension. The *kalas*, including all Muslims, became targets for verbal and even physical attacks by the Burmese nationalists.

Given all this, Burma was ripe for a nation-wide uprising by the late 1930s. Only the frontier areas remained by and large quiet; British policy had been to divide the country into 'Burma proper' or 'Ministerial Burma' —and the various hill states and districts where most of the country's ethnic minorities lived. As a general rule, these were left more or less alone and the British presence there was confined to a few political officers, forestry officials and army personnel guarding the frontier. Very few individuals from the ethnic minorities took part in the early pre-independence movement.

Two years after the second students' strike in Rangoon, the young nationalists spear-headed a mass-uprising and 1938 became known as 'The Year of the Revolution' or 'The 1300 Movement' in Burmese history; according to the Burmese calendar, it was the year 1300. It began with communal clashes between Buddhists Burmans and Indians near Rangoon's Theingyizay market, where the department store was burnt down in March 1988, and this was followed by a strike among the workers in Yenangyaung oil fields southwest of Mandalay. The workers decided to march on Rangoon — and the students went up to meet them half-way. Among them was a young radical called Thakin Soe who, apart from his prominence in the student movement also was renowned for his talents as a classical singer and violinist. The colonial police, however, stopped them at Magwe. A few, including Thakin Soe, were arrested.

In Rangoon, the students protested against the arrests. When the police charged the demonstrations, a young student suffered a bad head wound from a blow by a baton and died in hospital shortly afterwards. His name was Aung Gyaw and he immediately was proclaimed a martyr; the military title 'Bo' was added to his name although he had never served with any army. The incensed public all over the country joined in the protests. In Mandalay on 10th February 1939, the police opened fire on a huge demonstration, killing seventeen people of whom seven were Buddhist monks.

The mass uprising soon fizzled out, but it inspired a radical faction of the *Dohbama* to set up the Communist Party of Burma (CPB) on 15th August 1939. Its first general secretary was the student hero Thakin Aung San and many of its members also worked within the *Dohbama* as well as the *Sinyetha* party, or in the underground People's Revolutionary Party (PRP); no clear-cut distinction could be drawn between the various political parties in the rather confusing political kaleidoscope that emerged in the country in the wake of 'The 1300 Movement'. The only rightist party, if that term can be used in a Burmese context, was the *Myochit* (Love of Country) party, founded by U Saw, owner and editor of the *Sun* newspaper.

World War Two and the Japanese occupation interrupted the evolution of Burma's democratic process which, although still in its infancy and with immature and inexperienced politicians, was thriving by the end of the 1930s. Many students went underground and the now 25-year old Aung San secretly left Burma in 1940. He was actually sent to contact the Chinese communist party and tried to get on a ship to Shanghai where Mao Zedong's followers were strong and where it would be easy for him to hide.

But instead he took the first ship to China he could find in Rangoon's port and it happened to be destined for Amoy, which was occupied by the Japanese. He was taken to Tokyo and in the following year, he returned to Rangoon to fetch some more of the young *thakins* for military training in Japan. They arrived in batches, smuggled out on Japanese freighters from Rangoon's port. When the complete band was assembled, and one Burmese who studied drama in Tokyo had joined them, they added up to thirty dedicated young men. Consequently, they became known as 'the Thirty Comrades'.

After spending some months in Tokyo, the Japanese-held Chinese islands of Hainan and Formosa, they returned with the Japanese army when it launched an invasion of Burma from Thailand in December 1941. On the 26th, they had set up in Bangkok the Burma Independence Army (BIA), mixed drops of their blood in a silver cup, drunk it and sworn eternal allegiance to each other and their cause: freedom for their country.

While still in Japan, 'The Thirty Comrades' — who were all in their 20s or early 30s, had assumed *noms de guerre* to fit their personalities. Aung San became Bo Teza, or the Powerful General. His close friend Thakin Hla Pe, one of the founders of the CPB, assumed the name Bo Let Ya, the Right Hand Man. Thakins Aung Than, Shwe, Tun Shein and Hla Maung — all former student leaders from Rangoon University — renamed themselves Bo Setkya (General of the Flying Weapon), Bo Kyaw Zaw (the Famous General), Bo Yan Naing (the Victory General) and Bo Zeya (also the Victory General, but in Pali) respectively. Aung Thein, a young student activist, became Bo Ye Htut (the Bravest General). There was also Thakin San Hlaing, now Bohmu Aung (Victory) who at 31 was the oldest in the group. However, when they eventually reached the Thai-Burmese border, only 28 remained. Ko Saung (Bo Htein Win; the Bright Sun General), the Burmese who had joined the group in Tokyo, never went for military training in Hainan. Thakin Than Tin had died of malaria in Formosa; he never even assumed one of these new, revolutionary aliases.

In Burmese history, there is a certain mystique surrounding the Thirty Comrades and the close relationship that supposedly existed among them.

Some of that, however, is a myth; the tightly knit brotherhood actually consisted of two factions. Twenty-two of the young comrades were followers of the old writer and national hero, Thakin Kodaw Hmaing, and belonged to the deeply committed, main faction of the *Dohbama*. But eight came from the so-called 'Ba Sein-Tun Oke faction', named after two well-known *thakins*.

It should be noted that the connection with Japan was not established simply because Aung San had caught the wrong ship in Rangoon. Japan's secret activities in Burma were undertaken by various agents in Rangoon and elsewhere. As early as the 1930s a Japanese naval officer called Shozo Kokubu had made contact with the Ba Sein-Tun Oke faction. In 1940 another nationalist, Dr Thein Aung, had visited Tokyo on a trip arranged by a Japanese agent in Rangoon, Dr Tsukasa Suzuki. Thakin Kodaw Hmaing's followers, including Aung San, were suspicious of the Japanese, and the aborted trip to China should be seen as an attempt to find another source of support for the struggle for independence. While that failed, only the Japanese option was open to the young Burmese nationalists.

In Rangoon, the Ba Sein-Tun Oke faction had a certain reputation for trimming, so their arrival in Tokyo in July 1941 caused some concern among the others. But largely owing to Aung San's talent for compromise, any severe frictions between the two factions was averted. "Bo Setkya was the leader of the Ba Sein-Tun Oke group," related Bo Kyaw Zaw in an interview with this writer in January 1987. "Bo Yan Naing acted as a go-between and Aung San managed to keep us together."

However, the Ba Sein-Tun Oke faction also included an ambitious young man who had left Judson College in Rangoon without a degree in March 1931 to work as a clerk in a small, suburban post office. He was taller and more military-looking than the other intellectuals. His name was Thakin Shu Maung; in the Thirty Comrades he became Bo Ne Win, the Sun of Glory General.

"Aung San and Ne Win quarrelled quite often, and that was the only friction that actually did surface between us," says Bo Kyaw Zaw. "Aung San was always very straightforward; Ne Win much more cunning and calculating. But Aung San's main objection to Ne Win was his immoral conduct. He was a gambler and a womaniser which the strict moralist Aung San, and the rest of us as well, despised. But for the sake of unity, we kept together as much we could."

When they entered Burma, thousands of other young Burmese nationalists joined their BIA. They followed the Japanese army into Rangoon, when the capital was captured on 7th March 1942. The British retreated north, across the mountains into India, together with a large number of ethnic Indians from Burma. Only some of the national minorities, notably the Karens, the Kachins and the Chins, organised guerrilla forces to fight against the Japanese, and the BIA, in defence of Allied interests. As a general rule, the BIA regarded the Karens especially as British collaborators; after all, they had been favoured by the British and many of them had been recruited into the colonial army and police. On the eve of World War Two, only 1,893 of the soldiers in the colonial army were Burmans, compared to 2,797 Karens, 852 Kachins, 1,258 Chins and 2,578 Indians.

Many Karens in particular had been in the ranks of the force that crushed the Saya San rebellion in the early 1930s. Now, the Burmans took revenge. Shortly after the Japanese invasion, Bo Tun Hla, a BIA officer, shot seventeen Karen elders at Papun in the Karen Hills where guerrilla forces, organised by Hugh Seagrim of the Burma Rifles, were active. In Myaungmya in the Irrawaddy delta region, 150 Karens were slaughtered, including a former cabinet minister, Saw Pe Tha, his English wife and their children. The reprisals against the Karen civilian population was so brutal that Seagrim surrendered to the Japanese rather than see them continue. He was executed by the Japanese shortly afterwards. His self-sacrifice on the Karens' behalf is still a treasured memory. Many Karens even today talk fondly of their 'Grandfather Longlegs'.

A Japanese-sponsored puppet administration was proclaimed on 1st August and Dr Ba Maw, the *Sinyetha* leader, became its titular head. But many of the young nationalists had begun to have their doubts about the actual intentions of the Japanese. As soon as the 'government' had been formed, they disbanded the BIA and replaced it with the much smaller Burma Defence Army (BDA). This new outfit only had a token force of three battalions, led by Bo Ne Win, Bo Yan Naing and Bo Zeya respectively. Aung San was the overall commander with the rank of colonel.

Exactly a year later, on 1st August 1943, the Japanese granted Burma 'independence'. Dr Ba Maw was elevated to the post of *Adipati*, or Head of State. He also assumed the title *Anashin Mingyi Kodaw*, meaning 'Lord of Power, the Great King's Royal Person'. Burma's authoritarian traditions had surfaced again in the form of an Axis-sponsored *Führerschaft* with tendencies that clearly hinted at National Socialism. The BDA was reorganised once again and named the Burma National Army (BNA). Bo Ne Win became its commander after pressure from the Ba Sein-Tun Oke faction, which was favoured by the Japanese military authorities. Aung San's choice was actually his close friend Bo Let Ya, according to Bo Kyaw Zaw.

Frictions between the Burmese nationalists and the Japanese became even more apparent. Some of their more radical ex-fellow students, now in the CPB were already in the underground, organising armed resistance against what more and more people perceived as foreign occupation rather than Burmese 'independence'. The Allies were contacted secretly; Thakin

Thein Pe — a CPB member who journeyed so widely on clandestine missions that he was nicknamed 'the Wartime Traveller'—was sent to Calcutta. Despite his political affiliation, he was promised British support. In the hills in the north and the east, ethnic guerrilla forces were inflicting heavy casualties on the Japanese, who were retreating towards the south. On 27th March 1945, the final step was taken. The BNA declared war against the Japanese.

For strategic purposes, the country was divided into eight military regions. Ne Win was appointed commander of the No 2 region which included the strategic Pyapon District in the Irrawaddy delta region, close to Rangoon. His political commissar was the leftist firebrand Thakin Soe. Bo Ye Htut commanded the No 6 Pyinmana-Meiktila area in central Burma and Kyaw Zaw was in charge of the No 4 region around Toungoo and Hanthawaddy. Bohmu Aung led the forces in the No 7 region—Thayetmyo and Minbu in the central plains — with a young leftist, Thakin Tin Mya, as his political commissar. Down in the tropical jungles of Tavoy in Tenasserim Division, the political leader was a fiery young leftist called Thakin Ba Thein Tin. A broad-based popular front, first called the Anti-Fascist Organisation and later the Anti-Fascist People's League (AFPFL), provided overall political guidance to the struggle against the Japanese.

On 30th May, Admiral Louis Mountbatten at a meeting in Delhi recognised the BNA as the Patriotic Burmese Forces (PBF) and on 15th June, the red flag with a white star of the Burmese resistance flew beside the Union Jack in Rangoon. The war was over. The PBF was turned into a regular army with 4,700 troops. But about 3,500 ex-resistance fighters did not register for regular enlistment and instead formed the *Pyithu Yebaw Ahphwe*, which in English became known as the People's Volunteer Organisation (PVO). In effect, it was a paramilitary force controlled by Aung San.

The stated goal of the AFPFL was independence for Burma, and Aung San immediately began working towards achieving that objective. Despite his youth, and his past as a founder of the CPB as well as an ally of the Japanese, he had won the admiration of Mountbatten who persuaded the British government that he was the only political figure in Burma who could hold the country together. Despite Aung San's seemingly shifting character, Mountbatten was convinced that whatever the young nationalist leader had done and whoever he had allied himself with, it had always been for one goal only; independence for Burma. Therefore, he was immensely popular.

The main problem at this time was the position of the CPB. One radical action, led by Thakin Soe, argued that only a people's war against 'the imperialists' could deliver genuine independence for Burma. The moderates, led by Aung San's brother in law, Thakin Than Tun, wanted to work within the AFPFL for a socialist state, and he was the general secretary of the front. In March 1946, the CPB split and Thakin Soe soon afterwards went underground in the Irrawaddy delta with a small guerilla force, the Communist Party (Red Flag).

The main CPB joined Aung San's pre-independence cabinet and one of its members, the 'Wartime Traveller' Thakin Thein Pe, was appointed Minister for Forests and Agriculture. But he resigned after only two weeks in office when Aung San refused to include more CPB members in his cabinet. Than Tun declared a general strike against the AFPFL government — with the result that the CPB was expelled from the front in October. Than Tun was succeeded as the AFPFL's general secretary by Kyaw Nyein. The gap between Aung San and the communist camp widened in January 1947 when the Red Flags were declared illegal following a number of sabotage raids in the delta.

By then, Aung San's efforts had began to bear fruit. On 27th January, he had signed an agreement in London with British labour prime minister Clement Attlee, promising full independence for Burma "within one year". On 12th February, he travelled to Panglong in the Shan States and signed an agreement with leaders of the Shans, Kachins and Chins, paving the way for their joining the proposed Union of Burma under a federal constitution.

Only the Karens, deeply suspicious of the Burmese nationalists, remained outside the constitutional process; their main political organisation, the Karen National Union (KNU), led by Saw Ba U Gyi, decided to boycott the elections in April to the new Constituent Assembly. The CPB also refrained from participating, although seven individual communists were elected to the 255-member assembly; the AFPFL captured the remaining 248 seats. The new constitution, which was being drafted, had borrowed heavily from those of Ireland, Yugoslavia and India. It was democratic and federal in character and safeguarded basic democratic liberties.

Totalitarianism, which had briefly re-surfaced during the first stages of the Japanese occupation, had been left behind. The only really controversial clause in the 1947 constitution was its Chapter X, which provided for the right of secession for the Shan and Kayah (Karenni) States after "ten years from the date this constitution comes into operation". The only other constitution in the world that has a similar clause is that of the Soviet Union in 1936. Presumably, the right of secession for the Shan and Kayah States was included in order to appease the national minorities and thus facilitate the amalgamation of their areas with the Union as a whole. It was, as in the case of the Soviet Union, a right that was not truly expected to be exercised.

Everything appeared set for Burma's independence when a totally unexpected event took place. In the morning of 19th July, two military jeeps sped down the streets of Rangoon. They stopped outside what was then the

Secretariat in Dalhousie Street — now the Ministers' Office on the renamed Maha Bandoola Street. Some young men in uniform, armed with sub-machine guns, jumped out and rushed into the old, colonial red-brick building. On reaching the room where Aung San was holding a cabinet meeting that fateful morning, they pointed their guns at the assembled ministers, shouting: "Remain seated! Don't move!" Aung San rose to his feet — and the men opened fire. The shooting continued for about 30 seconds, and then the uniformed men left the building, jumped into their jeeps outside and sped off.

It was 10.37 am. Other occupants of the building were soon jostling in the open doorway. The pungent smell of carbide and fumes of heavy smoke filled the room. Tables and chairs were overturned and soiled with blood. Nine corpses lay on the floor: Aung San; his close friend Thakin Mya, one of the leaders of the 1920 students' strike; Ba Choe, a former editor of the nationalist *Deedok* journal and now a prominent AFPFL leader; Razak, a Muslim school principal and politician; Ba Win, the chairman of the AFPFL unit in the Yenangyaung oil field area and Aung San's elder brother; Mahn Ba Khaing, one of the few Karen leaders who had sided with the AFPFL government; and Sao Sam Htun, the *sawbwa*, or prince, of the Shan State of Möng Pawn who had taken part in Aung San's efforts to amalgamate the frontier areas with 'Ministerial Burma', or Burma proper. There were also Ohn Maung, a deputy secretary of the Ministry of Transport who had entered the meeting room to submit a report when the assassins arrived, and Ko Htwe, Razak's bodyguard.

The nation was plunged in grief. Its leaders, who had been preparing to take over Burma after the British, were dead before the country had even become independent. Aung San, the national hero, the *Bogyoke*, or General, was only 32 and left behind his wife Khin Kyi, and three small children, two sons and a two year old daughter. On the same day, the Rangoon police arrested U Saw, the right-wing politician who had been Aung San's main rival for the premiership of independent Burma, and charged him with murder. U Saw was convicted and hanged in May 1948.

The AFPFL's vice president, the former student leader Thakin Nu, now referred to as U Nu, took over as prime minister. In October, he travelled to London and a second agreement was signed with Attlee. Burma was going to become independent at the auspicious hour of 4.20 am on 4th January 1948. The timing had been carefully selected by Burma's famous astrologers, who even the Western-educated political leaders often consulted. The Union Jack was lowered and the last British soldiers marched past, accompanied by a military band playing 'Auld Lang Syne'.

While U Nu led the independent republic's first government, the presidency was given to Sao Shwe Thaike, the Shan *sawbwa* of Yawnghwe and one of the most prominent leaders of Burma's many ethnic minorities. Although there had been widespread discontent among the Karen minority, Lieut-Gen Smith-Dun, a Karen, became the commander-in-chief of the armed forces with two more Karens on important positions under him: Brig-Gen Kya Doe, a Sandhurst graduate, as chief of operations and Shi Sho as chief of the air force. They had been appointed on the insistence of Aung San, when he was still alive, in an attempt to hold the Union together.

But the promising Union of Burma was less than three months old when its very survival was being questioned. On 28th March, Thakin Than Tun's CPB went underground and resorted to armed struggle against the government. The first shots were fired on 2nd April at Paukkongyi in Pegu District north of Rangoon. Burma's 40-year long civil war had begun. In July, a faction of the paramilitary PVO also turned against the government. They were followed in August by a mutiny among the 1st Burma Rifles at Thayetmyo which spread to other units as well. Large parts of central Burma fell to the various insurgent groups.

The situation turned from bad to worse when Saw Ba U Gyi's Karen National Defence Organisation (KNDO), almost a private army of the KNU, began attacking government positions in the Thaton-Moulmein area in August. By January 1949, the Karen insurrection had gained momentum. They even took over the northern Rangoon suburb of Insein, captured the notorious jail there and released the prisoners, including Capt. Vivian, a British officer who had been charged with supplying Aung San's assassins with weapons.

In the Arakan area in the west, both Muslim *mujaheed* guerrillas and various communist groups established strongholds. The Red Flag faction was led by the notorious *Bonbauk* , or 'bomb thrower', Tha Gyaw while his no-less colourful comrade-in-arms Sein Da - a former monk known as 'the King of Arakan' — waged a guerrilla war in the western hills. Smaller groups of Mons, Karennis and Pa-Os in the eastern parts of the country also took up arms against the Rangoon government, allying themselves with the Karen rebels.

Although they had remained loyal to the government, the three top Karen officers in the Burmese Army were retired on 1st February. Smith-Dun's deputy, Lieut-Gen. Ne Win, immediately assumed the posts as Chief of General Staff and Supreme Commander of the armed forces, including the police and the paramilitary Union Military Police. On 1st April he was also appointed Deputy Prime Minister in charge of the Defence and Home Ministries.

Suddenly, Burma's dark horse, the ever-present but seldom seen Ne Win, had emerged as the most powerful man in the country; U Nu's civilian government was held hostage by the army and the insurgents at the same time. Dr Maung Maung, the historian, later wrote that Ne Win had no political ambitions at that time; "his pledge to the people was that he would work for the restoration of peace, law and order, so that the first general elections might be held in fair and free conditions". Other analysts observed with concern the rise of the ambitious general. Step by step, he was building up a power base within the military, mostly centred around a small circle of loyal officers from his old battalion, the 4th Burma Rifles, which he had commanded from its inception immediately after the war until December 1947 and who now were actively supporting Ba Swe's Burma Socialist Party (BSP).

Before the insurrections broke out, the tiny Burmese Army had consisted of only about a dozen battalions, several of whom were made up of Karens. They rose in revolt — and two more battalions were heavily infiltrated by the CPB. The whole country was threatened and the outside world sarcastically referred to U Nu's cabinet as 'the Rangoon government' since before long it controlled little more than the capital. Kyaw Nyein, U Nu's deputy, wrote some time later: "Very few people thought that the government could survive. Yet somehow it did...desperately, it fought for time to build up a new army, and to rally the people behind it, convincing them that the alternatives to democracy were either a military or a communist dictatorship, and that either would lead to chaos".

Disunity among the rebels, the KNDO was staunchly anti-communist and the PVOs fell out with the CPB, as well as generous arms supplies to Rangoon from Nehru in India also helped strengthen the government's position. Against most expectations, by 1951 the back of the insurrection was broken through a mixture of military pressure, a liberal amnesty policy for rebels who surrendered, and a determined social reform programme.

The Karen rebel movement had also suffered a substantial loss in August 1950. A unit from the 3rd Burma Rifles had stumbled upon the night bivouac of KNU and KNDO leader Saw Ba U Gyi and some of his troops in the eastern Karen hills, close to the Thai border. A fire fight broke out and Saw Ba U Gyi was killed along with Saw Sankey, another prominent Karen rebel leader (the Burmese Army for years thought that they had killed Capt. Vivian, who had retreated with the KNDO after his release from Insein; Capt. Vivian left Burma's jungles in the mid-1950s and settled in Swansea, Wales). One of the Burmese officers who led the attack on Saw Ba U Gyi's temporary camp was a 26-year old major, Sein Lwin, who previously had served under Ne Win in the 4th Burma Rifles.

While the task of fighting the insurgents were had been left to the army's field commanders, nearly all of whom had been battle-hardened during World War Two, Ne Win spent most of his time in Rangoon, consolidating his political power. The only military operation he actually participated in was 'Operation Flush' which was carried out in 1947, before independence, by British, Indian and Burmese (the 4th Burma Rifles) against communist rebels in the Yenangyaung oil field area.

In August 1950, Ne Win had to resign as defence minister since a non-elected cabinet member was not allowed to hold office for more than six months. But he was succeeded by his ally Ba Swe and Ne Win urged him to "start organising the socialist party (i.e. the BSP) on a strong and proper basis", according to Dr Maung Maung. Among the officers from the 4th Burma Rifles who had joined the BSP was colonel Aung Gyi, a Sino-Burman from Paungde who was also chief of staff.

The BSP was included in the overall AFPFL front but since it was so powerful, in effect it formed a 'party within the party'. Its ideology was a mixture of Western, socialist ideas and Buddhist thinking. Ba Swe wrote in 1951: "Marxist theory is not antagonistic to Buddhist philosophy. The two are, frankly speaking, not merely similar. In fact, they are the same in concept". Paradoxically, Ba Swe himself was a wealthy man by Burmese standards and his family owned mining and other industrial enterprises.

The relative stability which had been achieved after the first counter-insurgency campaign in 1949-51 was soon undermined. Mao Zedong's communists had come out victorious in the Chinese civil war, and the defeated nationalist Kuomintang (KMT) retreated to Taiwan. But thousands of KMT force from the southern province of Yunnan were cut off from the main force—and streamed across the border into Burma's northeastern mountain regions, primarily the Shan States. New bases were established there in an attempt to regroup and launch a 'war of liberation' against the communists. Air strips were built in remote areas and supplies were flown in from Thailand and Taiwan under cover of darkness and in close cooperation with US intelligence agencies.

The KMT also linked up with some of the ethnic rebel groups that operated along Burma's eastern border: the Karens, the Pa-Os, the Karennis and the Mons. Its influence spread along the border and within a year a line of communication had been established all the way down to the Tenasserim coast, near Amherst. Arms and ammunition for the KMT also entered Burma by sea. By 1952, the overall strength of the KMT forces in Burma had risen to 12,000. They were in firm control of the hilly region east of the Salween river, traditionally Burma's opium growing area.

Apart from launching cross-border raids into China, the KMT also built up an opium empire in Burma's northeastern border mountains. Through heavy taxation, the farmers were forced to grow more to survive, and the KMT infrastructure—which included C 46 and C 47 US-supplied planes—revolutionised opium transport. Across the border in Thailand, its police commander, Gen. Phao Sriyanonda, was the main buyer of opium from

Burma, and he paid handsomely. As a result, Burma's previously modest production of 30 tons annually rose dramatically to several hundred tons a year by the mid-1950s.

The Burmese Army launched a massive campaign against the KMT. The first target was the sea base near Amherst, from which the KMT was driven out in 1952. In the following year, an operation codenamed *Naga Naing* ('Victory over the Dragon') was mounted in the northeastern Shan mountains. A fierce battle was fought at the Wan Hsa-la ferry crossing on the Salween, the KMT retreated and soon their forces were pinned down in a string of camps along the Thai and Chinese borders.

The field commander who led the successful campaign against the KMT was Brig-Gen Kyaw Zaw of the Thirty Comrades. His battalion commander at Wan Hsa-la had been a young officer called Tin U. Kyaw Zaw was probably the Burmese Army's main strategist at the time and Tin U was popular with the troops; he soon became known as the commander who dug trenches with the privates and ate and joked with them. Together, they managed to contain the threat posed by the KMT after another successful campaign during the 1954-55 dry season — which also had been encouraged by a resolution adopted by the UN General Assembly on 22nd April 1953 demanding that the KMT lay down arms and leave the country.

While Kyaw Zaw was gaining admiration and respect for his performance in the battlefield, U Nu concentrated on the political side. The AFPFL was well entrenched and the opposition to it consisted of the Burma Workers' and Peasants' Party (BWPP), led by Thakin Lwin and Thakin Chit Maung, two leftist labour leaders. But the BWPP was too weak to pose any serious challenge to the AFPFL so in the absence of any actual opposition in the parliament, Burma's lively press served as public watchdog, especially in its frequent interviews with the prime minister.

The insurgents were still there, but badly organised and — with the sole exception of the foreign-sponsored KMT — poorly equipped. By 1955 it was obvious that they were not going to score any major victory over the Burmese Army, let alone capture Rangoon or any other town in the country.

Internationally, Burma emerged as one of the leaders in the non-aligned movement that was initiated during the Bandung conference in Indonesia in 1955. U Nu frequently visited foreign countries; he had charm and wit and was a well-respected statesman. Law Yone, the editor of the *Nation*, Burma's leading English-language newspaper in the 1950s, described U Nu as "a man who can be moved to compassion as well as to anger, he has matured with experience and with the practice of Buddhism, of which he is one of the most ardent supporters in Burma, devoting a part of each day to meditation and prayer. In politics, he has always been an independent."

In line with his deep religious beliefs, U Nu invited Buddhist monks and scholars from all over the world to a Sixth Great Buddhist Synod in Rangoon in 1953. A Buddha Sasana Council was set up to publish Buddhist scriptures and U Nu initiated the construction of the Kaba Aye, or World Peace Pagoda, in Rangoon's northern suburbs. While no one objected to these schemes *per se*, some criticised them for being too costly at a time when Burma needed capital for industrial development. Others accused U Nu of trying to use religion to provide legitimacy and attract international sympathy for his regime.

U Nu's version of socialist democracy was labelled *pyi daw tha* — 'the Happy Land' — and its many communal development programmes included the sinking of wells and the construction of irrigation systems, roads, bridges, schools, libraries and social welfare centres. It worked fairly well in central Burma, although many spokesmen for the ethnic minorities complained that the frontier areas were neglected. In the Shan States the situation was especially critical, mainly because the local peasants felt they were squeezed between the KMT and the Burmese Army that had entered the area to fight against the foreign intruders.

In the past, the Shan farmers had had almost no interaction with the majority Burmans and few could even speak Burmese. Now, 'Burman' became synonymous with the soldiers of the Burmese Army, and finding themselves in what they perceived as an alien land, their behaviour towards the local Shan and hilltribe population was far from exemplary. Separatist ideas began taking root among the Shans. They had also, after all, the constitutional right to secede from the Union.

Economically, Burma was still suffering from the devastation of World War Two. The country had been a major battlefield twice — first when the Japanese invaded and later when they were driven out — and then came the civil war. Even in the mid-1950s, the per capita output in Burma amounted to only 80% of what it had been in 1938-39. In order to undermine the CPB's propaganda that the government was an 'imperialist tool', U Nu had pursued an economic and social policy that was partly inspired by Scandinavian social democracy, for instance the *pyi daw tha* programme. Certain essential sectors were also nationalised — railways, river transport, electric power — and also rice and timber export. Domestic production was stimulated by state-sponsored plants for cement, textiles, jute, steel-rolling, sugar, brick and tiles as well as pharmaceuticals. Some of the old British enterprises, especially in oil and mining, were revived as joint venture.

A major problem, however, was that independent Burma, again as a political move to thwart the CPB threat, had sent the British civil servants and all other foreign technicians packing. Many Anglo-Burman subordinates, who worked for the railways, customs and other services, were either replaced or they emigrated, mainly to Australia. A large number of Indians had also left the country in the wake of the Japanese occupation and more followed after Burma's, and India's, independence. Although few were sad to see the *chettiars* leave, this departure also inevitably meant that Burma lost many skilled labourers, civil servants, small businessmen and experienced importers-exporters. As a result, Burma's national pride was boosted, but the economy suffered since there was not enough educated and experienced Burmans to fill the posts when the 'foreigners' had left.

Law Yone of the *Nation* wrote in an Atlantic Monthly supplement on Burma in 1958: "The loss in efficiency is incalculable, and Burma now finds herself obliged to bring in new and expensive Western technicians for positions which the earlier incumbents could have handled at far less cost". Law Yone also critically scrutinised Burma's political system: "Land allocations, crop loans, *pyi daw tha* development projects, welfare benefits, purchase of the harvests — all are controlled by AFPFL adherents. This is patronage. Intimidation sometimes occur too, the small ones still wield enough power, they have guns (i.e. the military/BL), to make the opposition to them distinctly uncomfortable. Thus our political life, which we hope one day to make completely democratic, is in reality still a compromise between one-party rule, strong-arm tactics, and a fully documented system of courts, elected legislature, and individual freedom. The insurrection is largely to blame...yet it cannot be denied that the forms of democracy are maintained, and are sincerely acclaimed by the AFPFL leaders, who declare that they actively desire freedom of speech, a strong, free press, impeccable courts, and a democratic opposition."

Burma's democracy was put to the test during the second national elections in 1956 (the first had been held in 1951 when civil war was still raging in the countryside). The leftist groups, of which the BWPP was the main party, as well as some moderate politicians, contested under the common banner the National Unity Front (NUF) and challenged the AFPFL juggernaut. The opposition did unexpectedly well and captured 36.9% of the votes and 48 seats in the 250-seat parliament. It also gained the support of some regional parties. The AFPFL maintained its majority, but it was reduced from 60% to 55%, or 173 seats compared to about 200 in 1951 — both including allied parties that supported the government. The rest went to independents or to some smaller, mostly regional parties.

The minor setback for the AFPFL would have posed no problem, had it not been for internal bickering and accusations of foreign meddling in the elections; the Soviet and Chinese embassies in Rangoon were named by critics as financiers of the new phenomenon, the NUF. Whether true or not, U Nu found it necessary to retire temporarily from his post as prime minister in order to rejuvenate the AFPFL. Ba Swe, the BSP leader became the new prime minister in June 1956.

When U Nu resumed office in 1957, the situation had undergone considerable changes. The transformation of the army from being a defender of the government to a political factor to be reckoned with had been completed. In the mid 1950s, it had even formulated its own policy which strongly resembled the *dwifungsi* ('dual function') doctrine of Indonesia's army which stated that the military has both a defence and a social-political role. A document entitled 'The National Ideology and the Role of the Defence Services' spoke of psychological re-generation which was the result of the "decisive leadership of the government and the clarity and conviction of the Defence Services".

Jan Becka, a prominent Marxist Burma-scholar from Czechoslovakia, wrote in *Archiv Orientalni* (Academia Praha) volume 49/1981: "Political and ideological work among the officers...was greatly expanded at that time (i.e the mid-1950s/BL), preparing the army to play the role of 'saviour of the nation'...the decisive criterion of the political and social prestige of any public figure in the Union of Burma was his participation in the resistance and/or service in the wartime national army. Consequently, those who headed the army considered themselves to be a part of the new post-war leadership and thereby implicitly claimed the right to participate in the decision-making process.

But even so, the army itself had also undergone substantial changes. Most of the original founders of the army, the Thirty Comrades, had gone into business or politics. One was an ambassador, some had died or faded into obscurity. Bo Let Ya suffered from tuberculosis. Bo Zeya, Bo Ye Htut and Bo Yan Aung had joined the CPB and gone underground. A second generation of ex-commanders of the wartime BIA-BDA-BNA-PBF commanders had taken over: Col. Aung Gyi, Brig-Gen Maung Maung, Brig-Gen Tin Pe and others, most of whom were close to the BSP.

Despite its socialist veneer, the army entered business under the aegis of the Defence Services Institute (DSI). The companies owned and controlled by the military included Rowe & Co which sold high quality foreign goods, the Ava Bank which was set up after buying out A. Scott Bank, the Burma Asiatic Company formed after buying up the former East Asiatic Company and, perhaps most important of all, the Burma Five Star Shipping Line, a freighter service company with a fleet of seven ships.

With profits from its own businesses, the army even funded a newspaper to convey its ideas to the public, the English-language *Guardian*, which was founded in 1955 by Aung Gyi and Dr. Maung Maung, a former army officer who had become a lawyer and a historian. The paper's editor, however, was Sein Win, one of Burma's leading and best-respected journalists.

Only two from the first generation of officers were still serving with the army: Ne Win and his serious contender for power over the armed forces,

Kyaw Zaw, who had become increasingly popular especially in view of his successful campaigns against the KMT. But then, in 1956, a mopping-up operation codenamed *Aung Marga* ('Victory Path') was mounted against the CPB in upper Burma and some secret defence documents were found in a captured communist camp. Without producing any evidence or direct connection, Kyaw Zaw was accused of being guilty for the leak. The public was shocked and many did not know what to believe.

However, Kyaw Zaw was dismissed from the army and briefly held in detention. In 1957, Kyaw Zaw was released since still no evidence had surfaced to substantiate the allegations against him. But his career was ruined and he settled down in Sanchaung in Rangoon with a modest pension from the army. Shortly after Kyaw Zaw's arrest, the army printed an information broadsheet about the campaign against the KMT. It did not even mention Kyaw Zaw. Instead, a smiling Ne Win in a bush hat was there inspecting the frontline troops "to personally direct operations against KMT agressors." Eyebrows were raised. Ne Win had not even participated in combat against the KMT; he hardly ever ventured outside Rangoon. Every Sunday, he could be seen at the race course in the capital where he had his own private box.

The rise in prominence of the army was immediately reflected in the AFPFL. U Nu, worried about the possible disintegration of the AFPFL, declared that it was no longer a front of various political parties and organisations, but a united political party. One faction, led by BSP leader Ba Swe and supported by deputy prime minister Kyaw Nyein — who had been pulled closer to the increasingly powerful military — favoured increased army participation in politics. In March 1958, they split from the ruling party. The Ba Swe-Kyaw Nyein faction called themselves the 'Stable AFPFL' — whereas U Nu's main faction was referred to as the 'Clean AFPFL'. The 'Stable AFPFL' even openly declared that they had the support of the army.

The political situation in Burma became totally confusing on 28th October when U Nu and the parliament handed over power to a so-called Caretaker Government, headed by the commander-in-chief, general Ne Win. This administration also included Brig-Gen. Aung Gyi, Brig-Gen. Tin Pe, Col. Kyaw Soe and several other close associates of Ne Win. In an attempt to explain the abrupt, and unforeseen, military takeover, Ne Win alleged in a speech before the parliament on 31st October that "the rebels were increasing their activities, and the political pillar was collapsing. It was imperative that the Union should not drown in shallow waters as it nearly did in 1948-49. So it fell on the armed forces to perform their bounden duty to take all security measures to forestall and prevent a recurrence". A propaganda leaflet, produced by the Caretaker Government a year later, claimed that the parliament had given him "the mandate to restore law and order in the country and also create the conditions that would be conductive to the holding of free and fair elections as soon as possible."

To most observers, this rhetoric was even more confusing than the squabbles within the AFPFL at that time. There had been a split in the ruling party, but the insurgents hardly posed a threat any longer and few were able to detect any serious decline in the overall law and order situation in the country. The only challenge to the government's stability had come during a vote of no-confidence shortly before the coup. U Nu had won by seven votes, but only by accepting the support of the NUF and the regional parties; the majority Burmans had rallied behind his rivals in the 'Stable AFPFL'. Unwilling to face the regular session of the parliament and recognising that the budget and other matters had to be settled, U Nu had turned to Ne Win and offered to resign in his favour.

Much later, U Nu in his autobiography *Saturday's Son* also claimed that he had heard about an imminent coup while travelling by steamer from Mandalay to Rangoon. It was not clear exactly who the plotters were — and one rumour had it that it was the paramilitary Union Military Police, another that a faction of the army was preparing to rebel — but U Nu, in order to avoid a confrontation, declared that he was willing to hand over power to the army on condition that a general election be held in six months. U Nu, pondering what the effect of the changes would be, said: "The army of course would rule over the country as a military establishment. At the moment the people regarded the soldiers as friends and protectors. After the takeover they would be looked upon with loathing. Politically, the party that had called in the army would suffer from the intervention. It was like putting a noose round one's own neck".

Despite the promise to "restore law and order" in six months, the Caretaker Government did not hand back power to a civilian government until December 1960, after the promised elections had finally been held. In the meantime, the army had been active in a way which was unprecedented. Claiming that "the insurgents were poised to take full advantage of the confused situation", the army soon began publishing lists and numbers of insurgents who supposedly had surrendered, of illicit arms that had been recovered, and reports of how the government machinery had been revitalised and the public's morale uplifted.

In a special notification, issued on 29th November 1958, the new military government declared that Rangoon had to be "cleaned up". Rubbish in the streets were ordered to be removed, houses painted and the about 165,000 squatters - mostly refugees who had streamed into Rangoon during the civil war and never left — who previously had been living in pockets all over Rangoon were re-located in a series of new 'satellite towns', including North and South Okkalapa, and Thaketa across the Pazundaung Creek, a tributary of the Rangoon River.

As a result, all the poor people who had been living close to the city — where most of them had jobs in the docks, as servants for rich families, as rickshaw pullers or day labourers — now found themselves living far out in new suburbs. While this made downtown Rangoon more pleasant to look at for the urban middle class, and foreign visitors, the move created other problems. Overnight it had become more expensive for those who had regular jobs to get to them; most of the day labourers found it almost impossible to survive. Hardly surprisingly, these new working class 'satellite towns' soon became breeding grounds for anti-army discontent.

In February-March 1960, the promised general elections were eventually held. Ne Win had ordered the army to "remain strictly neutral" in the process. U Nu, who all along had accused the military of supporting the 'Stable AFPFL', won, however. His 'Clean AFPFL' — which he had renamed the *Pyidaungsu* , or 'Union Party', got 52% of the vote, compared to 31% for the 'Stable AFPFL' and 5% for the NUF. Almost twice as many voted as compared to 1956.

Among the first tasks tackled by the new government were the problems that were undermining the democracy. Small groups of Shan students had gone underground in 1958 and 1959, demanding that their constitutional right to secede from the Union should be exercised. The Shan rebels, then organised in the *Noom Suk Harn* ('Young, Brave Warriors') numbered only a few hundred, based at Pangtawng near the Thai border. But the very fact that there was a new insurgency was cause for concern since other rebellions had been successfully contained.

The CPB still had forces in the Arakan Hills, the Pegu Yoma mountains north of Rangoon — which they once intended to turn into a Burmese Yan'an—and some areas near Mandalay and in Tenasserim in the southeast. Small skirmishes and bomb explosions occurred every now and then, but the CPB in the early 1960s was too weak to launch any significant attacks on the Burmese Army. According to figures released by Ne Win's Caretaker Government in 1958, the strength of the CPB had dwindled down to about 1,300. The actual figure may have been twice as high — still considerably less than the 10,000-15,000 armed fighters the CPB had during the height of the insurgency in 1949-50. And although about 140 CPB cadres had had a base in exile in China since the early 1950s, Peking's policy at this time was not to support the CPB insurgents inside Burma. Relations with U Nu's government were good, and a border agreement, for the first time demarcating the entire 2,180 kilometre Sino-Burmese frontier, had just been concluded.

In 1961, however, the Shans were followed by some Kachin tribesmen from the far north who set up the Kachin Independence Army (KIA). The mainstream ethnic leaders demanded greater autonomy, combined with development schemes for the neglected frontier areas, in order to solve the problem by political means. It was in view of these developments that U Nu had convened the seminar in Rangoon in February 1962 — and general Ne Win stepped in and seized power on 2nd March.

Since the mid-1950s, the army had been waiting in the background, consolidating its forces and preparing for the takeover. Immediately after the coup, it got down to work with military efficiency. After suspending parts of the constitution and dissolving the parliament on 3rd March, the 24-member Revolutionary Council vested Ne Win with full executive, legislative and judicial powers — privileges that he did not formally give up until 1974.

Within less than a month of the coup, Ne Win had achieved a power over the state machinery that nobody had had since the monarchy was abolished in 1885. In sharp contrast to the legalistic approach of the 1958-60 Caretaker Government, when Ne Win frequently had appeared in parliament to answer questions and even had petitioned it to allow him to rule for more than the six months the constitution allowed for a non-elected minister to stay in office, the military this time ruled by decree. It also introduced its own set of laws to formalise, rather than legalise, its omnipotence.

Burma's new power structure consisted of Ne Win at the top of the pyramid, and under him the stratum of loyal, second generation officers who had also participated in the 1958-60 Caretaker Government: Aung Gyi, Tin Pe and Kyaw Soe formerly of the 4th Burma Rifles, some officers from the 3rd Burma Rifles and others who had served under Ne Win in the high command in Rangoon. Among the few civilians in the council were Dr Maung Maung, the lawyer and the writer who always had been close to the military, and Ba Nyein, a dedicated Marxist who had left the BSP in 1950 and helped set up the BWPP. He now became Ne Win's main economic adviser.

Almost immediately, five 'State Supreme Councils' were also formed to take over the state governments. A Burma press council was set up on 30th April to control the hitherto outspoken media. "To uplift the morals" of the people, the Revolutionary Council banned horse-racing, beauty contests and popular dance competitions. The US Ford and Asia Foundations as well as the Fulbright programme were suspended along with US and British language training centres.

The state-control of the administration and the exclusion of outside influences seemed to be in line with the policy of any military dictatorship asserting its power. But the ban on racing and similar activities raised eyebrows throughout Rangoon; the general himself was not exactly renowned for an austere, puritanical lifestyle. This was the first example of the hypocrisy which came to characterise Burma's unique version of socialism. Though the old race course at the Kyaikkasan grounds in Rangoon was converted into a parade and meeting field, Ne Win was seen avidly betting at the Ascot races on his first trip to Britain after the coup.

The 'ideology' of the new military regime was published on the same day in a document entitled 'The Burmese Way to Socialism'. This was followed later by 'The System of Correlation of Man and his Environment', which again was an effort to provide philosophical underpinnings for the military government. These documents were written by a team of leftist Burmese theoreticians, including Ba Nyein.

Another staunch supporter of the new order was Thakin Thein Pe, who now called himself Thein Pe Myint and had left the CPB to publish the *Vanguard* newspaper in Rangoon. Basically, 'the Burmese Way to Socialism' was a hodgepodge of Marxism, Buddhist thinking and humanism which reflected an attempt by the military regime to give it a semblance of belonging to Burma's specific political traditions. On 4th July, the military announced the formation of the new Burma Socialist Programme Party (BSPP) which at first was a cadre party comprised only of the members of the Revolutionary Council.

The inclusion of the rabid ideologue Ba Nyein — and the clear drift towards leftist totalitarianism that followed — made most foreign business-men, who initially had welcomed the coup, change their minds about military rule. The stability the army envisaged clearly was not for them. The reaction among the public at large to the coup, and the transformation of Burma's political and economic system it resulted in, was one of shock and anger when the freedoms they previously had enjoyed were severely restricted.

The students, always at the forefront of any protest movement in Burma, were the first to demonstrate openly against the military takeover. Sai Tzang, whose father Sao Shwe Thaike had been Burma's first president 1948-52, was there on the campus on 7th July:

— The evening was cool and balmy, the atmosphere charged with excite-ment. In the past two or three days, there had been a series of confrontations with the police but these were largely indecisive until a student was shot and wounded. This infuriated and galvanised the student body and by the morning of the 7th, the police were finally evicted from the campus. Students had shut the main gate and declared the campus a 'fortress of democracy'. All day, speeches were held, condemning the coup and calling for the restoration of democracy. The Students' Union building, which had been an important symbol of Burmese nationalism since the 1930s, was alive with activities and filled with youthful laughter and cheerful banter-ing as students came and went.

The festive atmosphere changed later that evening when the students saw soldiers being deployed along University Avenue, armed with newly issued West German G-3 assault rifles. Soon, a small Fiat arrived and three officers got out to confer with their colleagues who were in charge of the troops facing the campus. The students booed and whistled. After a short while, the Fiat drove away. One of the remaining officers turned around to face the students, raised his arms and waved them above his head in a circular motion three times.

"We looked at each other, wondering what it all meant," Sai Tzang recalls. "Our questions were answered immediately and violently by gunfire. I dropped into a ditch and lay there not knowing what to do next. Then, the firing stopped. But when some students started running, gunfire resumed. There was a lull, soon followed by a volley as students started running again. While I myself was running, I tripped on a body lying on the ground and fell. There was a red flag of the Students' Union lying by the lifeless open palm of the dead student. Without thinking, I grabbed the flag and ran as fast as I could, praying frantically that I would not be hit. Finally, I reached the safety of the hostel building. Then, the soldiers began firing into the buildings and we heard bullets thudding into walls and the tinkling of glass as windowpanes shattered. It was clear that the soldiers were firing not merely to disperse the crowds, but were under orders to shoot to kill."

Officially, 15 were killed and 27 wounded. But both neutral observers and students who were present during the shooting say that the university looked like a slaughterhouse where not 15 but hundreds of potential leaders of society in many fields lay sprawled in death. The man in charge of the operation was Sein Lwin, one of Ne Win's closest lieutenants, and the orders to kill had come directly from the strongman himself.

In the early hours of 8th July, Rangoon residents were awakened by an explosion that reverberated through the city. The army had dynamited the historic Students' Union building, reducing it to rubble. David Steinberg, a US Burma scholar, commented in his *Burma - A Socialist Nation in Southeast Asia* on what he described as a gratuitous and unnecessary act: "[the building] had been as a familiar a symbol in the secular sphere as the Shwe Dagon Pagoda was a symbol of Buddhism...The student demonstrations and their tragic aftermath were harbingers of the continuous trouble the military experienced from the volatile student community".

Josef Silverstein and Julian Wohl wrote in *Pacific Affairs* 1/1964: "The General [Ne Win] defended the actions of his government on that occasion by declaring that the students had been prompted in their actions by certain political organisations (identified in an earlier communique as Communists) and said: 'I have no alternative but to meet *dah* [dagger] with *dah* and spear with spear'."

Burmese totalitarianism had returned with an unprecedented ferocity, and provoked an unexpected response from the country's young intellectuals. The army clearly had wanted to show just who was in charge — but the massacre on the campus in Rangoon also prompted hundreds of students to join the underground. Sai Tzang, who is a Shan, went to the guerrillas of his ethnic group in the northeast. Many, though, joined the until then almost depleted ranks of the communists in the Pegu Yoma mountains north of Rangoon.

Within the Revolutionary Council itself, rifts soon became apparent. Aung Gyi, whom most people considered Ne Win's heir apparent, had voiced criticism of the officially announced economic policies and suggested a much more pragmatic approach. On 8th February 1963, he was dismissed. Within a week, Ne Win announced state takeover of production, distribution, import and export of commodities. No new private enterprises would be allowed and on 23rd February all banks were nationalised. A new Enterprises Nationalisation Act was promulgated on 26th February, providing for all major industries to be government-run. Aung Gyi's dismissal was followed by the rise to power of brigadier-general Tin Pe, an orthodox Marxist like Ba Nyein.

Prior to these moves, Rangoon had been a booming and bustling international trade centre where a number of foreign banks were represented: the Hongkong and Shanghai Bank, the Chartered Bank, Grindlay's Bank, the State Bank of India, the Habib Bank and others. Several international airlines had Rangoon as a major destination in Southeast Asia and Mingaladon Airport was then considered one of the most modern in the region.

Before long, all that seemed to belong to a dim and distant past. The nationalisations wrecked the economy and measures were taken to root out private funds and deprive the old elite of power. On 17th May 1964, all 50 and 100 Kyat banknotes were demonetised, basically wiping out private savings. This, and the nationalisations, forced about 200,000 Burmese of South Asian origin, many of whom had lived in Burma for generations, to emigrate to India and Pakistan. Among them was Omar Farouk, whose family for decades had run a major Indo-Burmese enterprise in Rangoon. He arrived in Karachi in 1967, a city he had not even visited before:

— It was a tragic blunder. We felt, and still feel! — as Burmese as anybody else. We had been living in Burma for at least 200 years, and although some of our forefathers came from the Subcontinent, we are basically of mixed blood. Then, one day, somebody taps you on the shoulder and says: 'Hey! You are not Burmese. When are you going back home?' So we used to reply:

'This is home!' But the ordinary Burmese were not prejudiced. They couldn't understand why we had to leave. It was all a government trick to confiscate our property. We were accused of sending money abroad, but when the currency had been demonetised, we had nothing left. We arrived in Pakistan almost broke.

Aye Saung, a 41-year old ex-student from Toungoo recalls how the new economic policies affected life in his home town in central Burma:

— In 1963 all the shops were nationalised. I remember one morning some soldiers coming to the medicine shop next to our house. They came with green signboards, bearing the words 'People's Shop No.-' For the next few days the soldiers stayed in the shop. They seemed to be making a list of the goods. After a week, there was nothing on the shelves, and the shop was closed down. Our family was issued with a ration book, and for the first time we experienced shortages. When visitors came to our house we had to report them to the headman of the quarter. People travelling to other parts of the country found themselves being stopped at checkpoints, as the government attempted to curb the smuggling that had become rampant.

The infamous 'People's Shops' soon became a national joke. Initially, they were meant to function along the efficient lines of the DSI enterprises of the 1950s. By the time of the Caretaker Government, these had become the largest in the country and with the return of the civilian government in 1960 were renamed the Burma Economic Development Corporation. But without private competition and with more Marxist ideas being introduced by Ba Nyein and others, the entire system almost collapsed.

Distribution now became so badly organised that the few consumer goods which were now produced in the country reached outlying areas months after they had left the factories. Umbrellas appeared when the hot season set in and blankets when the rains began — if anything at all was available. But by adding the word 'people' in front of the new enterprises, and organs of state control, the military tried to give its rule an air of socialism, which they hoped would appeal to 'the masses'. Beer and alcoholic drinks came from 'the People's Brewery and Distillery'. Fashion-conscious ladies had their hair done at 'the People's Pride Hairdressing Saloon'. The public was supposedly protected by 'the People's Police Force' and ruled by a number of 'People's Councils' on different levels, while the judiciary was renamed 'the Council of People's Justices'. And, neatest of them all, pastries were sold by 'the People's Patisseries' while toothpaste came from 'the People's Toilet Industry'.

Burma's previously lively press was effectively brought under state-control within a few years of the coup. Prior to the military takeover, Burma had had more than 30 newspapers. Apart from the leading ones in Burmese and English, there were also five in Chinese, two in Hindi and one each in Urdu, Tamil, Telugu and Gujarati. The prestigious *Nation* had been closed already in May 1963 and Law Yone was arrested shortly afterwards for "hindering the implementation of internal peace". In September, the government set up the *Loktha Pyithu Nezin* to compete with the still existing private newspapers. An English-language version, the *Working People's Daily*, soon followed. At the same time, Thein Pe Myint's *Vanguard* was nationalised along with the *Guardian*, but the latter was already being secretly financed by the military.

The vitality of Burma's press was further undermined at the beginning of 1964, after the Law to Protect National Solidarity had been promulgated on 28th March, according to which all political parties, except the BSPP, were banned and all their property and assets confiscated. Five months later, the editor and owner of the mass-circulation *Kyemon* (Daily Mirror) was arrested for publishing an article considered seditious. The newspaper was nationalised on 1st September, followed by the *Botataung* on 11th September. Eventually, in December 1966, it was announced that private newspapers were to be banned altogether, and with immediate effect the government discontinued annual re-registration of all Chinese and Indian-language newspapers. Printing, the government said, must henceforth be done only in Burmese or in English.

The government did not stop there. A major irritant for the military had been the presence of foreign correspondents in Rangoon. The correspondent of *Reuters* was the first to be expelled after the coup — followed by the local representative for the *Associated Press*. Visits by foreign journalists were banned, although some managed to get in by posing as tourists and by giving a different profession on their visa application form.The foreign news agencies were forced to appoint Burmese citizens as their correspondents — and to have these approved by the government.

Although several of the local 'foreign correspondents' in Rangoon were competent journalists, they were restricted by government regulations and often compelled to write to please the authorities. Through this unique arrangement, the military regime managed to get its own version of the news from Burma out under internationally respected bylines such as *Reuters, Associated Press, Agence-France Presse, United Press International*, and the BBC. These agencies, presumably reasoning that it was better to have somebody rather than nobody in Rangoon, astonishingly agreed to this.

In the countryside, the situation also deteriorated rapidly. A Land Nationalisation Act had been introduced in 1954 to redistribute some of the land but landlordism had remained a major problem throughout the democratic period. Ostensibly to solve this, the Revolutionary Council in 1965 abolished tenancy rents and the sole arbiter of land use first became a village land committee and later the local People's Council. Many of the old landlords lost their former influence — and the ones who had been of Southasian origin, a considerable contingent, had left the country after the demonetisation.

But under a totally unrealistic procurement system, rural poverty was not alleviated. Rather than creating a class of free peasants, the new system delivered the power over the rice into the hands of retired army officers and corrupt officials who filled the posts in the local People's Councils; about 2,000 career civil servants from the old administration were retired by the Revolutionary Council during the first years of military rule and replaced by serving or ex-military men with little or no experience of how to administer rice procurement, distribution of consumer goods and how to build a workable civil service. According to Josef Silverstein's *Burma - Military Rule and the Politics of Stagnation*, the new military government "shows no signs of developing a new and creative bureaucracy. Indeed, policy seems directed towards replacing the professional with the amateur."

The outcome was gross inefficiency and rampant corruption. The regime's failure to distribute even basic consumer goods gave the farmers no incentive to produce more. According to the new regulations, the farmers were obliged to sell most of their crops to the government at prices well below the free market rates. Sometimes, farmers even had to buy rice on the black market to fill unrealistic quotas to feed their own families. Because of the official rice policy, many farmers switched to other crops and means of gaining an income.

During the period 1961-73, paddy production did increase from about 6.7 million tons to 7.2 million tons — but the population grew by 25% during the same decade. In 1961, Burma had exported 1.7 million tons of rice. By 1971, that had fallen to 0.7 million tons. In 1961/62, income per capita in constant prices had been 345 Kyats. In 1970/71, it had risen only slightly to 379 Kyats — which should be compared with the latest pre-war figure (1938/39) of 395 Kyats.

In 1967, there were acute shortages of rice and basic foodstuffs in Rangoon. At the same time, the Chinese community in the capital had been influenced by the Cultural Revolution in China and many young Sino-Burmans began wearing red Mao-badges. This violated an official Burmese regulation and the young 'Red Guards' were ordered to take their badges off. When some of them refused, anti-Chinese riots broke out in June and July that year. Chinese homes and shops were ransacked and looted, the

Chinese embassy in Rangoon was attacked and many Sino-Burmans were killed.

Commenting on that incident, Josef Silverstein wrote: "From interviews with residents of Rangoon, held less than a year after the affair, the author learned that the shortages in the spring of 1967 were so severe that the people were near revolt; the Red Badge affair, however, deflected their rage from their own leaders to the Chinese. When tempers finally cooled toward the end of the year, the new harvest was beginning to enter the market, and shortages began to disappear, the government quietly repaired Chinese restaurants and some shops, and the communal tensions diminished."

By the end of the 1960s, even the government admitted that its economic policies were not popular with most of the people. In a rare interview with Carol Goldstein in the *Far Eastern Economic Review* of 2nd January 1969, Ba Nyein admitted that "former landowners and businessmen...monks and workers...resent nationalisation...agricultural and industrial production, per capita income, and foreign trade have declined drastically in the past three years." A former finance minister, interviewed in the same article argued that "the economy has slowed down not so much because of unintended inefficiency, but because of a very conscious non-cooperation and passive resistance campaign on the part of the people."

Ba Nyein was eventually made scapegoat for the economic failures and dismissed. Tin Pe, the other main orthodox Marxist in the Revolutionary Council was also removed in 1970, which opened the way for a more liberal economic policy. That basically meant that the authorities turned a blind eye to the flourishing black economy which ironically was dominated by the two ethnic groups that government had targeted as "foreign manipulators": the Sino-Burmese and the Indo-Burmese.

Apart from the military there was only one other set of players in the country's political drama that benefitted from the military takeover and the new economic policies. Ironically, these were the insurgents. Almost immediately after the coup, Beijing — long wary of the ambitious and sometimes unpredictable general in Rangoon — decided to lend open support to its Burmese sister party.

Already on 1st August 1962, the Beijing-based CPB exiles published a document entitled *Some Facts about Ne Win's Military Government* — the first properly printed CPB publication in years. It was in English "for information abroad" and condemned the military takeover, the 7th July massacre at Rangoon University and urged the new regime "to guarantee the legal rights of the activities of the Communist Party of Burma, other parties and mass organisations". Intriguingly, it also suggested that peace talks be held between the new government and the various rebel groups.

Peace talks were indeed called for about a year later by Ne Win's regime. From 31st July to 14th November 1963, the CPB, Thakin Soe's Red Flag communists, the Karen, Mon, Kachin and some other smaller rebel armies attended the negotiations in Rangoon with guarantees of free and safe passage to and from the parley regardless of the outcome. The colourful Thakin Soe probably attracted the most attention when he arrived, accompanied by a team of attractive young girls in khaki uniforms, and placed a picture of Stalin in front of him on the negotiating table. He attacked the revisionism of Soviet leader Khrushchev, the opportunism of Mao Zedong's China — and called for free elections. On 21st August, the Revolutionary Council announced that Thakin Soe had been excluded from further peace talks.

But for the main CPB, the peace talks provided a rare opportunity to re-establish direct contact between its expatriates in China and the poorly armed bands of its once powerful 'People's Army' who were still holding out in the Pegu Yoma and other parts of central Burma. Twenty-nine CPB veterans returned to Rangoon from Beijing, purportedly to participate in the peace talks. Among the 'Beijing Returnees', as they came to be known, were yebaw (comrade) Aung Gyi (not to be confused with Brig-Gen Aung Gyi), Thakin Bo and Bo Zeya, the most prominent of the Thirty Comrades who had joined the CPB and gone to China in the early 1950s. There was also Thakin Ba Thein Tin, the veteran of the anti-Japanese struggle in the Tavoy area in Tenasserim, who did not officially take part in the talks, but who seized the opportunity to visit the then headquarters in the Pegu Yoma — bringing with him wireless transmitters and other aid from China.

Thakin Ba Thein Tin and another of the 'Beijing Returnees' went back to China after the peace talks broke down in November, but twenty-seven of them stayed in Burma where they assumed de facto leadership of the party at home. In the later half of the 1960s, the 'Beijing Returnees', inspired by the Cultural Revolution in China and supported by its own young Red Guards staged grisly mass trials in the Pegu Yoma. Many party veterans and especially intellectuals — many of whom had joined the party after the 1962 coup - were publicly humiliated and executed. Yebaw Htay, who had led the CPB delegation to the 1963 peace talks, was branded 'Burma's Deng Xiaoping' and shot. H.N. Goshal, a senior party member of Indian origin, was denounced as 'Burma's Liu Shaoqi', and also executed, and so was Bo Yan Aung, one of the Thirty Comrades. The third of the wartime heroes who had joined the CPB, Bo Ye Htut, had already surrendered in 1963.

Meanwhile, preparations were underway in China to launch an all-out thrust into the northeastern hills of Shan State and there establish a new base area, along the Sino-Burmese frontier, which the CPB hoped to link up with the old areas in central Burma. CPB cadres began touring the border areas from the Yunnan side in the mid-1960s to survey possible infiltration routes.

Other minority groups, among the Kachins and Shans especially, were contacted with promises of arms and ammunition if they joined forces with the CPB.

It was decided that the first attack should be launched on Möng Ko—and the military commander for the operation became Naw Seng, a Kachin World War Two veteran who had joined the early KNDO uprising, tried to march north to Kachin State but retreated to China from exactly the same place in 1950 along with a few hundred followers. In 1963 from his exile in Guizhou province, he had been taken to Sichuan, the base for the about 140 exiled CPB cadres, to meet Thakin Ba Thein Tin shortly after his return from Rangoon.

The anti-Chinese riots in Rangoon in 1967 provided the catalyst for the already planned China-sponsored CPB thrust into Shan State. Early in the morning of New Year's Day, 1st January 1968, Naw Seng staged his comeback. The Möng Ko garrison was overrun in 30 minutes and its commander lay dead. The local people, to whom Naw Seng was somewhat of a national hero, cheered his return. But when he had retreated into China 18 years before, he had been a Kachin nationalist; now, he was guided by leading CPB cadres who served as 'political commissars' in the 300-strong force that captured Möng Ko. A new era of Burmese insurgency had been ushered in.

During the decade that followed, the CPB received massive Chinese support. Everything from anti-aircraft guns and recoilless rifles to sewing needles and cooking oil came across the border from China. Even Chinese army personnel and individual volunteers — mostly young Red Guards from China — came to fight alongside the CPB. Radio Beijing denounced Ne Win as a 'fascist' — and he had already a few years before shown his displeasure by closing down the Chinese consulates in Mandalay and Lashio.

Within a few years, the communists had wrested control over a 20,000 square kilometre large area along the Chinese border, stretching from Panghsai (or Kyuhkok) where the Burma Road crossed into Wanting in China, down to the Mekong river and the border with Laos. The fighting in the northeast became so heavy that the Burmese Army realised that it could not defeat the CPB in Shan State. Instead, the military turned its attention to the considerably weaker CPB areas in central Burma, to prevent a link-up between the two forces. The CPB's official chairman, Thakin Than Tun, had been assassinated in the Pegu Yoma by a government infiltrator on 24th September 1968 and been succeeded by Thakin Zin. Bo Zeya, who had become the CPB's military commander after his return from China in 1963, had been killed in action in April 1968. The old Red Flag faction had almost vanished after its maverick leader, Thakin Soe, had been captured in November 1970 at his last stronghold, a tiny camp on the northern fringes of the Arakan Yoma mountain range. He was escorted to Rangoon and jailed.

Communists as well as Karen insurgents were forced to evacuate the Irrawaddy delta in 1970-71 and the Pinlebu area north of Mandalay was cleared of CPB influence by 1971-72. In early 1975, a major operation was launched against the Pegu Yoma, still officially the CPB's headquarters. The Burmese Army's crack 77th LID — which had been set up in 1964 as the first in a new series of special units set up to combat the insurgents — smashed the CPB's old bases in the Yoma and even managed to kill Thakin Zin and his secretary, Thakin Chit, on 15th March. The morale of the Burmese Army was boosted; the CPB had been isolated in the northeast. The new Chinese weapons only reached one old base area, which was located around Kyawkku in western Shan State, still outside Burma proper. But 'the new CPB' with more than 15,000 troops at that time was nevertheless ten times as strong as 'the old Party' — and much better equipped.

The Karen insurgents received no outside support, but benefitted in their own way from the new order in Rangoon. Following the collapse of Burma's own production of consumer goods and strangled imports in the wake of the introduction of 'the Burmese Way to Socialism' after the coup, enterprising black marketeers and smugglers soon made up for the short-comings. Most of the goods were brought in from Thailand — and the Karen units along the Thai border, led by a local hill-tribe commander in the eastern Dawna Range called Bo Mya, set up a series of 'toll gates' through which the contraband was funnelled. The first was Palu south of the Thai border town of Mae Sot in 1964. This was followed about a year later by Wangkha north of Mae Sot.

Links were established with Thai merchants and military authorities, whose interests often were intertwined. After a few years, at Wangkha alone, the sum of 100,000 Thai Baht was being collected by the Karen rebels per day in taxes — at the rate of 5-10% of incoming and outgoing merchandise. In other words, between 1-2 million Baht was in circulation every day only at Wangkha. Along the entire 2,100 kilometre Thai-Burmese border, dozens of similar gates were set up, by the Karen, the Mon, the Karenni and the Shan rebels. Consumer-goods, textiles, machinery, spare parts for vehicles and medicine went from Thailand to Burma and teak, minerals, jade, precious stones and opium in the opposite direction.

The total value of these unofficial transactions has never been thoroughly researched, but it is fair to assume that Thailand owes much of its rapid economic growth and development to the thriving cross-border trade with Burma. The Burmese government had to turn a blind eye to these smuggling activities along the border, given the choice of contraband or no goods at all, which would result in political and social unrest.

For the Karen rebels under Bo Mya, it meant that they could use the tax they collected on the trade to buy new US-made arms and ammunition and other supplies on what usually is euphemistically referred to as "the Thai black market." The rag-tag Karen guerrillas started to look almost like a regular army with smart uniforms, steel helmets and officers' insignia. But despite their increased financial strength and the new weaponry, the Karens also suffered the same fate as the CPB. The Burmese Army pushed the KNU out of its old base areas in the Irrawaddy Delta and the Pegu Yoma in the late 1960s and early 1970s.

The survivors — many of whom belonged to the educated class of Karens from the Delta — fled to Bo Mya's area along the Thai border, and more or less surrendered to him on his terms. Mahn Ba Zan, a Karen veteran, remained the official chairman of the KNU until 1976 when Bo Mya took over full control of the Karen movement. The KNU's area along the Thai border was considerably smaller than the CPB's territory, though, measuring about 5,000 - 6,000 square kilometers and forming a 400 kms long, narrow border strip from the areas opposite Mae Sariang in Thailand to the north and the Mawdaung Pass near Prachuap Khiri Khan in the south.

In Shan State, the CPB competed with ethnic Shan guerrillas from the Shan State Army (SSA) which was set up in 1964 by Nang Hearn Kham, the widow of Burma's first president, Sao Shwe Thaike, who had "expired in jail" a few months after his arrest in 1962. The SSA expanded its influence over the areas west of the Salween river and from a modest beginning of a few hundred disgruntled Shan students who went underground in 1958, the Shan insurgency had gained considerable momentum after the coup and soon counted several thousand guerrillas. Most of the state, apart from major roads and towns, soon were under the control of either the CPB or the SSA. In the northern Kachin State, the KIA also expanded rapidly after 1962. By the end of the 1960s, it controlled approximately 70% of Kachin State and also fielded several thousand armed jungle fighters.

The escalated civil war in the frontier areas had an immediate impact on the opium production, and the trade which the Kuomintang had initiated in the 1950s. Because of the fighting, many farmers who previously had been growing paddy in the valleys took to the hills where the opium poppy was the only viable crop they could grow — and the demand for the drug was increasing steadily.

Sai Tzang reflected on the situation twenty years later in an article published in the September 1982 issue of Chiang Mai University's *Political Science Review*: "The fast rolling opium bandwagon was further oiled by the introduction of the Burmese Way to Socialism following Gen. Ne Win's coup in 1962...all businesses and banks...were nationalised...in such an economic vacuum there arose a black market economy which for opium traffickers was a boon...opium was bought by them at very low price from ragged cultivators, transported in armed caravans to the border and refined into heroin. And on the return trip to get more opium, Thai goods and commodities were taken up and sold in Shan State...rather than creating socialism, the Burmese Way to Socialism delivered the economy into the hands of the opium traffickers. As such, opium became the only viable crop and medium of exchange. Thus, cultivation of opium, limited to east of the Salween prior to 1963, not only spread all over Shan State, but to Kachin, Karenni and Chin states as well."

Rangoon soon became incapable of overcoming the innumerable rebel armies, especially in Shan State. In order to fight the insurgents, Ne Win had in 1963 authorised the setting up of the *Ka Kwe Ye* (KKY) home guards, a local militia which was given the right to use all government controlled roads and towns in Shan State for opium smuggling in exchange for fighting the rebels. By trading in opium, Ne Win hoped the KKY militia would be self-supporting — there was hardly any money in the central coffer in Rangoon to support a sustained counter-insurgency campaign at this stage — and many local commanders actually became rich on the deal. The most famous were Lo I Ising-han, the chief of Kokang KKY, and Chang Chifu alias Khun Sa, who headed Loi Maw KKY. Lo Hsing-han fought alongside the Burmese Army against the CPB and established a close relationship with the Lashio-based Northeastern Commander in the early 1970s, Col. Aye Ko, who was later to become a prominent BSPP leader.

However, the entire KKY programme became a political failure from the government's point of view. Instead of fighting the insurgents, the KKY commanders had to negotiate tax agreements with them — since they controlled the countryside - in order to conduct the opium convoys down to the Thai border. In 1973, the KKY were disbanded. Lo went underground and briefly teamed up with the SSA, until he was arrested in Thailand in August and deported to Burma where he was sentenced to death, not for opium trafficking, but for "insurrection against the state."

Khun Sa had been jailed in 1969, but was released in 1974 after his followers had kidnapped two Soviet doctors at the hospital in Taunggyi. He returned to the Thai border where he built up a new working-relationship with both the Thai and the Burmese military authorities. After severe international pressure, the Thais launched a couple of spectacular attacks on Khun Sa's forces in 1982. But the absence of any significant fighting between Khun Sa and the Burmese Army has lent credence to the suggestion that the idea behind the KKY programme has not been abandoned, just reshaped. Khun Sa's forces on a number of occasions have attacked the ethnic rebel armies, and the CPB, in Shan State.

Central Burma was virtually cleared of insurgents by 1975, but dissent had simmered among the urban population ever since the 1962 demolition of the Students' Union building in Rangoon. Even Ba Swe and Kyaw Nyein, who had been considered close to the military, were arrested some time after the coup, which basically showed that any relationship the military previously had had with political parties had been mere marriages of convenience.

U Nu, Ba Swe and several of the other old politicians were eventually released in October 1966. Two years later, Ne Win began consultations with 38 politicians of Burma's democratic period who were officially constituted as the Interim Unity Advisory Board (IUAB), chaired by Mahn Win Maung, a former president of Burma and a Karen national. In June 1969, the IUAB submitted a report in which it proposed that the military regime be transformed into a national government including army officers, civilians, former politicians and representatives from the national minorities. It also recommended peace talks with the rebels and decentralisation of the economy. Twenty-two IUAB members, including U Nu, favoured a return to the old multi-party system, while eleven supported the socialist, one-party system. On the following day, Ne Win rejected the proposals arguing that the "time was not yet ripe" for such a change. He added, curiously, that the proposals were irrelevant since his Revolutionary Council "had no intention of retaining power indefinitely".

Disappointed over the outcome of the six-month experiment with the IUAB, U Nu left Burma the same year, ostensibly on a pilgrimage to Buddhist shrines in India. After spending a month in Bombay, however, he continued to London where he announced his intention to organise armed resistance against Ne Win's regime. In a speech at the time, the deeply religious U Nu declared: "It's a sin to kill, to be violent. But it is a greater sin to look on with folded arms when I see my countrymen suffering under tyranny. So in my case, I choose the lesser evil." After visiting the US, Japan, Hongkong and Cambodia to drum up support for his movement, U Nu was finally granted political asylum in Thailand on 29th October. From his secret headquarters in the seedy Sukhumvit Soi 22 in central Bangkok, U Nu began building up his Parliamentary Democracy Party (PDP) whose armed wing, the Patriotic Liberation Army (PLA) established a string of bases along the Thai-Burmese border.

On 25th May 1970, the PDP signed an agreement with Karen and Mon rebels and vowed to jointly overthrow Ne Win's regime. The PLA's strength at the time was estimated at 1,200, which quickly rose to about 3,000 by August 1971. Funds to buy arms and ammunition were provided by the Toronto-based Canadian oil company Asmara and beneficiaries in the Middle East, mostly old friends of U Nu's who sympathised with his cause. Asmara contributed US$10 million in exchange for sole rights to oil exploration in Burma after the expected victory.

A number of prominent Burmese leaders left Rangoon to join U Nu's Thai-border based resistance. The commander of the PLA was Bo Let Ya, the one of the Thirty Comrades who had been the closest to Aung San. Two other of the Thirty Comrades, Bo Yan Naing and Bohmu Aung, also joined in and so did Tommy Clift, an Anglo-Shan former Air Force commander who had been included in the initial Revolutionary Council after the 1962 coup; Law Yone, the former editor of the *Nation* who had been freed in 1968 and then gone abroad; and Brig.-Gen. Kya Doe, the Karen chief of operations who had been dismissed in 1949. U Win, a former Burmese ambassador to the US also left Rangoon secretly but died in the jungle on the way to the Thai border. His son, Tin Maung Win, made it, however and became one of the youth leaders of the PDP.

Frictions soon arose, however, between the anti-government Burman opposition and the ethnic insurgents. The most important bone of contention was the right of secession from the union, which had been afforded Shan and Kayah States under the 1947 constitution; now, even the Karens and the Mons demanded the same right "after victory". U Nu refused to accept that demand, arguing that constitutional safeguards for the ethnic minorities, not the right to break away from the union, was the best way of protecting their interests.

No agreement could be reached and, at last, in March 1973, U Nu handed over the chairmanship of the PDP to Bo Let Ya and left Thailand in July. After spending eight months in the US, U Nu settled with his family in Bhopal, India, where he devoted most of his time to meditating, studying Buddhist scriptures and writing his autobiography *Saturday's Son*. Bo Let Ya renamed the rebel movement the People's Patriotic Party (PPP) and continued the seemingly hopeless struggle from sanctuaries along the Thai border.

In Rangoon, however, the anti-government movement gained renewed momentum in 1974. On 13th May, the oil workers in Chauk went on strike demanding higher wages. The unrest spread from the oil fields, the origin of the historic anti-British movement of the 1930s, to Rangoon. The workers at a railway workshop in the northern suburb of Insein went on strike on 6th June over food shortages, rising prices and bad labour conditions. Soon, workers at the Thamaing Spinning Mill and the Sinmalaik Dockyard joined the strike and began pressing political demands as well.

Ne Win responded as he had done before when the students had demonstrated in 1962: he sent in troops who fired indiscriminately on the workers. Officially, 28 were killed and 80 wounded. Independent sources put to the death toll at about 100. Hundreds were arrested — and universities as well as colleges were closed since the students had demonstrated their support for the striking workers. The government blamed the unrest on "unscrupulous elements from the outside who had created disturbances"; no attempt was made to understand the deeper causes of resentment with the military authorities.

The superficial calm, sustained by the army's firepower, lasted until December. U Thant, the general secretary of the United Nations, had died in New York on 25th November. He was internationally perhaps the best-known and most respected Burmese citizen. Because of the long-standing animosity between the brilliant statesman and intellectual, U Thant, and the general who ruled at home, the Burmese government sent no official delegation to receive the coffin. When U Thant's body was flown back to Rangoon, the authorities planned to bury it in an obscure cemetery on the outskirts of the capital. The students, almost inevitably, seized the opportunity to launch large-scale anti-government demonstrations.

As the funeral procession moved towards the proposed burial site, the students snatched the coffin and carried it away to the university campus. Buddhist monks joined in and gave U Thant the rites for someone who had achieved distinction — and the students then buried him on the old site of the RUSU building, which the army had blown up in 1962. The students and the monks shouted "Down with the fascist government!" and "Down with the one-party dictatorship!".

An infuriated Ne Win sent out his troops again. The campus was occupied, the coffin with U Thant's remains recovered — and reburied near the Shwe Dagon. The violence and subsequent arrests of hundreds of students and monks provoked demonstrations all over Rangoon. The marchers, many of whom were very young, were cheered and applauded by ordinary townspeople as they chanted anti-government slogans. The government responded by declaring martial law on 11th December. When the students defied the ban, the troops opened fire. The official casualty toll was ludicrously low: 9 killed, 74 wounded and 1,800 arrested. Students who participated in the demonstration claim that 300-400 of their comrades were gunned down that day in Rangoon. Schools and universities were closed down once again and martial law was declared in Rangoon on 11th December.

After the December 1974 demonstrations, hundreds of young people took to the hills where they joined Bo Let Ya's PPP. But in Rangoon, the movement continued in the underground. In June 1975, on the first anniversary of the labour strike, students and workers decided to rise against the military regime. Kyaw Gyi, now 33, was one of them:

— Secret contacts had been established between us students and the workers. We had decided to march on 11th June and many of us gathered at the Shwe Dagon on the night before. We camped at the pagoda — but were awoken at 5 am the following morning when troops and policemen stormed in; 213 of us were arrested; half of them were under 20, some as young as 13. We were trucked away to Insein Jail where we were interrogated for about two months. I stayed there for four years before I was released.

Torture was a nearly everyday occurrence during his imprisonment. Kyaw Gyi says that he was forced to kneel on sharp pebbles while he was constantly hit and beaten. An almost perverted form of torture commonly employed was known as 'the motorcycle':

—A military intelligence officer would order me to "get on the motorcycle". When I said I couldn't see one, he'd beat me, point at an empty space on the concrete floor and shout: "There it is, don't you see?!" Then I had to stand at a half-crouch and pretend that I was riding a motorcycle, making all the engine noises and all that. Intermittently, the officer would rap me with his bamboo staff and shout comments such as: "You didn't stop at the red lights! What's the matter with you? You don't obey the laws!" It went on like that until I thought I was going mad.

A similar form of torture was called 'the helicopter' and was basically aimed at making the victim dizzy by forcing him to spin around with outspread arms. Whenever he lost his balance, he was beaten and then ordered to recommence spinning. More brutal forms of torture included electric shocks and forcing the prisoners to drink their own urine.

As soon as these young people were released, many of them took to the jungle where they joined the insurgents. The ones who remained behind in Rangoon began preparing themselves for the next round of anti-government activity, which was scheduled to coincide with the 100th anniversary of the birth of national hero Thakin Kodaw I Imaing. Tun Myat participated in that movement:

—Our intention was to launch a general strike on his birthday in March. But our underground movement had become so heavily infiltrated by military intelligence agents that the plans leaked out. There was only a relatively small demonstration on the campus in Rangoon; 130 of us were arrested before anything dramatic could happen. I spent two years in Insein Jail after that. We were all tortured. 'The motorcycle' was very common. A friend of mine was also stripped naked and told to climb a tree. Half-way up, a policeman poked a stick up his anus and ordered him to shout: "Release the arrested students!" and "Lower tuition fees!" — the slogans of our movement. It was all terribly humiliating.

Most political prisoners were kept at the infamous Insein Jail whereas hard-core oppositionists were usually detained at the *Yay Kyi Aing* near Mingaladon airport — where some of the young demonstrators had been taken in March 1988. The ones who were suspected of CPB sympathies were sent to Coco Island in the Andaman Sea, where a penal colony for political prisoners was maintained until the early 1970s.

The aborted 'Thakin Kodaw Hmaing movement' was the last attempt to organise student protests in Rangoon in the turbulent 1970s — and it seemed as if the government had gained the upper hand. After this, the only form of protest was that the students dressed in black on 7th July every year, to silently commemorate their colleagues who had fallen in 1962.

Many students had fled to the rebel side but frictions with the Karens had deepened rather than diminished. In November 1978, KNU forces attacked Bo Let Ya's camp opposite Prachuap Khiri Khan and he was killed. After this graceless death of the World War Two hero, the non-communist armed Burman resistance disintegrated and most of the remaining PLA soldiers either filtered back to their hometowns, or settled in Thailand.

The brutal suppression of the student movement, combined with the economic failure of the Burmese Way to Socialism, had, however, caused a rift within the top leadership and the military. Immediately after the Thakin Kodaw Hmaing demonstration in Rangoon, Ne Win surprised the nation by dismissing his chief of staff and minister of defence, general Tin U.

The officially announced reason was that Tin U's wife was corrupt. James Harriman provided a somewhat different picture in the *Far Eastern Economic Review* of 24th December 1976: "The split between the two [i.e. Ne Win and Tin U] first became apparent during the U Thant movement in December 1974 and the wildcat general strike in June the following year. Tin U refused to use troops to suppress mass demonstrations despite the orders of [Ne Win's close associate and later president of Burma] San Yu...general Tin U's restraint projected his popularity well outside the ranks of the army where he was already regarded with respect and affection." The final straw had been when Tin U openly had criticised the mismanagement of Burma's economy.

When the students had marched in March 1976, they had even shouted "Long live general Tin U!" While some of the students had taken to the Thai border when the demonstrations had failed to obtain their objectives, a few disgruntled elements within the armed forces began plotting against Ne Win. But when it became clear that the secret police was aware of the plan, the ring leader, a young captain called Ohn Kyaw Myint, on the evening of 2nd July appeared at the residence of the US ambassador in Rangoon. Ohn Kyaw Myint, surprisingly, was the personal assistant to general Tin U's successor as military chief and defence minister, general Kyaw Htin. The young man told the US officials about the abortive coup attempt and that he feared arrest, and asked for political asylum. He was turned away.

The government media made no mention of the attempted coup until the BBS on 20th July issued a bulletin stating that eleven captains and three majors had been arrested for plotting to assassinate Ne Win, San Yu and other state leaders. Also arrested were two colonels who were charged with dereliction of duty. The BBS said that the arrests of the implicated had begun on the 2nd — and that the leader was captain Ohn Kyaw Myint. Most of the 14 officers were graduates of the Defence Services Academy in Maymyo, 'Burma's West Point' which had been set up in the early 1950s to bring more professionalism into the country's tough but then ill-disciplined military machinery.

The trial began in September — and the greatest surprise was the appearance in the prisoners' dock of the dismissed general Tin U. He was charged with having prior knowledge of the plot but failing to inform the authorities. The trial was the last anti-government manifestation in the capital for many years; the testimony of one of the accused, captain Win Thein, reflected "the long smoldering discontent among the young and educated army officers whose experiences in the field had put them in touch with the grim realities of Burmese socialism," wrote James Harriman. Win Thein said that before the conspiracy came up, he had been thinking why the Burmese Way to Socialism had not been successful. The *leit motif* was bitterness over both "an economy in a shambles where prices are soaring and the only thing going down is public morale...and a corrupt party whose cadres cast lots among themselves to get motor cars at about 18,000 Kyats while the price in the market in about 150,000-200,000 Kyats."

Ohn Kyaw Myint was sentenced to death and later executed. The other officers, including general Tin U, got long prison terms. Another former Burmese army commander had already left Rangoon before the arrest of Ohn Kyaw Myint and the others had been announced: the hero of the anti-KMT campaign of the mid 1950s, ex-brigadier general Kyaw Zaw. On 18th July, he travelled with some family members across the Chinese border near Namkham.

About a month later, his voice was heard on the CPB's clandestine radio station, denouncing the Ne Win regime. The timing of Kyaw Zaw's disappearance was hardly a coincidence although no evidence was ever produced to link him — or his one-time lieutenant Tin U — to the plot; some of the arrested officers had, however, mentioned Kyaw Zaw and Tin U as their preferences for state leaders, if the coup had been successful. But why did Kyaw Zaw defect to the CPB? This became one of the many mysteries of Burma's shadowy political scene in the 1970s.

The abortive coup attempt, and the subsequent trial, prompted a major purge within the state apparatus as well as the armed forces. About 200 Tin U supporters were questioned, and in November Ne Win announced publicly that more than 50,000 BSPP members and cadres had been dismissed. During the party congress that followed in February 1977, 42 central committee members lost their seats, and the position of Ne Win's protégé San Yu was enhanced.

In the army, officers were shifted around and many of the professionals were transferred or retired. A fairly typical example of the kind of officers who rose to prominence after the 1976/77 purges was then colonel Saw Maung, commander of the 99th LID which has its forward headquarters at Kutkai on the Burma Road where fighting with ethnic Kachin as well as CPB guerrillas is a daily occurrence. He had only basic education and had risen through the ranks, but his posting in the middle of the battle-zones of northeastern Shan State was one of the toughest in the country. In 1976, he was promoted to brigadier general and put in charge of the Southwest command which encompasses the peaceful, rice-rich area in the Irrawaddy delta where any army officer can make a fortune. Naturally, officers like Saw Maung became immensely loyal to Ne Win and his other benefactors.

A second generation of officers who once had served with the 4th Burma Rifles also rose to prominence. Aung Gyi, Tin Pe and the others were gone — now, the one-time NCOs took over: Kyaw Htin, Tin U's successor, had as his deputy Aye Ko, also formerly of Ne Win's own battalion. There were also Tun Tin, the minister of cooperatives and, of increasing importance, Sein Lwin. However, the 4th Burma Rifles tradition had now undergone change; the new leaders had once been young, faithful subordinates of their much more senior commander Ne Win — rather than comrades-in-arms such as Aung Gyi and the others.

After the purges in 1976-77, Burma's armed forces were streamlined to the extent that it became impossible to distinguish interest groups within them, let alone factions or possible rivals to Ne Win and his inner circle of close associates. "The ones who stayed and did well had to prove their loyalty," according to Josef Silverstein. Any thought of challenging the supreme authority became out of the question.

The strength of the armed forces had been steadily increasing since the beginning of the insurgency in 1948. According to an agreement signed in September 1945 in Kandy, Ceylon, between the wartime resistance forces and the British, the independent Burma would be entitled to maintain an army consisting of 5,200 privates, 300 officers and 200 men in reserve — plus paramilitary forces. This was basically what the country needed for maintaining security along its frontiers; Burma then as well as now had no outside enemies.

But several battalions defected to the insurgents after independence and a new army had to be raised to fight the rebels. Consequently, its strength had risen to 40,000 in 1955. By the time of the coup, the army was about 100,000 strong and in 1976 it counted almost 150,000 troops. The first LID, the 77th, was supplemented with the 44th, the 55th, the 66th, the 88th and the 99th. These units were the elite corps which enjoyed special privileges and always had their home bases along major lines of communication, not out in the countryside as the regional battalions. In 1986, after a 33rd Light Infantry Division had been raised, the total strength of Burma's armed forces increased to 186,000.

Although the constitution said that it was the duty of every citizen to "defend the country", the enlistment in the Burmese Army has always been voluntary. But with a large pool of unemployed and virtually uneducated youths tin the countryside to draw upon, there has never been any shortage of recruits.

Defence spendings have always been high in Burma, partly because of the insurgency but also prompted by the central role the armed forces have played in Burmese political and social life. In 1985/86, 1,557.4 million Kyats, or 31.4% of the budget, went to the ministry of defence. In addition, the rather obscure "ministry for home and religious affairs", to which the country's intelligence apparatus is subordinate, received 412.2 million Kyats, or 8.3%. An additional 385.5 million Kyats, or 7%, was allotted for "monthly pensions, lump sum payments and rewards", mainly to the military and ex-armymen.

By comparison, education received 854.7 million Kyats, or 17.2% and health 395.2 million Kyats or 8%. But even the 'health' post was related to the military since it included army hospitals and the maintenance of Red Cross teams which operated closely with the troops during counter-insurgency campaigns. In all, it would be fair to estimate that Burma spent at least 40-45% of its revenue, directly and indirectly, on the military.

But actual salaries were kept deliberately low. A sergeant, for instance would earn less than 200 Kyats a month, a lieutenant nearly 500 Kyats and a lieutenant-colonel only 1,000-1,500 Kyats. But even so, many army officers were incredibly rich by Burmese and even regional standards. Apart from special privileges such as rations of imported whisky and 555 cigarettes, and the right to acquire vehicles and land cheaply after serving with the army for a certain period, military officers also got ample opportunity to earn 'extras' in the areas where they were stationed.

The most lucrative postings, naturally, were the jade mines in Kachin State and the opium growing areas of Shan State. As a matter of principle, officers and troops served there on a rotation basis — never more than six months — since so many others were waiting for their sojourn in these areas. This rotation, and a system of awards and punishments, also prevented local commanders from building up their own power bases.

While discipline within army ranks became impeccable, soldiers were given a free hand when on counter-insurgency operations in the frontier areas. Rape, beatings, looting and the burning down of villages were commonplace wherever the Burmese Army operated. The London-based human rights organisation *Amnesty International* concluded in a May 1988 report about Burma that it believed there is "a pattern of extrajudicial executions and torture of unarmed minority villagers...including elderly people, women and children, by members of armed forces on counter-insurgency assignments".

However, in the towns, a world apart from these minority areas, many people remained blissfully unaware of these practices. When the military paraded in Rangoon on 27th March every year — Armed Forces Day which commemorated the BNA's declaration of war against the Japanese — thousands of people usually showed up to greet their return from "the battle-front". But by indirectly encouraging corruption and brutality within the army, every soldier became part of the system and inherited a vested interest in maintaining the *status quo*.

The army also effectively controlled the country's sole political institution, the BSPP. In 1971, it had been transformed from a cadre party to a mass organisation, of which one simply had to be a member in order to enjoy social and political mobility in Burmese society. By 1977, the BSPP had 181,617 members and 885,460 candidates, over half of whom were drawn from past or present army and police personnel. Nearly 80% of the soldiers in the armed forces were party members.

Young children were organised in the *Teza* Youth — using the *nom de guerre* of Aung San — and at the age of ten, they could join the *Hse Hsaung* (Forward) Youth, before becoming full-fledged members of the BSPP's main *Lanzin* Youth Organisation when they turned 18. Several million Burmese belonged to these organisations, which prepared them for party membership later on. Other mass organisations included the Peasants' *Asiayone* with about 7.7 million members scattered in villages throughout the countryside. The labourers had their Workers' *Asiayone* whose more than 5 million members came from both state enterprises and private factories.

The civil administration was delegated to a number of 'People's Councils' on different levels. But everywhere, the omnipotent army-cum-party apparatus held the real reins of power. While the People's Council chairmen on state and divisional levels were civilians, or retired army officers, the corresponding party committee was usually headed by the highest army officer in the equivalent command area.

The legal basis for this set-up had been provided by a new constitution providing for a one-party, socialist state. It had been drafted by Dr. Maung Maung, the only intellectual who had always been close to Ne Win and the military. A referendum on the new constitution was held in December 1973. However, the 'voting' hardly met any acceptable, democratic standards. Nang Naw Kham, who at the time of the referendum was a 5th year middle school pupil in her home town Möng Hsat, Shan State, remembers:

— There were two boxes, a white one for the yes-votes and a black for the no-votes, which in itself indicated how the people were expected to vote. The two boxes were hidden behind a screen, but placed in different corners of the polling booth. And then, there was a 15-20 cms wide gap between the ground and the screen, so the officials could easily see how the people voted. But even so, some cast their ballots in the no-box. When we school kids, who had been mobilised to count the votes, discovered this, we put the no-votes into the yes-box anyway. We didn't want anybody to get into trouble. But the main thing for us was that we got five Kyats each for our work, so we didn't really care about the actual voting".

Officially, 90.19% approved the new constitution and it was promulgated on 3rd January 1974. Despite wordings such as "socialist democracy is the basis of state structure", the *tatmadaw*, or the armed forces, controlled the BSPP and its subsidiary organisations, and the *tatmadaw*, the BSPP and the administration were under the control of Ne Win. That was, in short, the actual power structure that had emerged. It was a highly centralised military dictatorship with a paper-thin, socialist veneer.

In effect, the military, after having done away with the old social and political power structure, had established itself as the new ruling class. The elevated position of the military in Burma far exceeded that of the armed forces of the Philippines, Pakistan, Bangladesh or even Thailand and South Vietnam, just to mention a few countries in the region which have also experienced military dictatorship of one form or another.

In the international field, this new regime benefitted immensely from its self-imposed isolation. Theoretically, the military continued the neural and non-aligned policy of U Nu's democratic government — even to the extent that Burma withdrew from the non-aligned movement at its summit in Havana, Cuba, in 1979. At the time, the Burmese delegate said that the movement no longer adhered to the principles of strict non-alignment - a statement which made a deep impression especially on Western powers who often felt the same.

But Burma's new 'neutral foreign policy' basically meant no foreign policy at all; its 28 embassies and consulates abroad did very little to improve relations with the host countries. Their main duties were to look after visiting, Burmese military officers and their families on shopping sprees or on trips abroad for medical treatment - and to keep a watch on the exiled Burmese community in the country in which the embassy was located.

Back home in Burma, the official newspapers always published endless 'messages of felicitations' to various foreign governments on the national days in their respective countries — or similar messages which had been received from abroad by the Burmese government. Since such messages are sent as a matter of routine and diplomatic courtesy, few countries in the world even bother mentioning them. But in Burma, the regime placed these messages on the front pages of the newspapers to show the public that it enjoyed 'friendly relations' with everybody and was a member of the world community.

In reality, the only relations Ne Win really enjoyed with the outside world were very personal contacts with a few selected foreigners, mostly private businessmen who had won the old strongman's confidence and trust. Contacts with foreign governments were kept to an absolute minimum. One Rangoon-based foreign envoy commented in 1988 on this diplomatic vacuum: "We had no meaningful contact with any element of the Burmese government. They had a designated group of foreign ministry types who would come to our dinners and talk about golf and tennis, the weather and what fruits were in season...during my first three months in Burma, by backhand improved immensely, and I even took up the game of golf, which I had thought was just a waste of time. But I had time to waste".

Burma was considered a sleepy backwater where nothing was expected to happen. The regime seemed well-entrenched, the people docile and the control mechanisms so absolute that a popular uprising appeared out of the question.

The man at the apex of this monolithic pyramid remained throughout his reign one of the most mysterious and reclusive personalities in modern Asian history. Although he was an absolute ruler of his country, he never created a personality cult around himself like Mao Zedong, Chiang Kai-shek or Kim Il-Sung. Unlike Indonesia's Sukarno and Prince Sihanouk of Cambodia, he shunned public gatherings and appeared for the outside world only twice a year, when he shook hands with foreign diplomats at the the 4th January Independence Day and the 27th March Armed Forces' Day celebrations in Rangoon. He never even tried to develop his country like Singapore's Lee Kuan Yew.

An *Associated Press* profile of Ne Win, dated 16th August 1972, was appropriately headlined: "Ex-playboy steered Burma to socialism — now lives like hermit." The article went on: "By all yardsticks of Southeast Asian politics, Ne Win should have been right-wing, conservative and anti-Communist like the military juntas that rule Thailand, Cambodia, South Vietnam and Indonesia. Before taking power he was widely known as a playboy, fond of girls and gambling...few people know Ne Win. Diplomats rarely see him."

Ne Win gradually established at his luxurious Ady Road residence on a peninsula in Inya Lake in Rangoon's northern suburbs an almost absurd, anachronistic replica of the old Burmese monarchy. In many ways it also resembled a Byzantine-style court with intrigues, deep distrust, nepotism and a mixture of bizarre characters and bright young officers. Significantly, one of the few men Ne Win really trusted was his old Indian cook Raju, who had served him since his 4th Burma Rifles days. Ne Win, fearful of being poisoned, entrusted only Raju with the task of preparing his food. But even

Raju had to taste it first, in Ne Win's presence.

Raju always accompanied Ne Win on his many trips abroad and his closeness to the general gave him unique opportunities to make a fortune. Whenever somebody wanted to buy land, build a house or needed a quick government decision on some urgent matter, a few banknotes in Raju's hands could open any doors. While tasting the day's meal in front of the general, Raju would casually remark on what he had been paid to say. A nod of approval from the general would mean that a deal had been struck. In this extraordinary way, the cook Raju became one of the most influential power-mongers in the country.

Despite shunning the public eye, Ne Win married seven times, twice to the same woman. His third wife, a socialite called Khin May Than — who was also known as Kitty Ba Than — was the women he admired the most. She raised their two daughters, Sanda and Kyemon, and a son, Pyo Wai Win, in the classic Burmese tradition. The daughters were taught to be polite and modest, like little princesses in the old Burmese court of the days of the kings. Sanda was the eldest and old schoolmates remember her as "sweet, unassuming and she never tried to take advantage of the fact that her father was the country's undisputed ruler".

But something must have happened when Khin May Than died in 1974. The state of Ne Win's mental health had always been a matter for speculation; in the early 1960s he regularly went to Vienna to receive treatment for an undisclosed mental disorder by one of Austria's most outstanding psychiatrists, Dr Hans Hoff. After Khin May Than's death, Ne Win never bothered going to Vienna again and he became a recluse whose only recreation was a round of golf, or yearly trips to an exclusive Swiss health resort, the *Clinique Lémana-Rustica* on Lake Geneva.

Ne Win's frequent visits to Switzerland had also other purposes. On one such trip, in June 1984, the *Far Eastern Economic Review's* 18th October issue quoted diplomatic sources as saying that his privately chartered jet "was delayed because chests of jade and precious stones carried on board...had been stacked incorrectly and had to be reloaded". Ne Win never made any distinction between private and state property; what belonged to Burma belonged to him. His personal fortune, according to most Burmese, rivalled that of Ferdinand Marcos in the Philippines. He owns property in London, West Germany and in Tokyo's most expensive business district, Ginza.

His next wife after Khin May Than was Ni Ni Myint, an academic who he divorced after less than a year. He then married Yadana Natmai, or June Rose Bellamy, a descendant of the last Burmese royal family. That marriage was seen as an attempt by Ne Win to forge a visible link with the old royalty; although he himself was a Sino-Burman from Paungdale near Prome he was personally convinced that the old Konbaung dynasty of Burmese kings were among his ancestors. Sometimes, he would even appear at state functions in full classical regalia, much to the embarrassment of some of his more astute ministers. He clearly viewed himself as an absolute monarch rather than a military usurper who had overthrown an elected government.

One of his obsessions was also a deep firm belief in astrology and numerology. Even the BSPP, although ostensibly a socialist party, had its own astrologer who was consulted before any important decisions were made. Already when he was young, he had taken up the study of *yedaya chay*, or a traditional Burmese exercise of attempting to control one's fate through the use of charms and combinations of lucky numbers. According to this notion, it was also possible to cheat one's fate by performing an act slightly related to the one that had to be neutralised. When Burma was threatened by a rightist uprising in the mid-1970s, Burma suddenly shifted driving from the left hand side of the road to the right — and the political threat was thus neutralised. When Burma was threatened by poverty, all government ministers had to eat *mohingka*, the cheapest Burmese market food, in order to thwart this menace.

Ne Win's marriage to Yadana Natmai lasted less than a year also — after which he remarried Ni Ni Myint. But by now, the most important woman in Ne Win's life was not his wife, but his favourite daughter Sanda who in many ways became a substitute for Khin May Than. He spoilt her with expensive presents, opened Swiss bank accounts for her and took her along when he travelled abroad. Her husband, Aye Zaw Win, had been a seaman when they got married. But soon after their wedding, he was appointed head of the government agency controlling the trade in pearls. Burma has some of the world's finest pearls, collected from oyster beds in the Andaman Sea, and the post is considered one of the most lucrative within the Burmese administration.

Significantly, North Korea was the first foreign country that acknowledged Sanda's increasing importance. During a state visit to Pyongyang in the late 1970s, the North Korean hosts referred to Sanda as 'the First Lady'. A flattered Ne Win developed warm relations with Pyongyang; North Korea presented bulldozers and tractors to Burma and a Burmese trade delegation visited Pyongyang in August 1978. In September of the same year, Burma's foreign minister was even sent to attend North Korea's 30th founding anniversary in Pyongyang.

The West did not realise Sanda's importance to her father until 1979 when she failed her English-test for admission to a British medical school — and Ne Win subsequently re-established English teaching in the school curriculum in Burma. Sanda's Burmese English teacher in Rangoon was blamed for her failure and fired; instead, native Englishmen were once again invited to teach at major universities in Burma.

In order to preserve this 'madhouse dynasty' — as many Burmese derisively called the ruling family behind their backs — Ne Win built up one of Asia's most efficient secret police forces, the Military Intelligence Service (MIS), which was known throughout Burma down to the lowliest non-

English speaking farmer as 'MI' (em-eye). Even if executions of political opponents was the exception rather than the rule, anyone suspected of having contacts with the opposition was likely to be arrested and possibly also tortured while in jail. The MIS kept a watchful eye especially on army officers with liberal ideas — which apart from rotations, corruption and brutality also greatly contributed to the cohesiveness of Burma's armed forces — and on the many politicised Burmese exiles living in Britain, West Germany, Thailand and the USA. Among the Burmese community abroad, no one was ever sure who was an informer or not; mutual suspicion neutralised them as a political force.

Ne Win's intelligence chief for many years was his devoted subordinate Brig-Gen Tin U — no relation to the jailed ex-defence minster with the same name. This Tin U had been trained by the US Central Intelligence Agency on the Pacific island of Saipan in the 1950s. By 1961, he had already became Ne Win's aide-de-camp and was almost regarded as the general's adopted son. Rodney Tasker characterised Tin U in the *Far Eastern Economic Review* of 7th July 1983: "He and his MIS colleagues were men of the world compared with other more short-sighted, dogmatic figures in the Burmese leadership. They were able to travel abroad, talk freely to foreigners and generally look beyond the rigid confines of the current regime...although known to be ruthless, he built up a reputation as a gregarious, open-minded, charismatic figure — a direct contrast to some of his mole-like colleagues in the leadership".

The bright Tin U, or 'MIS Tin U' as he was popularly known to distinguish him from 'General Tin U', was considered Ne Win's heir apparent and was looked upon as a successor who would possibly liberalise the Burmese system after Ne Win's departure. Among other achievements, he had written a series of books about the CPB, which remained some of the best sources on the communist movement in Burma. They were entitled *The Last Days of Thakin Than Tun* and *The Last Days of Thakin Zin and Thakin Chit* and became widely read throughout the country.

Ne Win managed to combine what appeared to be extreme idiosyncrasies with shrewd Machiavellian skills. Among other things, he also maintained his own intelligence files on close subordinates, which included information about their personal lives and weaknesses. Columnist Cho Lay in the Bangkok *Nation*, commented on 5th October 1988: "When Gen. Ne Win summons one of his top brass to a meeting, the official arrives well before the appointed hour, dressed in a spick and span uniform with his boots spit-polished. The officer arrives at least two hours before the meeting is to take place and spends his time nervously scanning through papers with anxiety written all over his face and sweat pouring down his neck. Never knowing what to expect, he marches into the general's office as the clock strikes the hour, and stands to attention to his boss... The outcome of the meeting is known by the tone of voice and the language Ne Win uses when he addresses the man on the carpet. When Ne Win lets go with foul and filthy language, the soldier before him knows he has survived the day and he continues to be in the good books of the general. But if the general begins with wishing one a good morning and enquiring after one's health...then another soldier bites the dust in Burma".

Ne Win's reputation as a ruthless despot was somewhat softened in 1980 when he unexpectedly called for a general amnesty for the country's insurgents. Peace talks were also held with Burma's two strongest rebel groups, the CPB and the Kachin rebels in the KIA. The light at the end of the tunnel of decades of civil war was, however, dimmed when the government demanded absolute surrender and offered no concessions. The negotiations with the CPB and the KIA broke down and almost no communist or ethnic insurgents accepted the amnesty offer. About the only one was Kyaw Zan Rhee, the leader of the flagging Arakan Communist Party, a local rebel group in Arakan State.

Officially, 2,189 'rebels' surrendered during the amnesty — but the vast majority of them were ex-PPP/PLA men from Thailand. Almost the entire ethnic Burman resistance returned home in 1980: Bo Yan Naing, Bohmu Aung and Kya Doe, the Karen who had joined U Nu, and all their followers. The former prime minister himself came back from his exile in India on 29th July. Some important prisoners were also released, for instance the opium warlord Lo Hsing-han, ex-general Tin U, the Red Flag leader Thakin Soe. Old army officers who had fallen from grace — Aung Gyi, Tin Pe and others — were rehabilitated and allowed to set up their own businesses in Rangoon.

Simultaneously, the government assembled 1,266 monks in Rangoon for a 'First Congregation for the Purification, Perpetuation and Propagation of Buddhism'. The emphasis, however, lay on the first element; the Buddhist *sangha*, or order of monks had always been one of Ne Win's main worries, next to the students. The 100,000-strong *sangha* was issued with government registration cards and henceforth a monk ordered to disrobe by religious authorities was liable to punishment by the civil 'people's courts' rather than ecclesiastical courts. A *State Sangha Maha Nayaka Committee* was formed along BSPP-lines to keep an eye on the monks and make sure that the country's thousands of monasteries did not become havens for political activists, as they had been so many times before in Burmese history.

Ne Win was clearly putting his house in order and preparing for his succession; one of his main obsessions had always been his place in history. He wanted to make a graceful exit from the scene and be seen as a benefactor to the nation.

On 8th August 1981, during the 4th BSPP congress, came the bombshell. Ne Win announced that he would step down from the presidency when his term expired in November. In the streets of Rangoon, there was a momentary, baffled pause in the pace of life. Hitherto unthinkable, change was now a prospect. But change, every Burmese knew, would come slowly as long as Ne Win was alive — and the old general declared that he would remain BSPP chairman. MIS Tin U was appointed joint general secretary of the BSPP to ensure a smooth transfer. Other loyal followers who retained high party posts included Aye Ko, now general secretary, and Gen. Kyaw Htin, the chief of staff.

In November, the colourless San Yu was appointed the new president. In his farewell speech, Ne Win sternly warned anyone who might have thought that he had stepped down from power: "Though I will not be in the *Pyithu Hluttaw* (parliament) or the state council, I shall be watching from the party and when I give advice as needed, do things with discretion. I shall continue to do things, but all those who would be directly concerned with the practical aspects of work should exercise utmost caution". Ne Win remained 'Number One', and that was what really mattered.

Burma calmed down again after a brief period of excitement. Nothing was really going to change, after all. But then, the next bombshell exploded. On 17th May 1983, the state council suddenly, and totally unexpectedly, announced that MIS Tin U had been "permitted to resign" along with the home and religious affairs minister and also a former intelligence chief, Col. Bo Ni. They had been purged ostensibly because their wives were corrupt — a charge that could be brought against any army officer in Burma.

The order, *Reuters* reported on 23rd May, "was given personally by Ne Win". The reason behind the move, however, remained a matter for conjecture. Tin U and Bo Ni were subsequently jailed — and the entire MIS apparatus purged as well. It was suggested at the time that the urbane MIS people had become too powerful for comfort and almost managed to establish a state within the state — which threatened Ne Win's inner circle of hand-picked, less-than-intelligent yes-men. Another explanation, ludicrous in an international context but quite plausible in Ne Win's Burma, was that Sanda Win was opposed to the idea that anyone should stand between herself and her father. The existence of a 'Number One and Half', as MIS Tin U had widely become known, was unacceptable.

The purge of the MIS had immediate effects on the security situation in the country. On 9th October a real bomb rocked Rangoon — and killed 21 people, including four visiting South Korean cabinet ministers. Two North Korean military officers, Maj. Chin Mo and Capt. Kang Min Chol were arrested for the bombing and a third, Capt. Sin Ki Chol, was killed by Burmese security forces during a series of incidents in which his two companions were seriously wounded. Kang lost a hand and killed three policemen when he detonated a grenade at the time of his capture — but signed a confession afterwards and cooperated with his investigators. Ne Win, who had always rated North Korea's friendship highly was infuriated and branded it a treachery. He expelled all North Koreans from Burma and broke off diplomatic relations.

However, observers at the time believed that the incident would never have taken place if MIS Tin U had still been in charge; it clearly indicated that the intelligence apparatus was no longer what it had used to be. A new intelligence chief, Col. Khin Nyunt, was appointed in 1984. His Directorate of the Defence Services Intelligence (DDSI), soon became almost as efficient as the old outfit. Khin Nyunt in many ways also resembled Tin U; he was fairly young, relatively bright and he could be exceedingly ruthless when ever this was considered expedient by the old strongman.

In order to prepare for his departure, 'Number One' became even more of a recluse than he had ever been, preoccupied with astrology and other metaphysical exercises. In 1984, he initiated the most extravagant construction project since he had seized power in 1962: he wanted his own pagoda, where he could be laid to rest. The formal name of the structure was the Maha Vizeya Pagoda, or the Pagoda of Great Victory — and it was being built next to the historic Shwe Dagon. *Time* magazine commented on 8th February 1988: "In ancient times, a Burmese king would try to build as many pagodas as possible during his lifetime, in order to make up for the bad deeds he might have committed during his lifetime. Whether or not he harbours similar notions, Ne Win...is obviously in a hurry".

Although the Burmese newspapers were filled with long lists of names of people who supposedly had contributed to the project, the construction of the pagoda progressed so slowly that the workers had to place the golden pinnacle, known as the umbrella, on top of its spire long before the building was completed. This enabled them to tell the strongman that the work was almost finished, since the umbrella is normally the last stage in the erection of a pagoda in Burma. But to the Burmese in the street, who see omens in most things, this inauspicious act confirmed the sad state of affairs in their country.

In more mundane terms, Burma's economy had reached rock bottom after 25 years of neglect and mismanagement. The country was compelled to apply for the UN-afforded status of Least Developed Country (LDC) to get some badly needed relief with its foreign debt, which had reached a staggering US\$ 3.5 billion at the same time as its foreign exchange reserves had dwindled to US\$ 20-30 million. The debt service ratio was already more than 50% of official exports, and it was rising rapidly.

In order to make up for the discrepancy and to secure rice for export, the government tried to increase production and collect more from the farmers at stipulated prices which were far below what they could get on the free market. In 1986/87, farmers in the Irrawaddy delta, Burma's granary, wore literally planting their rice at gunpoint — and in Daik-U north of Rangoon, four government officials were lynched by angry mobs. In Kyauktan southeast of the capital, enraged farmers stormed and burnt down a rice mill which belonged to the father of a member of the ruling state council.

On 21st July 1987, the retired Brig-Gen. Aung Gyi, who now ran a successful chain of tea and pastry shops in Rangoon, wrote an open letter to Ne Win. Aung Gyi reminded the chairman of the 1967 rice riots and warned of the possibility of spreading violence if nothing was done to resolve the situation immediately. Probably anticipating urban unrest, the Burmese Army in 1987 formed a special 22nd LID, headquartered in the Karen State capital of Pa-an, but specifically designated for central security duties in case of emergency.

Whether influenced by Aung Gyi's letter or not, Ne Win also made an unprecedented radio speech to the nation on 10th August. For the first time ever, he admitted that there might be flaws in the sacred principle of 25 years of the Burmese Way to Socialism, rather than in its implementation. He talked about failures and shortcomings in the present system, adding "we must also change with time, keep up with it, and work according to the changing times".

On 1st September, the government lifted restrictions on the trading of rice, maize, beans and pulses. The move allowed the people freely to buy, sell, process, store and transport the crops — and many were jubilant. Private traders withdrew large amounts of money from their bank accounts to begin the race to purchase the harvest. Then, in an extraordinary twist of policy, the official BBS radio only four days later announced the demonetisation of the country's three highest dominations of banknotes — 25, 35 and 75 Kyats. No reason was given.

The announcement came at a time when the final exams were approaching for the students in Rangoon. This is also when they have to pay their yearly fees — and, suddenly, they found that most of their money was valueless. At the prestigious RIT in Gyogon, there was a spontaneous outburst of violence minutes after the announcement had been made. Three hundred enraged students stormed out of the campus to Insein Road, where they smashed traffic lights and burnt government vehicles. It was all over in a few hours — but the government nevertheless was shaken. Not since 1976 had Burma's students demonstrated against the government. Its response was to close down the universities and colleges in Rangoon. The students who came from upcountry were bused back to their hometowns — where they were received as heroes by the local people who had heard the news.

After the brief September riots, the government declared that the demonetisation had been aimed at "insurgents and black marketeers", an explanation which few found satisfactory. Burma's insurgents are chiefly based in border areas and keep most of their funds in Thai or Chinese currency. The black marketeers might have suffered temporarily, but they were able to make up for the loss after a few more trade deals. The ones who suffered the most were the ordinary people, who lost their savings. In one sweep, 60-80% of Burma's money in circulation had become worthless.

The existence of odd 35 and 75 Kyat banknotes was one outcome of the superstition, which Ne Win had permitted to overshadow rational government planning; they had been introduced in 1985 and 1986 to replace the old 100 Kyat note. But more was to come. That month two new denominations were issued: 45 and 90 Kyats. The rationale behind the move was that both numbers added up to 9: 4+5=9 and 9+0=9. Ne Win's lucky number was 9, according to his chief astrologer.

Hardly surprisingly, discontent was brewing throughout Burma towards the end of 1987. The application for LDC status was perceived as a national insult and a final confirmation of the total failure of 26 years of Burmese Way to Socialism. Burma was a potentially rich country, not a basket-case like Bangladesh, or a tiny island nation like the Republic of Kiribati, other nations in the region who had won the dubious distinction of being an LDC.

The schools and universities had hardly re-opened on 26th October before underground student groups began their activities in Rangoon, Mandalay and other towns. At the beginning of November, students in the Arakan State capital of Sittwe went on a rampage and shouted anti-government slogans. On the 7th, students at the Ye Zin Agricultural College in Pyinmana in the central plains demonstrated against the government, pulled down portraits of Ne Win from the walls in their institution, and smashed them on the floor. Sporadic bomb blasts were heard in Rangoon, the targets being a cinema and, curiously, the Czech embassy on Prome Road.

Abroad, Burmese exiles now began organising themselves for the first time in many years. Emigrés in the US, Britain, Australia and West Germany had overcome their fear and set up a group called the Committee for Restoration of Democracy in Burma (CRDB). In 1987, some of their representatives travelled to the Thai border, where they met with the Karen, Mon, Shan, Kachin and other ethnic resistance armies of the umbrella organisation the National Democratic Front (NDF).

Years of frustrations with an inept regime were beginning to surface everywhere. It was 50 years since the Burmese people had risen against the British in the mighty '1300 Movement'. The signs now pointed in a similar direction; even a small incident — for instance a brawl over a cassette tape in a teashop — had the potential of developing into a mass movement. In January 1988, a Burmese had commented: "The play is over, but the audience is forced to remain in their seats, and the actors refuse to leave the stage".

Three WRATH OF THE CHILDREN

AFTER MORE THAN two quiet but tense months, the schools eventually re-opened on 30th May. Many students stayed at home since their parents feared there would be more unrest — but among the ones who showed up for classes, the re-organisation of the movement that had collapsed in March began almost immediately. Only one person seemed certain that nothing was going to change. On 11th April, only a few weeks after the most violent street demonstrations in Burma in more than a decade, Ne Win had left for a medical check-up abroad and a short rest at his favourite *spas* in West Germany and Switzerland, confidently leaving the running of day-to-day affairs in the hands of his trusted lieutenants, in particular his close protégé, the ruthless and widely hated Sein Lwin.

But at the RIT in Gyogon and the RU (Main) near Inya Lake, the young activists had not forgotten the brutality in March. The desire for revenge and the hatred of the government grew even more intense when batches of people were released in stages from the infamous Insein Jail north of Rangoon. They brought with them tales of beatings, torture and electric-shock treatment of jailed students. What seemed to upset the public the most were detailed reports of female students who had been gang-raped in custody by the dreaded *Lon Htein*. One of the alleged victims was said to be the daughter of an army major. Whether that particular case was true or not was actually irrelevant. The rumour had spread and people believed it. And if not even the children of army officers were safe from such atrocities, who could trust the regime? The seven violent days in March had changed the mood of the nation; it was obvious that it never was going to be the same again.

"We were thrown into a large cell which measured about 50 by 20 feet. But they stacked up to 200 to 300 people in each cell and in the beginning there was only room to stand up," says Maung Maung Thwin, the history student who had been arrested on 17th March. "It was almost impossible to sleep. The lights were on all night and our only toilet consisted of an empty petrol drum in one of the corners of the cell."

Each student was called in for questioning several times although the 'interrogations' mostly consisted of beatings and abuse. Students were forced to kneel on sharp pebbles, or to perform the bizarre 'helicopter' and 'motorcycle' acts, which had first been practised in the mid-1970s.

"If they asked any direct questions at all, they wanted to know who ourleaders were and who had organised us. There was no way we could answer these questions, since there were no leaders, or organisers, at this stage. We had risen spontaneously against the government. They hit me repeatedly in my ribs with heavy sticks for an hour and a half each time I was interrogated. But I had nothing to tell them since I didn't know anything," Maung Maung Thwin says.

Maung Maung Thwin had survived his tour in the jam-packed police vehicle, but 42 people in another van had suffocated to death after having to wait for several hours outside Insein Jail. The story of these unfortunate people soon became synonymous with the general perception of 26 years of BSPP-rule. "Like the student demonstrators who suffocated in the back of a police van in March, the country of Burma has been gradually choked by the grip of its intransigent rulers," a Burmese author in exile wrote shortly after the tragedy.

Yan Naung, who had been arrested at Inya Hostel on the same day, was himself spared from beatings, but he witnessed the cruelties from inside his cell: "Sometimes, the door would open and two policemen literally threw a young man into our cell. Most of them were bruised all over, some were covered with blood and came back unconscious. I remember one student especially well. He was so badly beaten that we had to carry him to the drum in the corner which served as toilet."

Aung Win, the organiser from RU's international relations department, was one of the few who was put in solitary confinement:

"I was beaten incessantly for three days and they wanted me to reveal who our leaders were. Fortunately, I have some rich relatives in Rangoon so they paid off the police and I was released after a week. By that time, I thought I was on the verge of becoming insane. I had to stay with my relatives for several days to recuperate."

Ohn-Ma Thwe, a girl student, majoring in Burmese, was beaten unconscious before her arrest on 17th March, when the *Lon Htein* entered the main campus:

— When I came to again, I found myself in a room without windows. I had no idea where I was. There were six policemen and an officer there. But they didn't ask me any questions. I was taken away to a place near a water-tank. There, I was raped, first by the officer and then by the policemen. I lost consciousness again, and when I woke up, a doctor was examining me. I know that this happened to other girls also. Some of them committed suicide.

Until the beginning of June, the atrocities in Burma had attracted almost no comment from prominent Burmese, and even less from the diplomatic community in Rangoon to whom the horror stories seemed literally incredible. The Enquiry Commission that the government had appointed in March to look into the death of Maung Phone Maw eventually presented its report on 6th May. It gave a totally distorted version of what had happened that week in March.

The report basically blamed the incidents on youngsters "who [had been] swayed by instigation of some students who wanted to create disturbances (sic!)". It claimed that two students, Maung Phone Maw and Soe Naing, had been killed by gunshot wounds and that no more than 625 had been arrested, of whom 141 were still in custody. The worst sufferers of all, according to the report, seemed to be the *Lon Htein*, 28 policemen had been injured by "rowdy students" who had thrown rocks at them. Rather than soothing the already inflamed tempers, the Enquiry Commission's report only added insult to injury — and whatever confidence the public had left in the country's judiciary was swept away instantly.

But then, on 8th June, Aung Gyi, the dismissed brigadier-general who had written to Ne Win about the economic crisis in Burma in July 1987, wrote another open letter to the old strongman. Aung Gyi's new letter was widely circulated in Rangoon and copies of it were even distributed upcountry; for the first time, a man of consequence spoke out against the human rights abuses. He dismissed the Enquiry Commission's report outright. "It is a malfeasance to issue this kind of statement", Aung Gyi wrote. He described the bloody incident at 'the White Bridge' on 16th March in forceful terms:

"The *modus operandi* of the police at the Inya Bund was to force the students into a corner and beat them to death...lecturers overheard such commands as 'Break their heads! Break them hard! The one who breaks the most heads will be rewarded!'...the *Lon Htein* berated the students for daring to demonstrate, beat the girls and raped them...the girls were so ashamed to tell anyone and some were in shock for four or five days. Some cried and requested to be sent to a nunnery without giving their parents any reason". Aung Gyi estimated that 282 people had been slaughtered in March. A large number had died at 'the White Bridge' but many were Muslims of Indian descent who had been rounded up on the 18th. Most of the Muslims died after being beaten in Insein Jail — and a controversy arose when relatives found out that they had been cremated in contravention of Islamic laws and Muslim beliefs.

In between the August 1987 and the 8th June letter, Aung Gyi on several other occasions also had tried to attract Ne Win's attention to the country's woes. Possibly because this first letter was believed to have influenced Ne Win to implement the reforms in August 1987, in January, he was approached by two Japanese envoys, Hitoshi Shozawa and Yenosuke Hara. These, Aung Gyi claimed in a letter which he wrote to Ne Win on 7th March, were sent by Japan's deputy prime minister and minister for finance, Kiichi Miyazawa.

The two Japanese, Aung Gyi said, told him that "though Japan has provided economic and technical assistance to Burma for many years, there had been no...success in any sector...Japan no longer has any faith in the present...regime and has decided to cut down on the assistance...unless you [Ne Win] change the 'whole team'. Since they believed that I was the only person who would report the true facts to you, these two Japanese requested me to do so accordingly."

Although Ne Win never even acknowledged receiving these letters, Aung Gyi persisted. On 9th May, he sent a voluminous, 40-page exposé, outlining Burma's political history since World War Two, his role in it and his position vis-à-vis Ne Win. Although he did indeed criticise major economic policies, he blamed the failures on bad influences. The gist of the message seemed to be that things went wrong in Burma because Ne Win did not listen to him but to his rivals Tin Pe, Ba Nyein and Thein Pe Myint.

So today, Burma was backwards, even less developed than a close-by LDC country, once sneeringly referred to as an "international basket-case": "On a recent visit to Burma by the Bangladesh president, I saw a programme about Bangladesh on TV showing about 50 textile factories in operation, and how ready-made clothes are now being exported. I think there are also about 100 to 200 jute mills operating. I saw an oil refinery plant with smoke billowing from its smoke-stack and other factories producing fertiliser and miscellaneous goods. In Burma, we have not yet even begun an experimental operation of the oil refinery at Thanbayakan but enormous sums of money have been spent on it. The Chauk oil refinery has had to halt operations."

Commenting on his own ouster from office in 1963, Aung Gyi mentioned that the authorities had "uprooted and overturned everything in order to discover any discrepancies or irregularities. I am grateful that they did not entrap me by throwing opium on my premises." Accusing almost every political opponent of being involved in the drug trade is a trick frequently used by Burma's military rulers.

However, there were no negative remarks about the old strongman himself, only a sarcastic remark about "a great member of the *Pyithu Hluttaw* of Bahan constituency" — an obvious reference to president San Yu. Even when Aung Gyi spoke out high and loud on 8th June against the atrocities, he carefully added: "Sir, may I request you...not to get involved or you will regret it. These violations of human rights will be infamous. You actually were not involved."

The main culprit, judging from Aung Gyi's letter was the BSPP's joint secretary general, Sein Lwin, who had directly, and unconstitutionally, ordered the Chief of Staff, General Saw Maung, to bring in the 44th LID from Pa-an without even informing the defence minister, Kyaw Htin. Presumably, this was a hint to Ne Win which direction he should take; Kyaw Htin was generally considered a moderate while Sein Lwin and his crony General Saw Maung were the supposed hard-liners.

Although Aung Gyi in no way became the leader of the dissident movement that was brewing throughout the country, the impact of his letters was considerable. The students felt more secure. At least, they had some backing from a person the government hardly could bundle up and send away to Insein to be tortured or summarily executed.

"Aung Gyi's letters affected our mood and we became braver," recollects Win Moe, a 24-year old student of international relations who later came to play an important role in the movement. "Shortly afterwards, we began writing leaflets and posters. Underground cells were set up on the campus, but there was no proper coordination and we were all afraid of informers from the DDSI. People loitered outside the Recreation Centre on the main campus, just waiting for something to happen."

Some students planned to hold a memorial service on 13th June for the ones who had died in March, but nothing substantial materialised. The vast majority was still hesitating, vividly remembering the horror of the White Bridge incident in March. But then, suddenly, on 14th June a student, masked with a handkerchief, stood up in front of the restless crowd outside the Recreation Centre and solemnly declared that a demonstration was going to be held on the following day. The lone agitator vanished as quickly and mysteriously as he had appeared. But the message had got through. Spirits were high again.

On 15th June, a Wednesday, an unusually large crowd had gathered in the open space between the Recreation Centre and the library. Some of the more daring students contrived a platform from chairs and tables. Wearing handkerchiefs as masks, one speaker after another appeared on the make-shift stage. Despite the disguise, some students recognised Maung Maung Kyaw, one of the leaders of the March movement. He condemned the government's brutality and demanded the release of those still in custody.

The thousands of students who had gathered to listen to the speakers finally marched off in one column, heading towards the empty plot of land where the students' union building had once stood before Ne Win's soldiers had dynamited it in the early morning of 8th July 1962. Next to it was the old site of a memorial dedicated to Bo Aung Gyaw, the student leader whose name had become engraved in Burmese history when he was killed by the British during the upheaval in 1938. The students halted briefly and saluted the first student martyr in Burmese history. Already this year, hundreds had died — and the casualties had not been inflicted by colonial troops this time, but by independent Burma's own armed forces, which made their deaths all the more sorrowful to bear.

The demonstrations continued inside the campus for several days. On the 17th, a Friday, an unusually large crowd had gathered between the library and the Recreation Centre. For the first time, some Buddhist monks and workers from a nearby textile factory participated in the meetings on the campus. The popular sympathy for the movement was best demonstrated when a speaker announced that 100,000 Kyats had been collected among the public in Rangoon to support the students. The initial tension between university students and townspeople had now transmuted into whole-hearted public support.

Teenagers from high schools all over Rangoon also flocked to the meeting ground outside the university's Recreation Centre; an increasing number of protesters were very young, and they were perhaps the fieriest of them all. For them, there was little future under the present system. They had only to look at their elder brothers and sisters who had gone through university just to be faced with mass unemployment, or at best, the chance to do occasional odd jobs in an effort to contribute something to their families.

In March, a students' union had been formed, but it had collapsed in the wake of the mass arrests on the 18th. Now, several underground groups became active. But because they coalesced spontaneously in isolation and secrecy, they had a variety of names and raised different demands; it was not factionalism as such, which many outside observers thought.

"However, there was a difference between those who wanted to confine the struggle to pure student demands; the release of the detainees, compensation to the families of the victims of the March massacre and so on. And then there were the more politically orientated students — and high schools pupils — who demanded democracy, human rights and cheaper consumer goods for the people," says Win Moe. "As for myself, I belonged to the former grouping. I thought it was premature to raise high-flown political demands at this stage. If we could force the government to make concessions on these basic issues — which actually had happened at the Institute of Medicine where four dismissed students had been reinstated — we would also be able to convince the public at large that we were powerful and political demands could follow more easily after a while."

Once again though, it was the government itself through its own ineptitude that became the catalyst for radicalisation of the student movement. On the 20th, the BBS evening news announced that classes had been suspended on all four campuses of Rangoon University. But by then, the unrest had already spread to the Institute of Medicine (1), whose main campus is located near Rangoon General Hospital in the centre of the city and the buildings for preparatory classes near the BBS building on Prome Road. The students, naturally, moved their activities to the Prome Road campus and the meetings continued. Students from the Institute of Dental Medicine also joined in. The movement was now bigger than ever before and it was becoming increasingly militant.

"We held a big meeting on the Prome Road campus on the 21st. Thousands of people were there and suddenly someone got the idea that we should march down to the main Institute of Medicine (1) in downtown Rangoon where another meeting was being held," says Soe Win, a medical student. "We marched off at 1 pm, a solid column of several thousand students. We took our peacock and student union flags and someone went inside the teachers' office. There were three portraits on the wall, of Aung San, Ne Win and San Yu. We let the latter two stay on the wall while one student brought out Aung San's portrait to be carried in front of the demonstration."

The column set off, along the tree-shaded avenue of Prome Road. "No violence! Peaceful demonstration!" the organisers shouted to the crowd of young but earnest-looking marchers. Most of them were university students, but some were younger, children barely in their teens. Suddenly, everyone glanced to the right. There were troops everywhere. Bren-carriers, positioned near the BBS building and the Hanthawaddy round-about, a stone-throw away from the by now notorious Kyandaw crematorium, pointed their deadly medium machine-guns in the direction of the demonstration. In front of the students, further down Prome Road, the road was blocked with lines of barbed-wire fences. Army units as well as *Lon Htein*-men were waiting with their rifles and clubs.

"At first, we thought it was going to be a repetition of the 'White Bridge' incident. But, fortunately, this was close to Myenigone market where there are lots of small houses and back-alleys. We fled in all directions before they could open fire and people readily hid us in their houses," says Soe Win who participated in the demonstration.

A army lorry roared up, loaded with soldiers, guns at the ready. They opened fire, but the only casualties were two 13-year old school children who were run down by the lorry. One was killed on the spot, the other severely injured, perhaps fatally. Out of sheer anger, people in the neighbourhood came out of their houses, picked up bricks and rocks and threw them at the soldiers and the *Lon Htein*. From nowhere, a slender projectile streaked through the air. One of the *Lon Htein* men slumped to the ground. He had been hit by a *jinglee*, a dart made from a sharpened bicycle spoke fired from a catapult. More followed, some were smaller and made from umbrella spokes. Both types were flighted with chicken feathers, and had been dipped in herbicide or cow dung to make them lethal. In the labyrinth of houses and lanes in the crowded Myenigone market, the soldiers and the *Lon Htein* were lost. They retreated in disorder, dragging their dead and wounded along with them.

Meanwhile, some of the young demonstrators had fled into the compound of the nearby Singapore embassy. From outside the locked gate, *Lon Htein*-men pelted the embassy with stones. The sound of gunfire rang out in the backstreets near the embassy; the streetbattle was not entirely one-sided. A girl who had been holding a students' union flag was dragged into a police station in the neighbourhood. A crowd stormed the building to secure her release — an incident which the official media later described as an unprovoked attempt to burn down the station. Enraged civilians hurled bricks or fired *jinglees* at any *Lon Htein*-man they caught sight of and at least ten were killed. The *Lon Htein* and the army fired back at random, killing or wounding dozens. But the public had fought back and the morale of the security forces was shaken.

The news of the clash at Myenigone market, and the *Lon Htein* casualties, spread all over Rangoon. Groups of students picked up some of the dead, young protesters and placed them on the roof of a Mazda pickup. With this macabre evidence of police brutality, they drove around town, shouting slogans, and public anger grew. Hardly surprisingly, there was considerably less sympathy for the *Lon Htein* who had fallen, hit by the new addition to the world's armoury, the deadly *jinglees*. On Bogyoke Aung San Street in the city centre, a truck carrying six dead policemen was stopped by an enraged mob and set afire. The lorry, and the corpses, were consumed by the flames to the applause of the on-looking crowd.

"I remember the incident clearly," says Sit Naing, a 23-year old medical student from Rangoon. "It was eerie. As the smoke rose in a dark column from the burning vehicle, we looked up in the sky — and we saw 21 wild geese flying in arrowhead-formation. It's not often we see wild geese in Rangoon and it was also 21st June. To us, it was a good omen; it encouraged us to continue our protests."

While the battle raged around Myenigone Market, the students' meeting at the Institute of Medicine (1) in downtown Rangoon was still going on. At about 3 pm, one of the students who had been in the demonstration came panting into the medical institute, gasping out the news.

"We sent out five groups of five students each to check if the security forces were coming our way," says Ko Lin, one of the organisers of this meeting. "One of the groups soon came across a DDSI agent. He was standing in the streets, staring around with a stern face, so he stood out like a sore thumb in the crowd of young students."

They pounced on him and grabbed his shoulder-bag. His ID card was in it — along with a Browning revolver. While waving the gun triumphantly in the air, one student read out his name and rank from the ID card: sergeant

Maung Pyone. The onlookers, who now also consisted of ordinary people from the area, were furious.

"Kill him with his own pistol!" somebody shouted.

"But we didn't want to do that," Ko Lin continues. "Soon afterwards, we caught one more DSI agent, who turned out to be the boss of this gang. He was carrying a camera and confessed that they had been told to infiltrate the meeting. In his bag, there was no weapon, but a complete, hand-written report on the meeting we had held on our campus on the previous day. While interrogating him, we learnt that his agents, for easy recognition, were dressed in white shirts and blue longyis. We caught two more agents also, but we almost made a mistake when we found a young man drinking water who happened to be dressed in the same way. When we searched his shoulder-bag, we found nothing more than a few movie magazines."

The apprehended DDSI agents were handed over to the institute's teachers. But the crowd was infuriated. As sergeant Maung Pyone was being dragged into the main building of the institute, someone in the crowd hurled a brick at him, hurting him badly. Later, all four of the DDSI-men were released — which turned out to have been a bad mistake. Over the next few days, several hundred student activists were arrested in their homes at night and taken away to Insein Jail and Yay Kyi Aing. The agents arrived at their doorstep with lists of names and sets of pictures; it was all carefully planned and executed in a manner totally different from the random mass arrests in the streets in March.

The melee of the 21st died out in the late afternoon. The official death toll, according to the Working *People's Daily* of 23rd June, was "six members of the People's Police Force...and three among those who caused disturbances and violence". Diplomatic estimates of the same incident amounted to 20 policemen killed and at least 80 civilians, possibly more than 100. All the universities and institutes in Rangoon had been closed down indefinitely and a dusk-to-dawn curfew was clamped on the capital.

However, in Pegu, 50 kms north of Rangoon, the anti government demonstrations continued. On 23rd June, police and army units opened fire on a crowd of protesters. About 70 people were gunned down near the old steel bridge over the Pegu River. One of them was a young student who died in the arms of an elderly and well-respected monk in the town; the youth had been poor and supported by one of the local Buddhist monasteries. The incident deeply moved the people of Pegu, and one more town in the country came out openly against the BSPP regime.

A few of the more militant students in Rangoon defied the curfew in the capital and retreated to the Shwe Dagon Pagoda, the centre of the historic student strikes in 1920 and 1936. A 'strike centre' was proclaimed one again. The police, however, dispersed the hundred-or-so students almost immediately, and a fragile calm returned to Rangoon. And the task of quelling the unrest once again had been delegated to Sein Lwin in his capacity of commander of the *Lon Htein* or, more specifically, because he was one of the few men Ne Win really trusted. 'The June Affairs' — as they later became known, were over.

The government's draconian emergency measures, which the *Working People's Daily* published on its front-page on 22nd June, included a total ban on "gathering, making speeches, marching in procession, agitation, exhortation, demonstrations and causing disturbances" between 6 pm and 6 am. The order, the announcement said, "shall be in force for 60 days from 21st June up to 19th August".

While this undoubtedly kept the increasingly restless students off the streets for a while, it resulted in other, unanticipated problems. Markets in Burma usually open before sunrise and are teeming with people at dawn. The vendors, consequently, spend the early hours of the day transporting their produce to market and setting up their stalls before the customers arrive. Now, that was impossible.

An old noodle vendor and his daughter, who ventured outside with their push cart before 6 pm, were gunned down by an army unit patrolling the streets during curfew hours. Other "curfew violators" were also rumoured to have been killed and the markets stopped functioning normally. Prices of basic consumer goods began skyrocketing. A *pyi* (eight empty condensed milk tins) of rice went up from three Kyats to nine whilst the wage of a manual worker remained static at 6.50 Kyats a day. The price of a *viss* (1.6 kgs) of fish in Rangoon's markets rose from 5-6 Kyat to 10-15. Even vegetables became increasingly expensive for the poor. On top of it all were rumours of another impending demonetisation. Burma, which despite its immense problems had always been able to feed its population in the past, suddenly had many hungry people.

The authorities obviously were caught in a dilemma. If the emergency measures were withdrawn completely, the students would take to the streets again. But if nothing were done at all, the entire population would rise in anger well before 19th August. In a feeble attempt to appease the public, the authorities announced on 29th June that curfew hours had been shortened to 8 pm to 4 am.

The effect of this undoubtedly welcome step was soured a few days later when Ye Win, the BSPP chief of Rangoon Division went on the air on the BBS and sternly warned the traders "not to manipulate prices...with greed solely for selfish interest." He went on to paint a rosy picture of the situation "when the state sold and distributed rice", that is, before the government had allowed free trade in a number of commodities in August the previous year. "If the prices soar exorbitantly with disregard for the consumer

WRATH OF THE CHILDREN

masses...the greedy ones will have to bear the main responsibility, and the state will have to take necessary action", Ye Win warned.

The authorities, sensing perhaps that this had not had the desired effect — the people were angry, not intimidated — then introduced a number of other concessions. On 7th July, the evening news of the BBS announced that all the students who had been detained in connection with the March riots were going to be released. Previously, the government had said that only 141 students remained in detention. Strangely, however, it now claimed that 240 people had been released of whom 139 were students and the rest was vaguely referred to as *ayatthas,* or 'locals'.

That was in Rangoon alone. In the southeastern city of Moulmein, where no disturbances had been officially reported in the first place, 73 detainees had been released, the BBS said. And that was not the end of the good news. 50 people had been set free in Pegu and 27 in Prome. It was in this incidental manner that the people of Rangoon learnt that they had not been alone while battling the *Lon Htein* and the army in Mycnigone market on 21st June.

The usual caustic wit, which generally met the authorities' announcements, gave way to excitement when the radio, totally unexpectedly, announced that the country's monolithic block, the omnipotent BSPP, was going to hold an "extraordinary congress" as early as 23rd July to "effect changes in the state and economic policies". Normally, the BSPP hold its congresses every five years and the next one was not actually due until 1989. Two days later, equally unexpectedly, the curfew in Rangoon was lifted altogether. Would things, this time, return to normal? Could the BSPP come up with a proposal that might satisfy the public?

Many people probably would have been prepared to settle for whatever concessions they could get. But, hardly by coincidence, a curious element in the agitation surfaced at about the same time as the anti-government demonstrations in June. A campaign was mounted against an extremely vulnerable sector of Burmese society — its Muslim population.

In 1967, the authorities had managed to divert attention from internal social and economic woes by instigating attacks on the Chinese community in Rangoon. For reasons which seemed very similar, there were widespread anti-Muslim riots in Moulmein, Martaban and in some towns in the Irrawaddy delta region southwest of Rangoon in June and July 1984 when there were new shortages of goods and local prices went up. Mobs stormed Muslim living quarters, looted houses and burnt down a number of mosques. The *kalas* became convenient scapegoats once again.

During the first wave of anti-government demonstrations in March, hundreds of Muslims had been rounded up and sent away to Insein Jail. The vast majority of them were ordinary people who unawarely had been caught up in the turbulent events of the 18th, but many were also young-sters of mixed Indo-Burmese blood, incorrectly referred to as *kaladaing*, which actually means low-caste Indians.

When the meetings at the main campus began again in June, nearly all the leaflets which were distributed had been hand-written. A notable exception was a stencilled series of leaflets, attacking the Muslims and purportedly issued by 'Nationalistic Buddhists of Burma'. The leaflets warned that "an organised gang of Indian Muslims in our native land" was planning to seduce Buddhist Burmese women in order to produce more Muslims. The 'Nationalistic Buddhists' claimed that they had discovered a secret docu-ment, signed by 'the Muslim League', which promised a monthly allow-ance of 1,000 Kyats to any Muslim who could make a Buddhist woman pregnant. If the woman in question was a university graduate, the allow-ance would be 2,000 Kyats and a record reward of 50,000 Kyats was promised for daughters of army officers. The leaflets exhorted the public to boycott Muslim shops and the final slogan was: "All Muslims — Leave our Country!"

"It was all so crude. We never had any doubts as to who was behind these ridiculous leaflets. We Muslims immediately discussed the matter with our Buddhist neighbours and there was never any misunderstanding between us," asserts Zaw Zaw, a Muslim student from Rangoon.

Communal frictions were, however, expected in the beginning of July when the Muslims were about to celebrate Idul Azah, an Islamic festival that usually includes animal sacrifices. The Buddhists were preparing for the Full Moon Day of Waso, the Buddhist lent, when any killing of living beings is considered a sacrilege by most Burmese. The US Embassy in Rangoon even issued a statement, warning its nationals not to travel upcountry during the time.

"We in the Muslim community feared that the authorities might try to stir up communal trouble. So we simply refrained from doing any *kurbani*, or animal sacrifices this year," says Zaw Zaw. "Calm prevailed between the Muslims and the Buddhists in Rangoon."

While the situation remained calm in the capital, communal unrest soon broke out in some provincial towns. The first to be hit by a violent wave of anti-Muslim rioting was Taunggyi, the normally tranquil hill station which is the capital of Shan State. In the early morning of 10th July, a young Buddhist novice was on his daily alms round in the town. When he passed a Muslim-run teashop, the Union Confectionery, near the central Myoma market, the son of the proprietor stretched a rubber band and aimed it in the novice's direction. Other stories claim that the novice was beaten and that the young Muslim smashed his alms bowl. Whatever the case, the novice returned to his monastery and some older monks went down to the teashop to talk to the owner. Since its was located in the crowded market area, some labourers, ethnic Burmans from the plains, were hanging around and they soon became involved in the dispute. They began throwing rocks at the teashop. The police arrived at the scene and the owner's son was arrested. Being a petty businessmen, the owner was comparatively affluent, at least by local standards, and he was able to pay off the police. His son was released.

Thus far, there was no evidence that even suggested official instigation of the clash. But at this stage, rumours began circulating in Taunggyi saying that the "Muslims control the police, that's why this could happen". In a strange twist of events, the police were, however, spared from public outrage. The mob went down to the teashop in Myoma market and burnt it down. On the following day, several other Muslim-owned teashops were destroyed. The young novice also mysteriously disappeared and a rumour began circulating that he had been abducted and killed by "the Muslims". According to the official reports over the BBS, the local authorities tried to defuse the situation. Taunggyi residents, however, tell a different story: "At first, we were all enraged with the Muslims. As Buddhists, we were deeply insulted by the way the novice had been treated and we took to the streets armed with clubs, swords and sticks to take revenge on the Muslims", says Sai Myo Win Htun, a 23 year old Shan student from Taunggyi. "But then some of us noticed that the police were just standing by. They weren't protect any Muslim property. They were only guarding the bank on the main road."

After two days of violent clashes, the situation at last got totally out of hand. On the 12th, the police opened fire with .303 Lee Enfield rifles — right into the crowd of rioters. Two people were killed and about ten wounded.

"After this, it became worse, not better," says Sai Myo Win Htun. "The crowd counter-attacked and someone fired a catapult towards the police-men. Sein Tun, the chief of the Shan State People's Police Force, was hit right in the eye. He died on the following day. For three days after his death, there was total anarchy. But by then, all the Muslims had left town so it all died down by itself. What was left was a deep anger with the local authorities and the police."

On 14th July, the Shan State People's Council issued an order prohibiting people in Taunggyi from assembling, making speeches, marching, demon-strating and "causing disturbances". But Sai Myo Win Htun and others went underground to organise anti-government groups and connections were established with local Buddhist monasteries. If the anti-Muslim riots in Taunggyi indeed had been orchestrated by the authorities to deflect the roots of dissatisfaction, the scheme had certainly backfired.

A few days later, more communal violence broke out in Prome, 290 kms north of Rangoon in the central plains. The official account said that the violence began when some allegedly drunk Muslim youth insulted a young Buddhist girl outside the Let Yway Zin Cafe in the town's market area and it all escalated into virtual street battles. Muslim homes and shops were attacked and burnt down.

A foreign diplomat in Rangoon described a slightly different scenario in his dispatch back to his government at the time: "Other reports, however, insinuate that the disturbances may have enlarged into anti-authority displays with their communal component being of less importance. It is evident from press reports that the police and security forces in Prome were unable to control the crowds."

Already after the March demonstrations in Rangoon, some people in Prome had begun organising underground anti-government groups. The DDSI, apparently, had got wind of it, and this, Prome residents say, was why their town was targeted for orchestrated communal clashes.

After six days of violence, martial law was declared in Prome on 22nd July. Especially disturbing from the authorities' point of view — and of significant symbolic value — was the fact that by then the unrest had spread from Prome itself to the small town of Paungdale about 20 kms to the east. That is where Burma's strongman Ne Win was born in 1911.

Burma by the end of July was so tense that any minor incident could be the spark that started a blaze. Every day, there were fresh rumours about impending disturbances. 26 years of pent-up frustrations with a military regime that had done nothing to improve the lot of the public at large had surfaced with a vehemence that had taken nearly everybody by surprise, the Burmese themselves included. And whatever the authorities had done to deal with the situation had proved counterproductive. That was the mood when the BSPP began its emergency congress in the Saya San Hall, next to the old British race course at the Kyaikkasan grounds in Rangoon.

During the days immediately before the emergency congress, the government had announced some unprecedented concessions, presumably aimed at appeasing the increasingly restless public. The BBS's evening news on 19th July had made the remarkable admission that 41 people had indeed suffocated in an overcrowded prison van in March. This was the first time the authorities had admitted that more than two people had died during the March riots. By sheer coincidence, this announcement was made on Burma's Martyrs' Day, which is held to commemorate the assassination of Aung San and his colleagues in 1947.

Min Gaung, the minister of home and religious affairs, was "permitted to resign" in connection with the affair — and two days later, Thein Aung, the director-general of the People's Police Force in Rangoon, was also given the same privilege and the national police chief, Pe Kyi, was demoted to the rank of deputy director and transferred. The man directly responsible for the deaths, Hla Ni, an ex-major who had been in charge of the riot squad, had his promotion postponed for two years.

The news of the students who had suffocated to death in March was widely known among Rangoon residents, but the figure usually given was 42 people. A source close to the Rangoon police told the following story:

"What Hla Ni did was to have 42 injured people thrown into the Black Maria, and since some of them were so badly hurt already, suffering from gunshot wounds and effects of tear gas, most of them were dumped flat inside the van. Even though it was nearly full, more bodies were piled up on top of each other and Hla Ni kept on ordering even more thrown in. When the van arrived at Insein Jail and was opened, dead bodies fell out instead of just injured persons. To make things worse, the truck did not get to jail for four hours after being loaded."

Even though the police officers were "punished", most people thought they got off very lightly. Home minister Min Gaung's role in the entire affair had been minimal; he had arrived at the RU (Main) in March and directed some operations over his walkie-talkie. And everybody knew that he, as well as the policemen, was doing little more than carrying out orders relayed to him from Sein Lwin, the de facto chief of the *Lon Htein*; it was obvious that convenient scapegoats had been selected and that the real culprits were not going to be purged or punished. Sein Lwin had been in full charge of operations, not only in March but in June as well.

Ne Win's own mood at the time was a matter for speculation. Following the March riots, he had been so confident that he had left the country shortly afterwards. But now, the unrest had spread all over the country, including his own hometown, and the opposition was not only gaining momentum but even beginning to raise very clear political demands. His own wealth and that of his family was now coming under scrutiny; an increasing number of people were comparing him with the deposed Philippine leader Ferdinand Marcos. While there undoubtedly were many similarities, developments over the next few days were to show that Ne Win was more than just an ordinary, corrupt Third World-dictator with tendencies towards megalomania.

Over a thousand delegates arrived at the Saya San Hall at 8.30 am and after the usual formalities, Ne Win entered the hall. Right behind him came a much younger, stoney-faced man, his confidant Col. Khin Nyunt, the chief of the dreaded DDSI. Ne Win rose to the podium: "Dear delegates to the party congress: I will explain the reason for convening this extraordinary party congress and the matters that will be submitted, deliberated and approved at this congress. My explanation will also include other facts that should be clarified," the now 77-year old party chairman began his half an hour long speech. "I believe that the bloody events of March and June show a lack of trust in the government and the party that guides it by the people who were either directly involved or were lending their support to the events. But it is necessary to find out whether it is the majority or the minority that support the people showing the lack of trust. Since it is our belief that the answer to the question — a multiparty or a single party system — can be provided by a referendum, the current congress is requested to approve a national referendum...if the choice is for a multi-party system, we must hold elections for a new parliament."

The people of Burma, who were closely following the speech over the BBS that night, were completely taken aback. But more was to follow. After Ne Win had suggested the referendum, the BSPP Central Committee headquarters secretary, Htwe Han, took over the microphone and read out a part of his speech, still in the first person: "As I consider that I am not totally free from responsibility, even if indirectly, for the sad events that took place in March and June, and because I am advancing in age, I would like to request party members to allow me to relinquish the duty of party chairman and as a party member." And not only Ne Win; five other top party leaders "have also asked to leave along with me and have entrusted their resignations to me". The five were no less persons than San Yu, the BSPP's vice chairman and the state president, BSPP general secretary Aye Ko, joint secretary general Sein Lwin, defence minister Kyaw Htin and finance minister Tun Tin — in other words, the entire inner circle of party and state leaders who had ruled Burma for years.

After Htwe Han's announcing the unexpected resignations, Ne Win took over again and resumed reading out the rest of the speech. He went on to comment on who had been responsible for the blowing up of the students' union building in 1962. He himself had had nothing to do with it, he said: "Only when I enquired, on hearing a very loud bang like the explosion of a big bomb on 8th July morning, did I learn that the union building had been dynamited." The main culprit, Ne Win discovered according to his own account, was — the now avid letter-writer and dissident voice Aung Gyi!

In reference to further unrest in the country, the old but still strong Ne Win did not mince his words: "In continuing to maintain control, I want the entire nation, the people, to know that if in future there are mob disturbances, if the army shoots, it hits — there is no firing into the air to scare".

When the speech was over, Ne Win promptly left the hall, climbed into his private Fiat and was driven off, back to his Ady Road residence by Inya Lake. The session recessed and did not convene again until the afternoon when Aye Ko delivered a speech, promising far-reaching economic reforms. In effect, he promised to open up the country to private enterprise and foreign trade. The state monopoly would only be retained over oil, natural gas, pearls, jade and gems.

The nation, and possibly even more so the diplomatic community in Rangoon, was flabbergasted. International wire service reports were euphoric. Public outrage in Burma had forced an end to 26 years of one-party rule and one of Asia's most rigid socialist systems!

Or had it? There were more surprises to come...

When the congress resumed on the following day, speaker after speaker went up to urge Ne Win to stay on. Lanang Bawk, a young representative from Kachin State, was one of the first to take the microphone. "The entire indigenous working people from our Kachin State Party Regional Committee area have absolute confidence in the party chairman and other state leaders," he said. "From past bitter experiences, I believe the multi-party system will not work at all...a single party system is most appropriate at a time when efforts are being made to build up the economy of the state".

Kyaw Hlaing from Kayah State warned that Burma would risk losing its independence if a multi-party system was introduced. Khan Mang, a Chin State representative, growled: "The national referendum on the multi-party system should not be held." Maung Maung Naing of the party unit in Tenasserim Division asserted that since the BSPP was "firmly established in Burma as the sole party, a one party system should continue to be practised. The party chairman should not resign from membership in the party." Khant from Magwe Division thought that a multi-party system would result in anarchy and disarray, causing "disunity between one state and another, between one class and another and even among one another in the same family, the same ward and the same town". Only a few, among them Than Tun from Mandalay Division, supported the proposal. San Tin from Pegu also gave his approval but added that "the party chairman is like a parent to the party...therefore, this congress should request [him] to continue to provide leadership". The congress seemed to be unanimous only on one issue; everybody expressed their gratitude to Ne Win because, at last, he had told the truth about the explosion in the students' union building in 1962.

On the 25th, the extraordinary — in more than one sense of the word — congress was over. Ne Win was "permitted to resign" as party chairman but not from the party. And there was not going to be any referendum. The task of developing the economy was all too important, the delegates had concluded. San Yu was also "permitted to resign", to repeat the official jargon, but Aye Ko, Sein Lwin, Kyaw Htin and Tun Tin, unfortunately, did not have their wishes respected. They had to serve on, the congress decided.

There was immediate confusion among all Burma-watchers both inside and outside the country. What was actually going on? Ne Win had left the congress on its first day and not showed up again. Normally, BSPP congresses are mere rubber-stamp functions which approve decisions that had already been made and the very thought of opposing a proposal from its chairman had been unthinkable throughout the 26 years of autarchic one party rule in Burma. But what was this? A rebellion against the old dictator from within the ranks of his own power base, the very party he himself had created?

There was febrile activity among the foreign observers. Several analysts tried to look at the vote in an attempt to detect any pattern. Some concluded that all the representatives from the minority areas — where there is ethnic insurgency — were against the proposal, presumably because stability and continuity were important hallmarks for them, while the few yes-votes had come from the more tranquil, Burman-dominated central plains. Ne Win's sudden departure from the meeting was also puzzling and maybe it indicated that he was not fully in control anymore? But observers abroad brushed aside such speculation in their enthusiasm over the promises of economic reforms. The moment they had been waiting for had come after so many years! The resource-rich Burma was about to open up!

The Burmese man-in-the-street, however, found such speculations and attempts at analysis bewildering in themselves. Surely, these observers weren't taking the performance in congress at its face value? Familiar with the ways of their old dictator, few ordinary Burmese saw any prospect for real change as long as 'Number One' was alive — which inevitably meant that he was also in charge; president or not , party chairman or not was of no significance. Ne Win was Ne Win and that was what really counted.

"It is unthinkable that the congress should vote against his actual wishes. By suggesting a referendum and then letting the congress overturn the proposal, Ne Win made it possible for himself to make a graceful exit from the scene — and to continue pulling the strings from behind it. It was one of his Machiavellian schemes to remain in power in a different form. Now, everybody would have keen memories of the old leader. After all, he had suggested a referendum, but the nasty congress had been against it! He had saved his place in history. Or, at least, so he thought," commented one Burmese friend at the time.

Subsequent events were also to prove that this was an accurate assessment. It was soon made clear that Burma was not entering a new era of liberalism. Towards the end of that dramatic week in July, a new successor to the posts of president and BSPP chairman was announced. The choice was Sein Lwin.

Four THE BUTCHER

In Burma, no day is holier than the Full Moon Day of Waso, which falls in June or July and marks the beginning of the Buddhist Lent. This is when the country's tens of thousands of monks remain in their monasteries for the following three months of the rainy season to study and meditate. On that day, every Buddhist celebrates the Buddha's conception, his renunciation of worldly goods and his first sermon after enlightenment: the *Dhammacakkappavattana-sutta*, or the Setting in Motion of the Wheel of Truth.

In the morning, people present robes and food to the monks. Devout Buddhists enter a period of fasting and, in the afternoon, almost everybody flocks to the temples to light candles, present flowers and sprinkle lustral water on gold Buddha images. In Rangoon, the Shwe Dagon always attracts thousands of worshippers and a serene tranquility usually prevails at the sacred mount just north of the city centre.

In 1988, however, even that had changed. Among the hushed worshippers, there was a taut foreboding, a tension like the sultry lull before a storm. Suddenly, some young people mounted water tanks near the pagoda and began giving speeches and shouting anti-government slogans. One of the four speakers, judging from his green *longyi* , was a high-school pupil. "The students and the people are oppressed," the young agitators declaimed. "We need your support to overthrow Ne Win and the BSPP government." Onlookers gathered and nodded approvingly. Some applauded the young orators; others shouted encouragements. Upcountry, there had been the disturbances in Taunggyi and Prome — and it had spread to the small town of Myayde where a few anti-government demonstrators had been shot by the police and a curfew imposed. But in Rangoon, the movement had been dormant since the June demonstrations. Now, it gathered momentum once again.

The extraordinary BSPP congress in July had been an unusual event in many ways, but even so, it basically reflected Ne Win's old policy of wielding the carrot and the stick in an attempt to bring the people into line. Economic reforms had been promised. But he had also appointed Sein Lwin his successor and, furthermore, threatened to "shoot to hit" if the people demonstrated again. However, not much materialised of the economic reform programme; the stick seemed to get top priority instead.

At the time of his appointment, Sein Lwin was probably the most hated man in Burma. He was considered a village ruffian of the worst sort, being virtually uneducated, barring a few years of primary schooling in his home village Kawkayin near Moulmein. He had joined the BDA as a private at the age of 19 and became an NCO under Ne Win in the 4th Burma Rifles after the war. His role in the unit that had managed to locate and kill the Karen rebel leader Saw Ba U Gyi had earned him Ne Win's confidence. In 1962, Ne Win, therefore, had put him in charge of the company that stormed Rangoon University and opened fire on the students.

During his tenure as strategic commander in Lashio, Shan State, 1969-70 his reputation as a ruthless commander had grown during several bloody campaigns against Shan guerrillas in the area. In 1970-72, while chief of Mandalay Division, he waged a determined campaign against the remaining political opposition, mainly the militant *Yahanpyo*, or Young Monks, who at that time formed a strong opposition force in the monasteries of northern Burma. In 1981, he was transferred to Rangoon and appointed member of the state council and rose to BSPP joint secretary general in 1983.

To most Burmese, Sein Lwin represented the corps of immensely loyal, less than intelligent henchmen Ne Win had surrounded himself with to sustain his power. The very thought that Sein Lwin's rise to the presidency and the chairmanship of the BSPP after the July emergency congress was the outcome of some kind of 'coup' was dismissed outright by astute Burmese. They perceived his appointment as a confirmation of the suspicion that Ne Win had publicly surrendered the reins of power only to become a puppet-master pulling the strings from behind the scenes.

Dissatisfaction among the public gave way to hatred. "That man is not going to be the ruler of Burma" was a common phrase repeated all over the country in late July and early August. Sein Lwin, the *de facto* chief of the hated *Lon Htein*, was already known as 'the Butcher' after his role in suppressing the March and June demonstrations. Nobody expected from him any leniency or willingness to listen to the people's grievances.

At 12.28 Bangkok time on 30th July, a brief telex message arrived at the office of the *Associated Press* in the Charn Issara Tower on Suriwong Road. It read: "Daddy has been taken away. He won't be available to answer your queries."

In a sweep on 29th July, the day after the demonstrations outside Shwe Dagon Pagoda, the police in Rangoon had arrested about a dozen suspected dissidents. Apart from the local AP correspondent Sein Win — whose daughter sent the telex to Bangkok on the following day — the police had, after several nervous weeks, netted Aung Gyi and about a dozen of his associates, including his nephew Zaw Win Oo, who had helped print and distribute the letters. Also taken away to Insein Jail that night were Aung Shwe, a retired brigadier-general who had been sent abroad as Burma's ambassador to Australia in 1961, when the military was planning the coup that followed the next year, Chit Ko Ko, a retired naval officer, ex-colonel Tun Shwe and Ba Shwe, a former ambassador to India. Two of them, Kyi Maung and Khin Myo, were retired colonels who had been included in the original Revolutionary Council of 1962. The rest were also former army officers who had been purged in the early 1960s for advocating liberal economic policies.

Aung Gyi now had to pay the price for writing his letters and criticising Sein Lwin's and general Saw Maung's decision to bring in the 44th LID from Pa-an. That Sein Win had been arrested along with Aung Gyi came as somewhat of a surprise, though. He was known as one of Burma's most professional journalists and had once been the editor of the prestigious *Guardian* newspaper which was nationalised after the coup. In 1965-68 he had been jailed, only two years after having been awarded the Golden Pen of Freedom by the International Federation of Journalists for his work in fostering a free press in Burma.

A year after his release in 1968, he was allowed to become the AP's Rangoon correspondent. Surprisingly, he was tolerated by the authorities, despite his independent reporting. In some ways, he had played the role of a Burmese Viktor Louis; his existence and the very fact that the government did not take action against him seemed to contradict the assumption that Burma was a totalitarian state, and it gave the regime some credibility abroad. But even that was over now. Sein Lwin seemed determined to crush the opposition with force and threats against any 'undesirable' individuals.

After the stick came the carrot. In a speech on 2nd August, Sein Lwin criticised the "almost deathlike immobility" within local units of the BSPP as well as government offices. He continued: "if there are any shortcomings in those places...point them out and report to the organisations above... corrupt practices such as bribery, deliberately keeping work pending for a long time, excessive lost and wastage, as well as malpractices are rampant in some offices and departments."

The contents of the speech would have been welcome and even ushered in a new era of *glasnost* in Burma — if it had been said a year before and by someone else but the hated Sein Lwin. At this stage, it was in any case certainly far too little, much too late. Even the countryside was turning openly hostile towards the government. "Sein Lwin's unpopularity could lead to serious trouble in Burma", a Rangoon-based Western diplomat reported back to his capital in the beginning of August.

Following the confrontation between demonstrators and the security forces in June, some student leaders had gone into hiding in Buddhist monasteries in Rangoon itself and in the working class suburb of South Okkalapa. In almost every ward and township in Rangoon, people had spontaneously begun organising citizens' committees. The Buddhist monks, casually strolling down the streets, kept a look out for army trucks or police contingents when meetings were being held. The 22nd LID was now more or less permanently based in Rangoon since the first units had been brought in to Rangoon from its home base at the Karen State capital of Pa-an in March. The teashops, as usual, were the centre of meetings and other anti-government activities.

While the economic hardships caused by the curfew, and memories of the brutalities in March and June, had led to widespread discontent, there were also two totally disparate persons who influenced the movement more than anybody else: the old strongman Ne Win himself — and a young Englishman called Christopher Gunness from the BBC's Eastern Service.

By first, as a tactical ploy, suggesting a referendum on the issue of a one-party or a multi-party system — and then letting the congress overturn the proposal — Ne Win had actually begun digging the BSPP's own grave. A Western diplomat based in Rangoon commented much later: "Up to then, the student movement and the sympathetic reaction of the masses was completely unfocused. It was in essence anti-government; protest against brutality, a frustrated reaction against the inane policies, the demonetisation, the hopelessness of the students, the lack of any future. There was no focus to it. Ne Win, unwittingly, provides a focus by calling for a multi-party system, and from there on in, the student cry is for democracy."

"Like everybody else, I listened to Ne Win's speech on the radio on 23rd July when he promised a multi-party system. Until then, I had considered that an impossible dream. Now, the thought of freedom and democracy came closer although we felt that we had been cheated when it was decided not to hold a referendum — and Sein Lwin was appointed new president," says Kyaw Thu, 20, from State High School No. 1 in Kemmendine. "My 18-year old sister, Win Maw Oo, became involved also like so many other high-school pupils all over Rangoon. Although everybody supported the movement, the youngest ones were always the bravest and the most daring."

On 22nd July, the day before the BSPP's emergency congress had begun, Christopher Gunness flew in to Rangoon on a tourist visa. He was on a reporting assignment in the Far East and his duty was to cover the extraordinary congress. Using the old, colonial-style Strand Hotel by the Rangoon River as his base, he achieved much more than just that. With Burmese newspapers being neither informative nor reliable, and foreign publications almost impossible to get hold of, the Burmese public relies on the radio, especially the Burmese services of the BBC and, to a lesser extent, of the VOA and All-India Radio.

However, until Christopher Gunness arrived in Rangoon, the BBC's Burmese service had been rather bland in its coverage of domestic, Burmese news and more often than not tried to avoid controversies — partly because its announcers were still Burmese citizens and had families back home. Christopher Gunness changed all that and infused a new vitality into the BBC's Burmese transmissions that made them the most popular, and the only reliable source of news in the country.

"My impression when I arrived was that the situation was extremely tense," says Christopher Gunness. "People were frustrated and angry and there was a feeling of 'unfinished business'; it was easy to sense that something big was about to happen. But there was a feeling of doom as well. I was enormously depressed by what I heard and what I saw."

Through a string of local contacts, Christopher Gunness was put in touch with the opposition. A car picked him up one night outside his hotel and took him to a small house in the outskirts of Rangoon, where they changed cars and continued to another secret location. Cars were changed a third time and, eventually, he reached a safe house in the outer suburbs. The interviews he recorded there later shocked and infuriated the Burmese public. Some students related their experiences from Insein Jail of beatings and torture. A girl claimed, in a calm but firm voice, that she had been raped by *Lon Htein*-men while in custody.

Through other contacts, Christopher Gunness interviewed an army officer who had just returned from the Karen front near the Thai border. The story he had to tell differed considerably from the bombastic victory bulletins which were usually published in the *Working People's Daily* and broadcast over the BBS. According to this officer, his soldiers were dying like flies from both malaria and fighting on the battlefront in the country's frontier areas: "We don't engage the enemy [the ethnic insurgents] unless we absolutely have to. There's never enough rice and medicines. It's a struggle for survival and the morale is very, very low among the troops."

"Nothing of this was actually new to the Burmese. Everybody knew it. But to hear it over the radio, on the BBC, related by Burmese people themselves was an entirely different matter. For the first time, people spoke up in public," says Christopher Gunness. "I think that had a tremendous impact on the morale of the Burmese people."

One of the students who Christopher Gunness interviewed had also been farsighted enough to announce that the student movement was calling for a nation-wide general strike on the auspicious day of 8th August; 8.8.88. A cartoonist for the popular monthly *Cherry* magazine had earlier drawn a picture of the Statue of Liberty breaking a chain which resembled a series of four 8s. Now, the message spread to radio listeners in every town across the country — and it was met with cheers and jubilation: "Let's rise against the government!"

OUTRAGE

On 1st August, the underground student organisation *ba ka tha* — the Burmese abbreviation for the underground All-Burma Students' Union — began distributing leaflets, calling for a general strike. The proclamation was signed 'Min Ko Naing' — obviously a *nom de guerre* since it meant 'The Conqueror of Kings' as well as 'I shall defeat you'. Rumours had it that a committee of six leading student activists were behind the signature. Students suddenly appeared in teashops and at bus stops, distributed the leaflets — and quickly vanished into crowds of people. Some leaflets were mimeographed on rough, brownish paper while others were hand-written. On 2nd August, monks joined the students outside the Shwe Dagon and fiery appeals were made for a strike against the BSPP regime. There was also a widespread awareness that this also marked the 50th anniversary of the mighty 1300 Movement of 1938, the beginning of the end of British rule in Burma.

The government's official response to the mass movement that was brewing throughout the country was the usual mixture of lies and prevarications. The *Working People's Daily* under the headline 'Unsavoury activities by young students at Shwe Dagon' on 3rd August published its own version of the events on the Full Moon Day of Waso in a quaintly jumbled English:

— Those young students carried on with such activities as sticking leaflets on the pagoda platform, inciting novices and members of the Buddhist Order to deliver speeches in opposition, providing false information to foreign tourists and having them take pictures, and perpetrating physical harassment to some working people coming to worship at the pagoda. Moreover, at about 5 pm yesterday, they took away donation money after breaking open the donation box kept in front of the...upper terrace of the Pagoda...when these elements swelled to a strength of 100 or 200 they were seen going in a procession on the pagoda platform, flying a peacock flag. The young students in the group were mostly of gullible age, and as they were carrying on so, at the instigation of those taken to be destructive elements, there can come about undesirable disturbances. So, it is necessary for parents and teachers to most carefully keep their children and pupils from getting into wrong ways, it is learnt.

"When we read that nonsense, we said enough is enough! On the same day, more than ten thousand students and high-school pupils marched down to the Sule Pagoda near the City Hall," recalls Wa Wa, a 23-year old female medical student from Rangoon. "Actually, it was the police's own mistake that the demonstrations spread to central Rangoon. They had sealed off the Shwe Dagon so the Sule became the obvious alternative."

The 3rd August demonstration attracted about 10,000 marchers and was the biggest thus far in Rangoon. Support and encouragement came from everywhere: people in windows and on balconies applauded, vendors of sweets, snacks and cheroots distributed their goods free to the marchers — and some spontaneously joined in the demonstration. Others offered water and handkerchiefs — welcome in the afternoon heat. The atmosphere was carnival-like, and the police and the few troops that were stationed near the City Hall did not interfere as the young demonstrators danced along the streets, cheerfully chanting:

be u talone ta kyat khwe — Sein Lwin khoung ko khwe!
hsan ta pyi hse kyauk kyat — Sein Lwin khoung ko pyat!

a duck's egg is 2 Kyats 50 — break Sein Lwin's head!
a *pyi* of rice is 16 Kyats — chop off Sein Lwin's head!

Apart from being a rhyme and a rhythmic chant, the slogan also alluded to rising prices of basic foodstuff and it ridiculed the new, hated "Butcher, Sein Lwin". The on-lookers laughed, cheered and clapped their hands. One *pyi* of rice had risen even further from nine Kyats after the curfew had been imposed in June to twelve in July and now 16.

"The people seemed to appreciate it and they clearly were proud of us," Wa Wa says. "When we dispersed, we said to each other: 'Let's meet tomorrow again, at the Sule Pagoda!'"

That night, the BBS announcer read out two formal declarations, signed by Sein Lwin and Gen. Saw Maung respectively. Martial Law had been declared in Rangoon. The jittery move, however, had no intimidating effect on the public at large — if anything, it just made them angrier and even more determined to oppose a regime that seemed both unwilling and unable to understand the sensitivities of its own people. Over the next few days, the demonstrations continued although they were not as large as on the 3rd; the objective seemed to be to keep the flame alive in preparation for the general strike. Meetings were also held here and there in the capital. In Yankin, a 29-year old dentist, Thu Ra, who is more commonly known by his comedian's stage-name Zagana, 'the Forceps', entertained gatherings with biting satires, ridiculing the one-party system and the ruling elite.

The wave of anti-government sentiments also swept upcountry; curfews were imposed on Pegu, Thanatpin and the oil town of Yenangyaung on 6th August following outbreaks of public unrest there and police firing into crowds of demonstrators. That, however, did not prevent masses of people from journeying down to Rangoon in private cars, trains, buses and by the lorry-load. They arrived in batches, shouting slogans and waving the old Union of Burma flag from the pre-coup era; thousands camped in the university, outside Rangoon General Hospital and in the lush Bogyoke

Aung San Park near the Royal Lakes.

The whole country was gearing up for the great 8.8.88. Christopher Gunness had left Burma on 29th July, when his 7-day tourist visa was up, but continued reporting from Dhaka, Bangladesh. Droves of other journalists arrived in Bangkok, posed as tourists at the Burmese Embassy there, and managed to get into Rangoon on the thrice weekly Thai International flight. The mosquito-infested rooms of the run-down Strand were full for once and the waiters in the hotel's high-ceilinged restaurant — which, in the tropical heat and 40 years after the British had gone, still offers oats for breakfast and cucumber sandwiches for afternoon teas — were unusually busy serving a crowd of odd-looking 'tourists'. All of them were equipped with notepads, cameras and portable tape-recorders; they scrambled for the telephone and hotel telex, eager to report back to their editorial desks that they had indeed made it into hermetically sealed Burma. Everybody was poised for the big day.

Peter Conard, a Bangkok-based Buddhist scholar did not belong to the journalistic crowd at the Strand, but happened to be in Rangoon anyway that week in August. He was staying at the more centrally located Dagon Hotel on Sule Pagoda Road, near the old Globe Cinema:

"I was standing on the balcony of my hotel room just before 9 am when I spotted some masked youths on bicycles racing down the almost empty road outside, calling out something in Burmese. Apparently they were announcing that the demonstrators were coming. A few minutes later, some students came and formed human chains around the soldiers who were posted at the main intersections. I was told that the students intended to protect the troops from possible, violent attacks from the demonstrators. And then the first marchers arrived. I saw them coming in a massive column across the railway bridge on Sule Pagoda Road with flags and banners heading for the city centre. There were thousands of them, clenching their fists and chanting anti-government slogans. People came out of their houses, applauding and cheering the demonstrators on."

Soon, various groups of marchers appeared from all directions and everybody seemed to be on their way to the City Hall and the nearby Bandoola Square. There were young and old men, women and children, Burmans, Indians, Chinese and people from nearly every other ethnic group in the country with flags, banners and portraits of the national hero Aung San. Strikingly evident was a disciplined column of hundreds of Buddhist monks carrying their alms bowls upside down to indicate that the entire nation was on strike. Within an hour, the entire city centre was solidly packed with tens of thousands of people. The balconies on the surrounding houses were crammed with spectators and some even went up to the rooftops. About ten makeshift podiums were erected outside the City Hall and one speaker after another went up to denounce the government. It was a clear and sunny day.

"We want democracy! Down with the BSPP government! Down with Sein Lwin! Release Aung Gyi and the other political prisoners!" the tens of thousands strong crowds chanted. Street vendors handed out cheroots, sweets, bread and snacks to the demonstrators and people stuck wads of banknotes into the hands of the ones who seemed to be the organisers. The foreign journalists from the Strand were cheered when they raised their cameras to take pictures of the marchers. Placards in English were turned in their direction while the demonstrators called out, also in English: "Let the world know that Burma has risen against the tyranny! We want democracy! Welcome foreign journalists!" Quite a few Caucasian reporters were asked: "Are you Christopher Gunness?"

Ko Lin was one of the hundreds of thousands of people who demonstrated against the government that day: "There was actually no central organisation for the demonstrations. We had only agreed on some basic principles, the main one being that every march should converge outside the City Hall. In Yankin, where I live, we met in a teashop on the night of the 7th to draw up plans. Similar meetings were held in every township in Rangoon."

At 8 minutes past 8 on 8.8.88, the dockworkers in Rangoon port had walked out. That was the auspicious moment, and as soon as the word spread that the strike was on, people began marching towards the city centre.

— At first, there were only twelve of us in a teashop in Yankin. We had gathered old pre-coup Union of Burma flags, student flags with the fighting peacock and portraits of Aung San which we had collected from government offices and people's homes. Then we set off, soon after 8 am, down Kaba Aye Road. Other groups of people joined in and before long, our column was several thousand strong. We marched past the zoo and the ministry of defence. At every intersection, marchers from other townships appeared and we joined hands and continued down Sule Pagoda Road to the City Hall. It was unbelievable; the entire population of Rangoon seemed to be out in the streets. The different columns had banners indicating which township they came from: Yankin, Bahan, North Okkalapa, South Okkalapa, Thaketa and Thingangyun. It was almost like a competition; which township would have the most participants and the most daring slogans? When we reached the City Hall and the nearby Bandoola Park a couple of hours later, there were hundreds of thousands of people.

A festive mood prevailed all day — and the army remained in the background at the intersections, protected by rings of students. Spontane-ously, some demonstrators struck up the the national anthem, the army song and shouted: "The *pyithu tatmadaw* (people's army) is our army!" The soldiers were addressed as *akogyi* , or elder brother; there was a widespread belief that the soldiers would join the uprising and help overthrow the gov-ernment. To show the soldiers that they would have to kill their own people if they didn't, some young demonstrators even walked up to the lines of troops, which were positioned here and there, unbuttoned their shirts and shouted: "Shoot me if you dare!"

"But it was also easy to see the psychological isolation of the soldiers," observed Peter Conard. "Nervously clutching their automatic rifles, they seemed swamped in the sea of people and taken aback by the massive demonstrations."

The *Associated Press* reported: "Marching behind red flags, symbolising courage and waving portraits of 1940's national hero Aung San, young students, women, monks and other Rangoon residents...called for democ-racy and economic reform. 'You couldn't see the end of it,' said a 22-year old British student...Georgina Allen said she saw 'solid flanks' of organised, unarmed demonstrators clenching their fists, cheering and clapping their hands as they marched along a main street in Rangoon."

The massive demonstrations were by no means confined to Rangoon. In nearly every town across the country — Mandalay, Sagaing and Shwebo in the north, Bassein in the Irrawaddy delta, Pegu, Toungoo, Pyinmana and Minbu in the central plains, the oil towns of Yenangyaung and Chauk along the Irrawaddy river, Moulmein, Mergui and Tavoy in the southeast, Taunggyi in Shan State and even as far north as the Kachin State capital of Myitkyina — masses of people took to the streets to vent 26 years of pent-up frustrations with the BSPP regime. Min Win Htut, a 20 year old chemistry student, participated in the demonstration in the southeastern port city of Moulmein: "About 100,000 people gathered outside the Kyaik-touk Pagoda in the morning. There were students, monks and ordinary people. Peasants from the countryside had arrived in lorries and bullock-carts to participate in the demonstration. We marched through the city to the Maidan grounds." For the first time, the slogan *dimokresi apyei-awa ya shiye do-a-ye! do-a-ye!* — we want full democracy, that's what we want! reverberated between the walls of the old colonial-style houses of Moul-mein. Columns of local Mon people, brandishing their own banners, mixed with the Burmans in a unique display of ethnic solidarity between two of the country's main national groups.

However, in central Rangoon, the military at last showed some kind of reaction at about 5.30 pm. Brig-Gen Myo Nyunt, the Rangoon commander, appeared on the portico of the City Hall along with several other high ranking army officers. Over a loud-speaker, he firmly told the people to disperse, or the troops would open fire. Across the street on a balcony was Hnwe Hmwe, a 25-year old woman: "But nobody reacted in the way that the military had expected. The crowds only grew bigger and bigger. Myo Nyunt repeated his threat twice after the first announcement and each time, his voice seemed to get weaker as the demonstrators responded in unison: "This is a peaceful demonstration! Be disciplined! No provocations!"

The euphoric atmosphere prevailed all day. In the evening, thousands of people moved to the Shwe Dagon where a meeting was being held. Meanwhile, Bren-carriers and trucks full of armed soldiers were parked in the compound of the City Hall — and in the nearby Barr Street. But nobody really thought that the troops would be called out.

"We almost thought we'd won and that the government had given up," says Ko Lin.

At 11 pm there were still thousands of people outside the Sule Pagoda. At 11.30, trucks loaded with troops roared out from the behind the City Hall. These were followed by more trucks as well as Bren-carriers, their machine-guns pointed straight in front of them. Spontaneously, the demonstrators began singing the national anthem. Two pistol shots rang out — and then the sound of machine-gunfire reverberated in the dark between the build-ings surrounding Bandoola Square. People fell in droves as they were hit. The streets turned red with blood as people "scattered screaming into alleys and doorways, stumbling over open gutters, crouching by walls and then, in a new wave of panic, running again," Seth Mydans wrote in the *New York Times* of 11th August.

Almost simultaneously, trucks loaded with soldiers pulled up close to a column of about 2,000 people who had gathered on Shwegondine Road northeast of the Shwe Dagon Pagoda. Ko Lin was there:

— Some soldiers got down from the trucks and aimed their rifles towards the crowd while others stayed on the trucks. They fired on automatic right into the thickest part of the crowd. We ran for our lives. Two young men in front of me fell to the ground and died instantly. My friend next to me was hit in his leg and I helped him along. People ran for cover in all directions as bullets flew through the air. We reached our house safely, but my friend was too scared to go to hospital; we treated him at home the best we could. Luckily, he survived.

Richard Gourlay, who was in Rangoon on that fateful Monday, wrote in the *Financial Times* two days later: "Eye-witnesses saw armoured cars driving up to groups of demonstrators and opening fire indiscriminately, challenging official claims that they were using only moderate force. Some witnesses reported seeing demonstrators carrying bodies of dead protesters over their heads as they marched through the streets."

Nobody knows how many people were killed that night, but the shooting continued until about 3 in the morning. Sit Naing, the medical student who had participated in the June demonstrations, went to Rangoon General Hospital (RGH) as soon as he heard that the army had opened fire on the demonstrators: "I thought they needed volunteers. But that night, only two wounded were brought to RGH. They came from Shwegondine and were twins. One of them died almost immediately. We heard that the army was picking up the dead bodies outside the Sule Pagoda and taking them away. I have no idea where".

James Coles, an Australian tourist from Sydney, told *Reuters* on his arrival in Bangkok that he had given a lift in his hired car to a young demonstrator that night. With tears in his eyes, the young man produced two cartridge cases from his *longyi* and said he had picked them up at a spot where four of his colleagues had been shot when the army smashed one of the many scattered marches round the city.

Shooting also occurred in the northern town of Sagaing on 9th August. Two frequent visitors from Japan were in the area when the local police opened fire on demonstrators:

— On that day, students were marching towards the police station in Sagaing to demand the release of other students who were being detained there. The demonstrators were joined by a large number of peasants from surrounding villages. By the time they reached the police station, the crowd had swelled to about 10,000.

At the police station, someone in the crowd — believed by local people to have been an agent provocateur — threw stones at the police, who responded with gunfire. When a male student stood up to urge the crowd not to react violently, he was immediately shot and killed. A monk repeated the student's plea. Five bullets hit him before he died and fell to the ground. "When the monk fell, a female student shouted: 'Be calm! We're not afraid to die!' She was shot as well. There was a moment's silence and then an automatic gun fired into the crowd. The the one who began shooting indiscriminately into the mass of people was *Thura* Kyaw Zwa, the chairman of the Sagaing Division's People's Council. He was blasting away with his Sten gun and hundreds of people were hit."

Another source on the massacre in Sagaing was a 53-year old man from Manchester who then was teaching at the Mandalay Teachers' Training College. In an interview with *The Times* on 23rd September, he related the incident that had taken place more than a month before:

— 200 to 300 died on the spot, others died in hospital and elsewhere. Two weeks later, I asked a doctor who was involved how many wounded he was still treating. He said 100, many with hideous wounds. Most of the wounds had been inflicted from behind as the crowd rushed away.

The two visitors from Japan claim that the police threw bodies into the Irrawaddy river to destroy the evidence:

— Some of the injured managed to swim to safety and to report the massacre. All locals know that anything thrown in the river from the Mandalay side will float all the way downstream. But from the Sagaing side, because of a bend in the river, objects will get caught on Naukchinkyun Island a few miles away. Sure enough, bodies began washing up there soon after. A few days later, the army, who had taken over the police station, noticed a strange smell there. Upon investigation, they found twenty bodies which had been thrown into the well of the compound.

The title *thura* in front of Kyaw Zwa's name means 'hero'; a distinction he had earned when he was an army lieutenant fighting communist insurgents in upper Burma. Local people in Sagaing say that he used to kill even small children, arguing that they were "the seeds of communism". *Thura* Kyaw Zwa was but the most extreme example of brutal, autocratic ex-army officers who filled the posts of the BSPP administration out in the provinces. The BBS described the incident in Sagaing on 9th August as an attack by 5,000 demonstrators against the town's police station: "In order to prevent the police station from falling into the hands of the mobs, shots were fired. It was learnt that 31 people were killed and 37 others wounded in the incident."

On Tuesday 9th August, the demonstrations continued in Rangoon, but on a smaller scale — and the euphoria of the previous day had turned into anger and deep bitterness. On Monday, all major roads had been divided with concrete blocks to separate them into one 'security lane' for the army and the other for civilians. These blocks were now overturned as barricades had been built all over the city, or they had been broken to pieces by people who threw chunks at the soldiers. Pieces of concrete had also been laid out in the streets to mark the places where people had been gunned down. And it rained almost all day.

Peter Conard went out from his hotel in the morning and met an old man who was literally trembling with fury. "This is a murderous government", the old man said. "This is a Hitler government. Let the world know what is happening in our Burma!" Peter Conard continued down the streets into the Indian quarter behind the Sule Pagoda and some people, who noticed his camera, summoned him into a back alley: { They carried out the dead body of a 15 year old Muslim boy into the street for me to photograph. They had hidden him in their house since they feared the army would snatch the corpse and take it away for cremation, which goes against Muslim beliefs. I had to hurry up, since there were troops only a block away. Then a plump little 8-9 year old boy appeared and pointed down the street, screaming in broken English: 'Fuck army!'"

Army trucks raced past crammed with soldiers, their guns pointed outwards. Inside, Peter Conard glimpsed civilian prisoners who were being taken away, presumably to Insein. Several thousand people were arrested that day, many to disappear forever. But remarkably, thousands of others were still demonstrating, albeit in a more cautious manner than on the previous day. A group of flag-waving people would appear in a street corner, shout a few slogans, and then disappear when heavily armed soldiers arrived with their guns at the ready.

A Western diplomat, who was out in the streets of Rangoon at the time, reported: "There were disciplined bursts of automatic riflefire into the crowds and snipers picked out the people holding flags and portraits of Aung San. It was awful, like rabbit shooting. I know a 15 year old boy who participated in a march on the 9th. When they encountered the troops, they sat down in the street. The soldiers opened fire but this boy was lucky. A bullet hit right between his legs. Then the soldiers began bayonetting the kids. When a soldier was about to thrust his bayonet into this boy, another trooper said: 'No, he's too young'. He was saved but many of his friends were bayonetted to death in front of his eyes."

Win Moe from RU (Main)'s international relations department, who had been active in the June movement, participated in a demonstration of about 20,000 people who marched from Thingangyun on Tuesday. The leader of the march was a charismatic student in his early twenties, Moe Thi Zon.

"At the junction of Kaba Aye Pagoda Road and the road leading to the Japanese embassy, we met up with another demonstration, also carrying flags and portraits of Aung San," says Win Moe. "Monks walked in front of the column; we thought that would inhibit the troops from firing on us. But then we discovered that soldiers from the 22nd LID and the 16th Regiment were closing in from behind and in front of us. They charged us, shooting into the demonstration and bayonetting the ones who fell, or ran too slowly. 30-40 must have been killed there; hundreds were arrested. We survivors fled into private homes, where people gave us shelter."

The shooting in downtown Rangoon on Monday night had cleared the actual city centre, but the demonstrations continued on Tuesday and, particularly, Wednesday in the suburbs where it was easier to escape when the troops arrived. The working class suburbs of South Okkalapa, North Okkalapa and Thaketa were the most active; army discontent had been rampant there ever since these "satellite towns" were founded during the time of Ne Win's 1958-60 Caretaker Government. Rising food prices during the curfew and martial law had deepened the resentment in the poorer parts of Rangoon. Instead of being able to buy one *pyi* and still have a few Kyats left over, as the case had been in April or May, a labourer, earning 6.50 Kyats per day now had to work almost three days to buy the same quantity of rice. "Some of us had marched down to the City Hall on the morning of the 8th," a North Okkalapa resident relates. "But at 8 pm, people from all the wards of North Okkalapa gathered in the streets of our suburb and staged a local demonstration. Long processions of people marched back and forth all night, shouting anti-government slogans. Workers, students, housewives, Buddhist monks — literally everybody participated. Troops cordoned off our suburb, but some columns of demonstrators managed to break out and marched downtown".

Early on Tuesday morning, thousands of people gathered outside North Okkalapa's Thazin theatre, near the Tatakalay exit, leading down to Rangoon proper. Troops blockaded the way; at 7 am they opened fire and killed four demonstrators. The crowd retreated, and speeches were made on makeshift stages: "At 11.30, an army major ordered one of his soldiers to fire into the crowd. He refused — and was taken away. The officer made a phone call from a nearby private house. The house-owner overheard the conversation. An order to shoot to kill demonstrators had been given."

The slaughter began soon afterwards. The first to be hit were a young Buddhist novice and an 18-year old girl. She was still tightly holding a portrait of Aung San when she fell dead to the street. Troops and Bren-carriers rumbled into the winding backstreets of North Okkalapa — and fired indiscriminately into crowded market places, teashops and people's ramshackle homes.

The people fought back with *jinglees* , swords, clubs, molotov cocktails and whatever they could grab. The people in North Okkalapa even managed to overman a Bren-carrier and kill its driver with a *jinglee* . But not knowing how to operate the machine-gun, the people burnt the vehicle. Monks also participated in the counter-attacks, and they soon became dubbed as 'the Yellow Army'. Many monks were also shot and killed when government troops fired into crowds and neighbourhoods: "I saw a monk standing in a meditation pose on a sidewalk. He was shot in his head by a sniper and died instantly. In that incident, at least four other monks were killed as well as five demonstrators. The people fled helter-skelter to escape from the shooting," claims Aung Kyaw from North Okkalapa.

Gone now were the high spirits, obliterated by the army's ferocity.

OUTRAGE

Hatred of all in authority raged through the city. In the evening of the 9th, a suicide squad of protesters drove a fire engine into the local *Lon Htein* headquarters in North Okkalapa. The police station was trashed and burnt. On Wednesday morning, a DDSI agent on a motorbike — easily distinguishable with his stern face and sunglasses — was spotted near the suburb's hospital. *"Em-eye! Em-eye!"* the crowd roared, and a rock knocked him off his motorbike. An enraged crowd beat him to death and set the corpse afire together with the vehicle.

The shooting continued on Wednesday as well — and now the crowds stormed around in blind fury. An outraged mob of several hundred people overran a local police station in North Okkalapa, torched it — and dragged four kicking, struggling policemen out into the street. A young man came forward with a rusty sword and decapitated them in turn to cheers and applause from the crowd. The policemen's weapons were carried off to be hidden. Trees were felled to build barricades around North Okkalapa to prevent army trucks and Bren-carriers from entering the congested, vulnerable suburb.

"The troops that remained inside our suburb, mainly at the local party unit office, were totally blockaded by crowds outside. The soldiers radioed for help from their headquarters. At 5 pm, three military aircraft were hovering at a low altitude over North Okkalapa for nearly an hour. People shouted and waved swords into the sky to show that they were defiant, not afraid," Aung Kyaw says. "Then the aircraft dropped leaflets, which ordered us to disperse and remove the barricades — otherwise they'd bombard North Okkalapa. We shouted even louder, and, at last, the aircraft disappeared. The soldiers escaped but that night, we positioned our own sentries at the main entrances to the suburb. They kept vigil all night. The police had already disappeared as well and we had confiscated lots of rifles from their abandoned stations. We were prepared to fight if the army dared enter North Okkalapa again."

Mun Awng, a 28-year old singer from the Kachin minority, participated in the demonstrations in the northern suburb of Insein:

— The army had blocked the way so only a few of us could get down to central Rangoon. But there were demonstrations every day near Insein bus station. We marched around with flags and banners and shouted anti-government slogans. Thousands of people showed up and the mood was jubilant. However, at 3 pm on Wednesday the 10th, the troops opened fire. Demonstrators as well as people who were shopping in the market were killed. The soldiers were very, very young and seemed to regard any civilian as an enemy. Whenever they saw a crowd, they shot into it without hesitating. Both wounded and the corpses were taken away in trucks by the army.

Sit Naing spent the entire week at the RGH, working as a volunteer and assisting the doctors and the nurses in operating on the wounded that the army dumped in the hospital compound: "When the staff saw all the wounded students and children, they cried but carried out their duties with meticulous care. They were so furious with the army that they even refused to accept the few injured soldiers who were brought there. The wards were filled with crying and moaning youths".

On the 9th, over 100 wounded demonstrators were brought to the RGH, according to Sit Naing. Many of them came from the working class suburbs: North and South Okkalapa, Thingangyun and Thaketa where troops from the navy had opened fire on demonstrators who had tried to march across the bridge on the Pazundaung Creek. Most of the victims were young, between 16 and 22. The youngest he saw was a boy of 15 who had been kept in the ministry of defence almost all day. When he eventually was sent on the back of an army truck to the RGH, it was too late. He died of loss of blood after about an hour.

A group of high-school students had marched out of Thingangyun on the 9th. Before leaving, their teachers had told them that if they ran into troops they should ask them to join in. The school children did exactly that when they spotted the first line of soldiers blocking their way. The troops ordered the teenagers to kneel down on the road and raise their hands above their heads. Then, riflefire rang out — and several youngsters were killed. The survivors fled; one wounded made it to the RGH and related the story to the outraged nurses and doctors:

— The worst day was Wednesday the 10th. Army trucks dumped both dead and wounded from all over Rangoon outside the hospital. Some kids had a bulletwound in their arms or legs — and then a bayonet gush in their throats or chests. Some were also totally disfigured by bayonet cuts. Several corpses were male and stark naked — with shaven heads. Those were the monks whom the soldiers had stripped off their robes before dumping their corpses outside the RGH. I counted 160 dead and hundreds of wounded at the RGH alone and there were many more at other hospitals throughout Rangoon. At least 1,000 people were killed by the army during the period 8th-12th August.

The most horrific incident took place right outside the RGH on the 10th. Ko Ko, a 22-year old medical student, came there at about 1 pm and saw a large crowd outside the emergency unit:

— Someone put up a big white banner above the entrance. On it, it was written in blood: "Doctors, nurses and hospital workers who are treating the wounded urge the soldiers to stop shooting!" There was not enough staff to take care of all the wounded, the the hospital was rapidly running out of blood plasma, anaesthetics and even bandages. Shortly afterwards, a group of nurses emerged from the hospital, carrying the national flag and placards with the same message. I decided to join them, believing that it would be safe to march together with the nurses. We walked around the quarter — and saw an army truck approaching. I never thought they'd shoot. Some enraged people climbed the fence outside the hospital and shouted abuse at the soldiers. Then I heard a single shot, and another — followed by automatic riflefire. They were firing into the column of hospital personnel! I saw dead and wounded sprawling in pools of blood outside the RGH. I helped carry them inside, where people cried at the sight of the nurses, their hospital white sullied with blood.

Two female and one male nurse were severely wounded, two others only slightly hurt. Several civilians — blood donors and relatives looking for their kin — were killed. The shooting occurred at 1.30 pm — and half an hour later, the soldiers returned and fired their rifles at the hospital. No one was hit this second time, but the hospital staff and others erected small, makeshift shrines of flowers, wreaths and monks umbrellas in the compound outside the RGH. News about the hospital shooting spread all over Rangoon. The very thought of shooting hospital staff, whose duty is to save life, was horrendous and the public was further inflamed: "The hospital shooting was a major turning point. The rift between the public and the military was now total; there could be no way back to the days when serving with the army was an honour. We worked overtime throughout the nights and slept wherever and whenever we could. Everyone was upset. Some wept openly. We were unable to understand why the soldiers, who we'd thought would join us, could do this to their own people," says Sit Naing.

On the 11th, Peter Conard visited the RGH:

— Everyone was outraged. The staff had carefully circled the bulletmarks on the walls of the hospital with white chalk. There were also lots of posters pasted on the walls, denouncing the regime and the killings. Inside, the wards were full of wounded people, who were being treated with whatever was left of the almost depleted stocks of medicines. But we were also told that many people didn't dare bring their wounded relatives to hospital for fear of being arrested, or registered by the military. Many died in their homes, without medical care.

That fear was not unjustified. During the nights of the worst killings, rumours abounded that cars belonging to the US embassy in Rangoon were picking up wounded and sending them to hospital. While that, according to several sources, did happen in a few cases, Sit Naing recalls a curious incident that took place one of the nights he was staying at the RGI I: "Four white vans came to the hospital to collect both dead and wounded. The drivers claimed they came from the US embassy and said: 'the Americans are going to treat the wounded at the embassy.' I found the whole thing peculiar and noted down the registration numbers of two of these vans." The numbers were Z-1448 and Z-4227. When asked later, the US embassy in Rangoon made it clear that it had no cars with these registration plates. But Rangoon residents recall that every night during the week of terror in their city, smoke billowed from Kyandaw crematorium — and that whole area was sealed off by the army.

The massacres and street fightings eventually came to an end when people listened to the BBS on Friday night. The announcer read out a brief message, signed by Kyaw Htin, the secretary of the state council:

— U Sein Lwin has submitted a letter of resignation as chairman of the state council, from the position of the president of the state and as representative from Mon State's Moulmein constituency-2. In accordance with Article 4 on resignation, replacement and election, U Sein Lwin has been allowed to resign from the position of chairman of the state council, president of the state and member of the *Pyithu Hluttaw* effective today — 12th August 1988.

Within minutes, people were streaming out of their houses, embracing each other, laughing with tears in their eyes and dancing down the streets. Inside, the housewives banged pots and pans in their kitchens; it was a night of joy after five bloody days in Rangoon which had claimed scores of young lives.

Five THE PUPPET

FOR A FEW days immediately after Sein Lwin's resignation, Rangoon remained in a state of shock. Since the night of the 8th, the streets had reeked of blood and cordite; at home, many families still wept in mourning for their dead relatives. Several government officials had fled their homes in Rangoon's posh northern suburbs to take refuge in the Rangoon Command headquarters near the airport. Calm and confidence seemed to prevail only in a heavily guarded residence on the tree-studded shores of Inya Lake. Protected by 700 troops, Ne Win was celebrating a brief honeymoon with a 25-year-old Arakanese beauty. It was not a formal marriage, but a magic act of *yedaya chay* to prevent the country from disintegrating.

On the night of the 10th, while the most brutal killings were going on in the streets of Rangoon, Ne Win had convened his closest associates for a relaxed game of scrabble at his magnificent villa on Ady Road. Sein Lwin, Aye Ko, Dr Maung Maung and the others in the inner circle around the old strongman had laughed and joked as usual; there was nothing to indicate that they were affected by the bloody events or really thought their positions were being threatened by the nation-wide outburst of public outrage with their rule.

In the streets and ordinary people's homes, however, almost everyone was waiting for someone to take the first step for renewed protests; despite the massacre, the spirit of defiance had not been quelled. In Rangoon's Barr Street, where private law firms are located, a group of advocates and attorneys met to deliberate upon the situation. On the 15th, they released an official statement. The message, though in dry legalese, was clear:

— After careful scrutinisation of the people's general demonstration that started on 8.8.88 and the work performed by the organs of power prior to that date, the members of the Central Bar Council, advocates and lawyers, give their findings as follows...the demonstration that started on 8.8.88 by the people did not exhibit any violence, was peaceful and the people were merely asking for their rights according to the constitution. As the authorities started using violence against these peaceful demonstrators, undesirable events have now followed...the shooting and bayonetting to death of young children, students and the people by the security forces in Rangoon, Sagaing, Pegu and other big towns in Burma since 9.8.88 is acting totally against the Constitution of the Socialist Republic of the Union of Burma and international human rights law. The shooting of...personnel of the Rangoon General Hospital without any provocation, of people sitting peacefully at their homes, of the people sitting peacefully at tea shops by the security forces...is a totally unlawful act.

The communiqué was signed by Myint Myint Khin, the secretary to the bar council. It was hardly surprising that Burma's lawyers were the first to speak up against the violence. As is the case in neighbouring India, the Burmese traditionally have a strong legalistic approach to life and society, which was further reinforced by the introduction of British justice during the colonial period. Moreover, few but the lawyers had observed at first hand the gross injustice of 26 years of military rule.

On the same day, another letter was delivered to Kyaw Htin, who in his capacity as state council secretary had become the officiating head of state after Sein Lwin's resignation. It was signed by Aung San Suu Kyi, the daughter of independence hero Aung San, and was supported by a number of former state leaders, including the erstwhile prime minister U Nu and ex-president Mahn Win Maung. The letter stated that "a situation of ugliness unmatched since Burma regained her independence arose throughout the country" — and it suggested the formation of a "People's Consultative Committee" to solve the crisis.

Until then, the uprising had been completely spontaneous and it had lacked proper leadership. Many people had privately expressed hope that Aung San's son, Aung San Oo who now lived in the US, would return and lead the struggle. But despite his family background, Aung San Oo had shown little interest in politics; he had settled quietly in San Diego, California, and taken US citizenship. The second son, Aung San Lin, had drowned in a pond near to the family compound when he was still a child.

Aung San Suu Kyi had left Burma in 1960 when her mother, Khin Kyi, was appointed ambassador in New Delhi. Khin Kyi was one of Burma's most outstanding public figures in her own right. She had succeeded her assassinated husband as MP for Lanmadaw constituency but resigned in 1948 to become the director of the Women and Children Welfare Board and later chairman of the Social Planning Commission and the Council of Social Services. She had travelled extensively in Europe, the US, China and Southeast Asia before becoming the first Burmese woman to be given an ambassadorial post.

Aung San Suu Kyi was only 15 when she arrived in India together with her mother. She attended high school and later Lady Shri Ram College in New Delhi, where she always was at the top of her class. The bright girl furthered her studies at St. Hugh's College in Oxford and earned a BA in philosophy, politics and economics in 1967. Five years later, she married Michael Aris, a British Tibetologist. She joined her husband in Bhutan where he had been employed since 1967 as private tutor to the Royal Family of the Himalayan kingdom and head of the Translation Department. She took the post of Research Officer in the Ministry of Foreign Affairs with specific responsibility for advising the Minister on UN Affairs. They returned to Oxford in 1975.

Roger Matthews summed up her career in the *Financial Times* of 24th October 1988: "She lived in Bhutan, Scotland and Oxford, gave birth to two sons, learned to speak Tibetan, took her younger son to live in Kyoto where they both learned Japanese, met up with her husband again in Simla, India, and had just started a postgraduate thesis at the School of Oriental and African Studies in London when in April this year [1988] her mother suffered a stroke."

Khin Kyi's condition was getting worse, and Aung San Suu Kyi returned to Rangoon in April to look after her. For nearly four months, she tended Khin Kyi in hospital, residing there herself. She just managed to bring Khin Kyi to the family home on University Avenue in Rangoon when Michael Aris and their two sons, Myint San Aung (Alexander) and Htein Lin (Kim), arrived in late July and the whole situation in Burma exploded with Ne Win's resignation and subsequent events. Unlike Khin Kyi, Aung San Suu Kyi had never been politically active. But she had regularly visited Burma, maintained her Burmese citizenship, sent her sons to become novices in monasteries at home — and also written a children's guide book to Burma in 1985. Titled *Let's Visit Burma* it was written in simple language but revealed a deep devotion for the country she had left when she was a teenager. One of the chapters concluded: "The economy has not been well managed and Burma is not a prosperous nation. However, with its wealth of natural resources, there is always hope for the future. And that future lies in the hands of its peoples."

Unintentionally, she herself came to play an important role in that future. While the uprising was gathering force she had stayed neutral, but after the August massacre pressure was building up that she should take an active role in the resolving the crisis. Thousands of protesters had carried portraits of her father in demonstrations all over the country; his name was almost mythical and symbolised all that Burma was not but should be — free, democratic and prosperous. Aung San Suu Kyi continued the legacy of her father and her appearance on the political stage in Burma in August was met with excitement and high expectations.

After these first moves, more and more people began to speak out again. On the 16th, the Burma Medical Association issued a statement saying that "we felt great sorrow when shots were fired at the Rangoon General

Hospital (RGH) compound on 10th August 1988, in which incident nurses Ma Sein Sein Yi, Ma Thaung Khin, special nurse Ma San San Aye and male nurse trainee Maung Myo Thant were injured and two persons from the crowd were killed...we earnestly request that similar incidents will not take place at all in hospitals where health staff are serving the people".

In a feeble attempt to contradict the staff at RGH, the BBS on the following day broadcast a claim that the statement had been issued "by unknown persons" and not the Burma Medical Association. The RGH staff immediately issued a new, stronger statement condemning the hospital shooting, adding "we [also] feel deep and great sorrow for the unarmed monks, children, students and pedestrians who were killed and wounded".

That afternoon, more than 5,000 people rallied outside the RGH. The monks held a Buddhist ceremony outside in the compound to honour all those who had been killed during the demonstrations. Troops nearby watched the crowd nervously — but did not interfere. Almost simultaneously, another crowd gathered outside the US embassy in Merchant Street, opposite Maha Bandoola Park. On 10th August, a powerful US senator, Daniel Moynihan, had tabled a resolution condemning the slaughter in Rangoon and called for an end to the one-party system in Burma. It had been supported by five other senators including Edward Kennedy, unanimously approved by the senate on the following day — and reached the people in Rangoon and elsewhere in translation over the VOA's Burmese Service. People had cheered in their homes as the shooting continued outside. It was the first international condemnation of the carnage in Burma.

In a peculiar twist of historical accidents, the democratic movement in Burma, as well as pro-American sentiments among the public at large, grew even more intense when Arnold Raphel, the US ambassador in Islamabad, died in a helicopter crash together with Pakistan's president Zia-ul Haq on 17th August. US embassies all over the world — including, of course, the one in Rangoon — lowered their flags to half mast as soon as the news came in. The crowd outside the embassy in Merchant Street, however, immediately assumed that the Americans were showing sympathy for their countrymen killed during the recent bloodbath.

The crowd was standing outside the actual embassy while a group of government troops, their guns at the ready, were positioned at a nearby intersection. They stared at each other apprehensively. Then, a young boy, aged about 14, split from the crowd holding high an unusually large peacock flag — and strode with firm steps towards the line of soldiers. He planted the flag in the street just in front of them and unbuttoned his shirt. A soldier raised his rifle. The boy stood there resolutely, his hands holding his shirt open, chest bared to the challenge of bullets. The soldier aimed, hesitated for a few seconds — and lowered his gun. The boy waited motionless for another minute. When nothing happened, the entire crowd surged forward, cheering and waving banners. The demonstrations had begun again.

During the first days following Sein Lwin's unexpected resignation, the government did its utmost to give the impression that the situation in Burma was returning to normal. On the 14th, the BBS claimed that "residents" in North Okkalapa had "requested assistance" from the army to "restore law, peace and tranquility" in their ravaged suburb. Two days later, the state-run radio broadcast an interview with an alleged student leader who "confessed" that the hundreds of thousands of people who had demonstrated against the regime on the 8th actually had been "forcibly recruited". Consequently, the "student leader" begged for forgiveness for his "misdeeds".

The daily minimum wage was raised from 6.50 Kyats to 8.50, the previous stringent regulations for issuing passports were relaxed and Burmese seamen were granted permission to open foreign exchange accounts. Most startling of all, the *Working People's Daily* on 17th August proudly announced that "personnel concerned from Japan, Australia and Singapore" were planning to build a string of hotels in Rangoon, Mandalay and Pagan to accommodate all the foreign tourists who presumably were going to flock to Burma now that the 'disturbances' were over.

But the most urgent task for Burma's rulers was to elect a successor to Sein Lwin. Troops backed by Bren-carriers rolled into central Rangoon to hold in check the crowds that had taken to the streets again while the BSPP's central committee and the *Pyithu Hluttaw* were convening their respective emergency sessions in the capital. After a hasty, one-day meeting on the 19th, a new party chairman and state president was elected. Since the hardline approach of Sein Lwin had failed, the choice this time was a supposed 'moderate': the chairman of the council of people's attorneys, Dr Maung Maung.

The new leader was a 64-year old, Western-trained lawyer, journalist and writer who had held several high posts in both the state and the party since the 1962 coup. He was sometimes described as a 'unique species' — a rare civilian intellectual among hard, military powerbrokers. But it was often overlooked, especially among foreign observers, that he was actually an ex-army man who always had maintained close ties with the military. He had joined the BDA in 1942 and also attended an officers' training school during the Japanese occupation. Although he left the army after the war to become a scholar, he remained close to the inner circle of officers who later took over state power in 1962.

Significantly, when his oldest son graduated from the Defence Services

Academy in Maymyo in 1971, Dr Maung Maung published a book called *To a Soldier's Son*. In this autobiographical tribute to the army, Dr Maung Maung referred to the *tatmadaw* as "my second home". Sai Tzang, the Shan scholar, describes Dr Maung Maung as "one of the few Burmese intellectuals who sincerely and deeply admired Gen. Ne Win". That admiration had been clearly expressed in a flattering biography, *Burma and General Ne Win*, which Dr Maung Maung had written in 1968. And everyone knew that he had also been the main author of the 1974 Constitution, whose abrogation now had become an almost universal demand. 'Dr Maung Maung the Moderate' was a ploy that no one accepted. He was seen as just another, powerless frontman for the old 'Number One' on Ady Road. Sein Lwin had become publicly known as 'the Butcher'; the new leader's popular nickname was simply 'the Puppet'.

No sooner had his appointment been made public than the streets of Rangoon were once more packed with protesters. Tens of thousands of people of all ages, respected professionals and monks rejected Dr Maung Maung's nomination and demanded an end to the one-party rule. Day by day, the strength and the intensity of the demonstrations increased. It had become clear that it did not matter who the ruling elite chose to represent them; the public's unequivocal cry was for democracy and the ouster of the BSPP regime. On the 22nd, a nation-wide general strike was proclaimed to press the demands for the formation of a new, interim government that could rule the country pending general elections. The entire country ground to a halt.

Before long, the people were back in the streets in towns and cities right across the country. Strike centres were established everywhere from Kawthaung, or Victoria Point, at the southernmost tip of Tenasserim Division up to the Kachin State capital of Myitkyina in the far north. In Mandalay, 100,000 marched through the city and joined in the demands for the ouster of the BSPP regime. Thura Kyaw Zwa, the BSPP official who had fired into the crowd outside the police station in Sagaing across the Irrawaddy, was sentenced to death by a court of militant monks in Mandalay and a 300,000 Kyat reward was offered for his head.

The renewed demonstrations went on peacefully almost everywhere. The only exception was Moulmein, where a large crowd had gathered outside the Mon library on 21st August. Two representatives from the ruling elite — the township people's council chairman, Soe Hlaing, and Han Yin, the leader of the local party unit — appeared heading a section of troops.

"Soe Hlaing and Han Yin ordered the soldiers to shoot into the crowd," asserts Min Win Htut, a 20-year old chemistry student from Moulmein.

"We counted 47 dead, including four monks, and about 20 wounded when the firing was over. By then, the people were furious and thousands of us stormed the homes of the two officials — who managed to escape to a nearby army camp. We confiscated 900,000 Kyats worth of property from their houses: TV sets, video equipment and all sorts of black market goods. These we sold in the streets of Moulmein afterwards at very low prices to raise funds for our local strike committee."

Moulmein was one of the first towns in the country to be taken over by its own people. Outside the town's main cinema hall, a brightly painted poster was put up. It looked like an advertisement for a new film and depicted two frightened men being chased out of town by a huge crowd of angry people. The supposed movie was called 'Running Away' — and the two fugitives strikingly resembled Soe Hlaing and Han Yin.

In Rangoon, the authorities' new approach was somewhat less aggressive. An 11-man commission, headed by Tin Aung Hein, the chairman of the council of people's justices (the chief justice), was formed to "ascertain the aspirations of the people" and questionnaires were printed and distributed in the city. The idea was widely regarded as being copied from Aung San Suu Kyi's proposal for a People's Consultative Committee, which she had submitted on the 15th. However, Tin Aung Hein's commission suspended its operations after only five days; its office was besieged daily by tens of thousands of people bombarding the commission with complaints about the BSPP regime.

Then, unexpectedly, on the 24th, martial law was lifted in Rangoon and Prome. The soldiers who had been patrolling the streets in the capital were withdrawn to the loud cheers of thousands of demonstrators. Jubilant people chanted in celebration, waved flags and sounded horns as the army trucks pulled out of the city.

On the following day, the dissident Aung Gyi was released together with the *Associated Press* correspondent Sein Win and all the others who had been arrested on 29th July. Aung Gyi returned in triumph to address a crowd of 30,000 people at the Padonma Grounds in Sanchaung, close to his home. Beside him on the stage was one of the Thirty Comrades, Bohmu Aung. Aung Gyi was cheered and applauded but puzzled his listeners when he declaimed that "we must have complete trust in president Maung Maung and the chairman of the council of people's justices, Tin Aung Hein...we must not feel bad about the army either, not even in our minds". The crowd fell silent; but when Aung Gyi, presumably sensing the changed mood, interrupted himself by shouting pro-democracy slogans, cheers filled the air again.

In downtown Rangoon, the protesters became more and more daring.

They began removing the handkerchiefs from their faces and makeshift stages were erected at almost every street corner where various speakers got up to denounce the government. Soon, different professional groups joined and formed their own sections in the marches. There were the lawyers in their court robes, doctors and nurses in hospital white, bankers, businessmen, labourers, writers, artists, film actors, civil servants from various ministries, housewives banging pots and pans to voice their demands, long processions of trishaw drivers, Buddhist monks in saffron robes, Muslims brandishing green banners, Christian clergymen chanting "Jesus loves democracy" — and even fringe groups such as columns of blind people and demurely simpering transvestites demanding equal rights. To demonstrate their unity, most demonstrators wore red headbands with a white dove, symbolising peace. It was a true "parliament of the streets" in the striking phrase of Cardinal Sin of the Philippines.

In Taunggyi, Shan State, policemen, doctors, local merchants, government employees and farmers with bullock carts joined the demonstrations which attracted nearly 100,000 people and resembled a lively country fair. In Henzada and Bassein in the Irrawaddy Delta, in the oil fields of Chauk and Yenangyaung, in Prome, Magwe, Toungoo, Pyinmana and Meiktila in the Burmese heartland, altogether millions of people marched against the BSPP government. Strike centres were established in more than 200 of Burma's 314 townships. Rice farmers from the countryside around nearly every town arrived in lorries, bullock carts and on foot to participate; it was an entire population, rural as well as urban, who in unison demanded an end to the military-dominated one-party rule that had held the country in its suffocating grip for more than two decades.

Communal frictions and old grudges were forgotten and, maybe for the first time ever, all national and political groups across the country joined together for a common cause. In Arakan State in the west, where tension between Buddhists and Muslims have long been prevalent, these two religious groups now marched hand in hand chanting anti-government slogans. The yellow banner of Buddhism fluttered beside Islam's green flag with the crescent moon.

A mass rally was held in the state capital of Akyab on 22nd August — and a number of younger people as well as old, almost forgotten politicians appeared and voiced flaming appeals for the success of the 'revolution'. There was the legendary *Bonbauk*, or 'bomb thrower', Tha Gyaw, who had waged guerrilla warfare in the Arakan Yoma almost forty years before; Kyaw Zan Rhee, the Arakan Communist Party leader who had surrendered during the 1980 amnesty; Bogri Kra Hla Aung, the commander of the regional BIA unit during the Japanese occupation; and lawyers, teachers and school headmasters. In Man-aung on Cheduba Island, also in Arakan State, local farmers and fishermen carried two coffins, which were decorated with demonetised 75-Kyat banknotes and labelled Ne Win and Sein Lwin, to a mock funeral pyre by a riverside.

In Rangoon, the rallying points for the daily mass demonstrations were still the RGH and the US Embassy. But in the afternoon of the 25th, thousands of people began gathering on the open ground to the west of the Shwe Dagon Pagoda. Some had brought their own bed rolls and entire families squatted in circles around their evening meals. They were all there well in time to get a good viewpoint for the meeting that had been announced for the following day: Aung San Suu Kyi was going to make her first public appearance. By mid-morning of the 26th, the crowd had swollen to at least 500,000 people of all ages, and national and social groups in Burmese society. Aung Win, 23, was there: "The mood was festive but there were several bomb scares before the actual meeting began. We arrived at 7 am but spent more than three hours searching the stage and checking out suspicious-looking characters. The ground outside the Shwe Dagon was jam-packed. Even U Wisara Road and all the other approach-ways to the meeting place were full of people. We students and the monks were taking care of the security and formed human chains around the stage where she was going to appear."

A huge portrait of her father, Aung San, had been placed above the stage alongside a resistance flag from World War Two. Loud-speakers were directed towards the enormous crowd. Eventually, she arrived. Her car had to stop outside the meeting ground since there were so many people and she walked the remaining stretch up to the stage amidst deafening applause and cheers. Htun Wai, a well-known Burmese film actor, introduced Aung San Suu Kyi and told the restive crowd to sit down and listen to her speech. After taking the microphone, her initial message of democracy through unity and discipline gave way to a more personal note: "A number of people are saying that since I've spent most of my life abroad and am married to a foreigner, I could not be familiar with the ramifications of this country's politics," she said over the loudspeakers. "I wish to speak very frankly and openly. It's true that I've lived abroad. It's also true that I'm married to a foreigner. But these facts have never, and will never, interfere with or lessen my love and devotion for my country by any measure or degree. People have been saying that I know nothing of Burmese politics. The trouble is I know too much. My family knows better than any how devious Burmese politics can be and how much my father had to suffer on this account."

Hundreds of thousands of people cheered and applauded and the roar reached its crescendo when she concluded: "The present crisis is the concern of the entire nation. I could not, as my father's daughter, remain indifferent to all that was going on. This national crisis could, in fact, be called the second struggle for independence."

Most of the people who had come to see and hear her outside the Shwe Dagon had probably done so out of curiosity. But during her speech, the 43-year old daughter of Burma's foremost hero won the hearts of her audience. She emerged as the leading voice for the opposition that demanded the restoration of democracy in the country.

"We were all surprised," Aung Win says. "Not only did she look like her father, she spoke like him also: short, concise and right to the point."

On the following day, the 27th, another prominent Burmese appeared in public: Tin U, the former minister of defence who had been dismissed and jailed in 1976. About 4,000 people listened to his speech outside the RGH. He quoted Dr Maung Maung's old thesis from the 1950s: "Democracy calls for 'justice, liberty and equality' which are the eternal principles of the [1947] constitution. That's what our president wrote 30 years ago. But now, I don't know what's happened to that man." The crowd roared with laughter and applauded.

Following his release from jail during the 1980 amnesty, Tin U had done a correspondence course in law. Privately, he had also expressed sympathy for the elements within Burmese society who were beginning to organise resistance against the BSPP regime. His public re-appearance roused optimism in many quarters. On 8th August, the demonstrators had tried in vain to woo the soldiers over to their side. But now, a former defence minister and chief of staff had joined the movement for democracy and it was widely believed that he still had many followers within the armed forces — which, if it proved true, could exert an important influence on events.

One by one, several ex-politicians also began issuing statements in support of the movement. The octogenarian U Nu, became active again despite his age. On 28th August, he defied the one-party constitution and set up Burma's first independent political organisation in 26 years, the League for Democracy and Peace (Provisional). Several of his old colleagues from the democratic period of the 1950s declared their support for the ex-prime minister. Thakin Chit Maung, Thakin Lwin, Thakin Tin Mya, Bo Ye Htut and other leftist leaders also re-emerged from oblivion and obscurity. The fighting spirit of the once fiery Thakin Soe was re-born as well. From his hospital bed, the ailing 83-year old former Red Flag communist leader issued a flaming appeal in support of the uprising.

Throughout the country, people resigned from the BSPP en masse. Almost daily, stacks of membership cards were turned in to the local BSPP offices. Within weeks, the entire BSPP empire collapsed. Ironically, some of the most efficient student organisers were actually former *Lanzin* Youth leaders: "It wasn't a big step, really," says Ko Lin who had been a *Lanzin*

Youth organiser for several years. "Few of us had taken the BSPP ideology seriously in any case. The *Lanzin* Youth had been more like a boy scout organisation. It had enabled us to go on summer camps in the hills, attend various training courses and simply socialise with other young people."

The traditional creativeness of the Burmese psyche flourished again after 26 years of silence. By the end of August, Rangoon alone had almost 40 independent newspapers and magazines, full of political commentaries, witty cartoons, biting satires and cartoons ridiculing the ruling elite and the BSPP. Even the official newspapers, including the *Working People's Daily* and the *Guardian*, began publishing outspoken political articles and pages full of pictures from the demonstrations.

The new, lively papers, some daily and others intermittent, had fanciful names such as the *Light of Dawn, the Liberation Daily, Scoop, New Victory, the Newsletter* and so on. Some were hand-written and photocopied or mimeographed while others had had access to professional printing presses, often free of charge since their owners wanted to show that they also supported the movement. The authorities seemed to tolerate this — but, significantly, the state-run radio, the BBS, and the government television station remained unchanged. Their employees protested and demanded the same rights as the journalists working for the print media were dismissed. Others went on strike saying they would "no longer broadcast propaganda."

At night, people tuned in to the BBC's and, to a lesser extent, the VOA's Burmese language programmes. The BBC especially remained the most reliable outside source of information for the Burmese public and its popularity was undisputed. However, in the army camps on the outskirts of the towns, leaflets and even booklets were distributed by the DDSI, denouncing the BBC and urging the soldiers "not to believe rumours". Intriguingly, one rumour that seemed to be deliberately spread by the ruling elite was that Ne Win was about to leave the country. One version was traced back to Aye Zaw Win, Sanda Win's husband. A detailed report claiming that Ne Win had flown to Coco Island en route to Singapore and West Germany turned out to have originated with the son of the former minister of defence, Kyaw Htin.

While the public was waiting for the old leaders to leave the country, the humorist Zagana continued entertaining his audiences outside the RGH with biting sketches. In street corners all over the capital, popular rock bands and singers played and sang for the demonstrators who marched past chanting slogans. And although everyone was on strike, employees in factories, offices and other work sites formed their own independent trade unions — something that had been unthinkable for 26 years. The unionists of the Burmese Railways declared that they would no longer provide special trains for "dictators of the one-party system." The staff at the meteorology department announced that, henceforth, weather forecasts would be "for the people and not for the one-party dictatorship".

To prove the unanimous support for the pro-democracy movement, one of the new newspapers, the *Phone Maw Journal* which was named after the first student to be killed in March, published in late August a report from the cemetery in Tamwe, a northeastern suburb. After the killings on 9th-12th August, many corpses had been dumped there without being cremated or the holding of appropriate Buddhist funeral rites. Consequently, the cemetery was haunted and after midnight, the newspaper claimed, the ghosts were shouting pro-democracy slogans. Recently, the *Phone Maw Journal* reported, a new unusual chant had been added to the ghosts' repertoire: "Corpses of BSPP members are not allowed to be buried in our cemetery! Stay out! Stay out!"

In North Okkalapa, where large numbers had been killed, the local people built a concrete pillar to commemorate their dead friends and relatives. In consonance with the historic date 8.8.88, the pillar measured 8 feet and 8.8 inches in height. The old union flag of the pre-BSPP era flew from a mast that topped it. Every day wreaths of fresh flowers were laid at its base.

BSPP rule had collapsed everywhere, the army and the police had withdrawn from the city — and the dreaded *Lon Htein* simply vanished from sight, which probably meant that they had been issued new uniforms and absorbed into the army. The first steps towards forming an alternative civil administration had been taken already during the days immediately after the August massacre. In several neighbourhoods in central Rangoon, people had decided to donate one blanket and one pillow per household to the RGH which was running short of all kinds of supplies for the wounded who were still being treated there. Even the black marketeers had handed over, free of charge, the contraband medicines they had in stock.

From this spontaneous effort emerged local citizens' committees, usually consisting of monks, community elders and students. Having taken over the administration, a major problem was the maintenance of law and order. Bamboo fences with guarded gates and even watch-towers were erected around the various localities to keep a close watch of movements in and out of the respective areas especially at night. Crime was increasing and monks often functioned as interrogators and judges whenever a culprit was caught.

Funds for these new administrative organs were raised through collections among the citizens. But during the turmoil immediately before Sein Lwin's resignation, an enraged mob had also stormed the Mittamon warehouse in Tamwe, where imported luxury goods were being stored awaiting distribution to army officers and BSPP officials. TV sets, video machines, foreign whisky and other items soon appeared for sale in Rangoon. Popularly called "Sein Lwin markets", they offered the goods at give-away prices and the profits went to the strike committees.

Public confidence grew as more and more well-known Burmese dared to speak out openly against the regime — and as most people really thought that the old leadership was about to go into exile. On 28th August, the All-Burma Students Union, also known by its Burmese abbreviation *ba ka tha* , had been officially established in Rangoon. Its elected chairman was a charismatic, 26-year old 3rd year zoology student, Baw Oo Tun. He assumed the *nom de guerre* with which the students previously had signed many of their underground statements: Min Ko Naing, the Conqueror of Kings. Moe Thi Zon was another prominent student leader in his mid-20s who also appeared at mass meetings and rallies in Rangoon in August and September.

There was also a rival students' union — which in English had the same name as the ABSU but used *Myanma* instead of *Bama* for Burma and therefore was abbreviated *ma ka tha* . It was headed by Min Zeya, a 5th year law student who at 30 was a bit older. He had participated in the movement since the beginning, been arrested in his hometown Kamawek in Mon State on 27th March and taken to Insein Jail in Rangoon. He was released on 7th July, re-arrested on 6th August and then released again on the 25th together with Aung Gyi, Sein Win and the other political prisoners. It was not only former politicians who had resurfaced; a new generation of young leaders had also emerged and they became as influential as the old ones.

But young and old people often worked together and there was never any real generation gap. Hmwe Hmwe, the young woman who had watched the 8th August demonstrations outside the City Hall from her balcony and later joined the movement, spent a week at the beginning of September travelling upcountry to coordinate the activities there with those in the capital. There were 15 young students in her group, but the leader, Thakin Kyi Shein, was a veteran of the anti-British struggle. They went by van and pick-up truck to Pegu, Toungoo, Pyinmana, Meiktila and Mandalay: "Since everybody was on strike, there was no train service or other regular transport and it was difficult to buy petrol as well," Hmwe Hmwe says. "But spirits were high and we attended meetings all along our way. We slept in the strike centres and there was one in every town we passed through. The people had often taken over the local BSPP offices and government premises and managed their own administration from these. There was feverish activity everywhere: people printing leaflets, making posters, publishing their own local newspapers and preparing meetings, rallies and demonstrations."

In Mandalay, the young monks' association, the *Yahanpyo* movement which Sein Lwin had forced underground in the 1970s, had resurfaced. The monks organised day-to-day affairs like rubbish collection, made sure the water supply was working and, according to some reports, even acted as traffic policemen. The maintenance of law and order was also in the hands of the monks — and the criminals who had been caught were often given rather unorthodox sentences. One visitor to Mandalay in August saw a man chained to a lamp post outside the railway station who shouted all day: "I'm a thief! I'm a thief! I'm a thief!"

What had actually happened? Had the government given up? Opinions seemed to be divided. Since the old BSPP administration had collapsed almost everywhere, the army was no longer in evidence and many government officials had left their homes to take refuge in military camps, some people assumed that this was the case. Others, however, were more cautious. A series of unusual events had taken place parallel to the emergence of the 'people's power' movement throughout the country, beginning with the unexpected lifting of martial law on 24th August and the release of the political prisoners on the following day.

At night on the 25th, a truckload of armed soldiers had entered central Rangoon and, at gunpoint, removed 600 million Kyats from the Myanma Foreign Trade Bank. The bank's newly formed trade union had protested against the action — but all troops stationed in the capital had been given six months' pay in advance. Then, on the 26th, even the prisoners in Insein Jail held an anti-government demonstration. A fire broke out, and panic broke out. The guards in watchtowers opened fire and gunned down droves of people as they tried to escape the flames. About 1,000 people were massacred and another 500 wounded crammed into the nearby Insein hospital, appealing for medical supplies. The remaining prisoners were released on what the BBS in a broadcast termed 'parole'. Political prisoners were held in communal cells with convicted criminals and it was unclear how many anti-government activists died in the bloody incident. The state radio gave the death toll as 36 and claimed 100 had been wounded.

But by strange coincidence, similar riots occurred simultaneously in nine widely dispersed towns throughout the country and nearly 9,000 convicts escaped or were released — without food and money. In Rangoon, there was almost panic. The local citizens' committees set up a temporary reception centre at the central railway station to feed the released prisoners to prevent them from resorting to crime.

There seemed to be little doubt that the "escape" of all the convicts had been orchestrated by the authorities. A few days before the prison uprising, three inmates had even been quietly transferred from Insein to Yay Kyi Aing. They turned out to be Burma's three best-known top security prisoners: MIS Tin U, his associate Bo Ni, and captain Kang Min Chol, the sole survivor of the North Korean bombing mission in Rangoon in 1983.

It also became clear that the DDSI was still active even if the regular army had evacuated Rangoon. A most remarkable incident had taken place at 4 o'clock in the morning before Aung San Suu Kyi was going to give her

Previous: student procession, Rangoon, Sept 1988
Up left. Kawthaung, Sept 1988 (Conrad Swan)
Lower left: Kachin tribes' people visit Mandalay to demonstrate on 26 (2+6=8)/8/ 1988
Above: Peoples' Railway Police demonstrate in Rangoon, Sept 1988
Next: the flag of the 'Socialist Republic' is flown upside dow, Rangoon

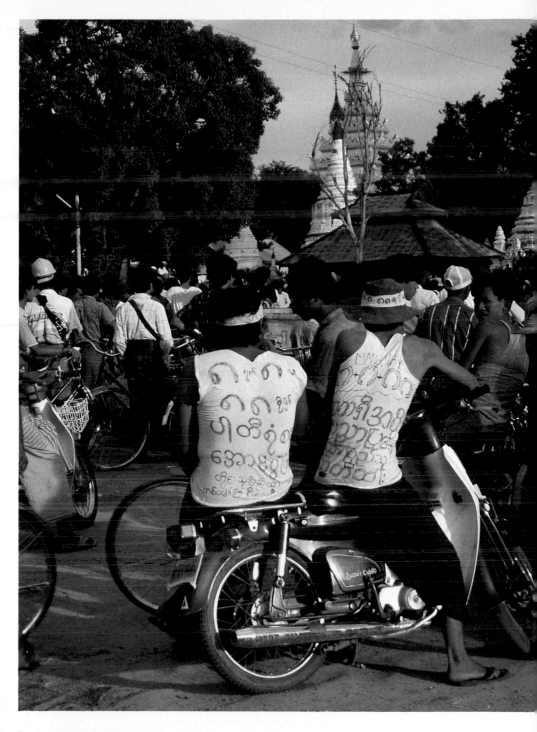

Previous: scenes from Rangoon, Sept 1988
Up left: officials from the immigration, police and customs march for democracy, Sept 1988
Lower left: government workers march in Kawthaung (Conrad Swan)
Above: at the Mandalay Mahamyamuni Shrine, the vests are sloganed '8 8 88'

Left: the *sangha* policing Mandalay after the collapse of government there, Sept 1988 (J Abbott)
Right: Light Infantry attempt to hold back a nation, Aug 1988

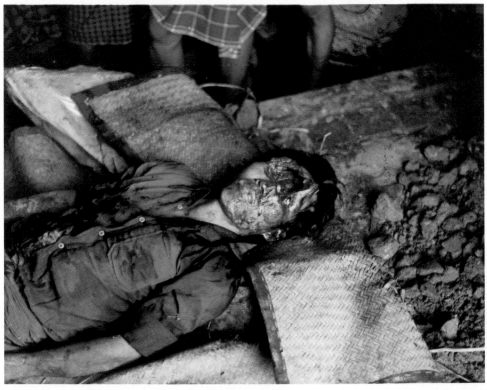

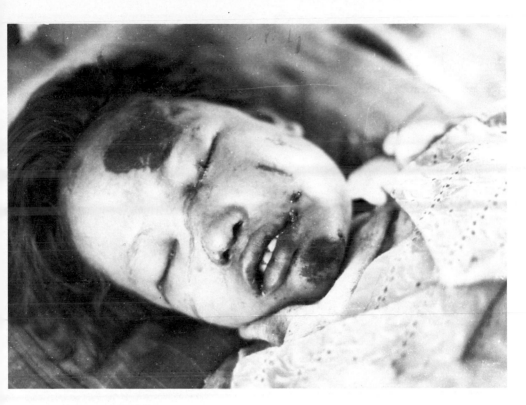

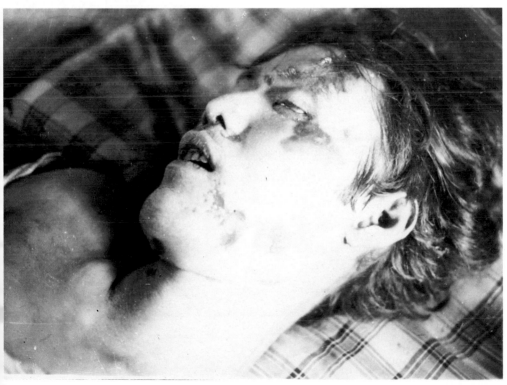

Victims: a new generation of martyrs in Burma

Up left: Gen. Ne Win, 'Number One'
Up right: Daw Aung San Suu Kyi (S Tucci)
Down left: U Nu, Daw Aung San Suu Kyi and U Tin Oo (S Tucci)

speech outside the Shwe Dagon. Two Toyota pick-up trucks carrying between them six people had been stopped for a routine check in 29th Street in central Rangoon by local vigilantes. While searching the vehicles, the vigilantes found, to their astonishment, a whole stack of leaflets defaming Aung San Suu Kyi and her British husband, Michael Aris. The hand-written leaflets contained crude drawings of the couple and slogans such as "Call your bastard foreigner and buzz off now!" and "Genocidal Prostitute!" Some of the slogans and drawings were startlingly obscene.

The vigilantes immediately apprehended the six and tied them up. A pistol was found in one of the pick-up trucks together with the ID cards of two of the prisoners. One was corporal San Lwin and the other private Soe Naing, both from the DDSI. The six were taken to Thayettaw monastery where the monks had set up a court and a temporary prison. The interrogation was filmed on video and the identities of the other DDSI agents were also established. The leader of the team was a DDSI captain, Si Thu, a trusted officer who earlier had accompanied Ne Win on trips abroad. Their pictures were displayed on notice boards all over Rangoon before they were released. During their interrogation, they claimed that they had been sent by Ne Win's powerful daughter, the ubiquitous but seldom seen Sanda Win.

The initial euphoria over the new and unprecedented freedom the people in Rangoon had enjoyed since 24th August soon became mixed with fear and paranoia. A main feature in the streets during the daily mass demonstrations were earthenware water-jars where the marchers, hoarse from shouting slogans for hours, could stop to refresh themselves. Rumours now spread that DDSI agents were poisoning these water-pots. Although it was never actually proven that this was taking place, the now outspoken *Working People's Daily* reported on 3rd September: "Members of the *sangha* [the Buddhist order of monks] yesterday stopped two suspicious-looking men near Mingun Kyaungtaik in Insein township. They fled, but one was caught. It is learnt that a bottle containing a liquid believed to be poison...was seized from the man. He reportedly claimed that the bottle contained a harmless chemical solution. He was reportedly made to drink the liquid and died soon after."

On 5th September, four men and one woman were caught outside a children's hospital on Halpin Road. After a rough interrogation, two of them confessed that the gang had tried to poison the water tank outside the hospital and they were released. But the remaining three refused to say anything and an angry crowd beat them in the street. A man came forward with a sword, decapitated the three and held up their blood-dripping, severed heads to the applause of the mob. Public executions — mostly beheadings — of suspected DDSI agents became an almost daily occurrence in Rangoon. What had started as a carnival-like, Philippine-style 'people's power uprising' was beginning to turn nasty and coming more and more to resemble the hunt for the *tonton macoutes* in Haiti after the fall of 'Baby Doc' Duvalier in 1986. Aung San Suu Kyi constantly sent her people, mostly young students who were camping in her compound on University Avenue, to try and intervene in the beheadings. In some cases they were successful in saving the lives of the suspected agents, but public anger with the military intelligence was so intense that it was almost impossible to prevent the lynchings.

Arson and looting of government warehouses and factories also were becoming more and more common. The most widely reported incident — and the most disturbing as well — took place during the first week of September in South Okkalapa. At 9.30 pm on the 4th, the local citizens' committee got a phone call from someone who claimed a mob was looting the Kyi Kyi biscuit factory in the township's Ward No. 14. Nine monks and twelve students were sent to investigate the matter. When they did not come back, a several hundred people went down to the factory — only to learn that the monks and the students had been captured by the "looters", beaten and taken away to an enclave for ex-military officers in South Okkalapa.

The crowd gradually swelled to nearly 1,000 people, and they demanded the release of their colleagues. Jingle*es* were fired at the crowd, who in turn was armed with daggers and catapults and stormed a godown inside which "the looters" had barricaded themselves. The battle lasted all night and left nearly 100 people wounded on both sides. Eventually, 67 of the "looters" were captured. Three of the ones who had been held hostage were freed while the others were missing, presumed killed.

There was uproar in South Okkalapa for several days afterwards. On the 6th, those captured stated that they had not been involved in any looting, but been sent as a ploy to lure monks and students to be killed. They claimed their "leader" was a DDSI sergeant whom they named as Htun Thein. Allegedly, he had offered rewards for the head of each student or monk in the local citizens' committee. Min Min, 22, from South Okkalapa was there during the trials and the executions that followed:

"About 20 of the captured were beheaded. They seemed drugged and showed no signs of pain during the executions which were carried out by local residents of South Okkalapa. The monks and the students tried to stop the killings and managed to have some of the prisoners ordained as monks. That saved their lives. The people were furious with them."

Early in the morning of 6th September, looters were seen carrying construction material, papers and office furniture from the compound of a German-sponsored rodent control project in Gyogon-Insein. At the same time, two army lorries were parked in the yard of the nearby People's Land Settlement Department. The soldiers did not even attempt to stop the looting — instead, they were loading their own lorries with goods from the warehouses. Two hours later, after the army lorries had left with their loot, about 200 people invaded the offices and the godowns and took almost everything that the soldiers had left behind.

In the wake of these incidents, U Nu's new league on 7th September issued a statement accusing *agent provocateurs* from the military of instigating looting and other criminal acts. But the tactics seemed to have changed since the debacle on 26th August, when a prominent DDSI officer, captain Si Thu, had been caught red-handed and publicly exposed.

On 9th September, a woman in her thirties, Ma San, was caught in Dawbon township in Rangoon while trying to commit arson there. She turned out to be a prostitute and a former inmate of Insein Jail. She had been released on 23rd August, given a large sum of money by a DDSI officer and, according to herself, also made to swallow some "medicine" before being sent out to set fire to houses in Dawbon. Ma San did not know what kind of pills they were, but they made her "high" and unable to feel any pain or remorse, she told her interrogators. The unfortunate woman was decapitated by an angry mob.

Another bizarre incident, which added to the paranoia among the public at large in Rangoon, occurred on 10th September. An 11-year old boy, Sein Han, was caught shooting *jinglees* at some demonstrators in South Okkalapa. The boy appeared drugged and had several needle marks in his arm. During questioning, he claimed that he and several other youngsters had been picked up by a "lance corporal", whose name he did not know, and shown how to use *jinglees* and catapults. The ends of the boy's eyebrows had been shaved off "so that we can recognise each other — and be identified by our bosses", he said. Sein Han's life was spared because of his admissions, which were video-taped and also published in the independent *Warazein* newspaper on 11th September.

Was it all part of a plot to destabilise the situation and deliberately foster chaos and anarchy? The ones who believed this pointed at copies of a document, stamped "top secret", which circulated widely in Rangoon at the time. According to this, an emergency meeting had been held at Ne Win's Ady Road residence on 23rd August when it had become clear that the public had rejected the 'moderate' Dr Maung Maung as well — and other methods were needed to reassert the power of the ruling elite. Present at this purported meeting were Ne Win, the supposedly ousted Sein Lwin, Dr Maung Maung, the chief of staff Gen. Saw Maung, other top state and party leaders, plus Sanda Win.

The scenario the 'leaked minutes' from the alleged meeting outlined seemed too absurd to be true and were, consequently, met with scepticism by foreign observers at the time. The first step would be to spread the rumour that Ne Win had left, or was about to leave, the country. Attempts would be made to drive a wedge between the students and the monks on the one hand and the people on the other. In the meantime, DDSI agents should "be responsible for creating anarchy and staging covert operations on as large a scale as possible". This would include "poisoning water supplies, instigating looting of government warehouses and blaming it on the people, committing arson and beginning defamation campaigns of the opposition leaders". Some superficial concessions should be made at the same time as these actions continued, such as giving promises of a multi-party system and democracy. Certain student leaders should be earmarked for assassinations and, eventually, the army would use the "deteriorating conditions in the country" as a pretext to stage a coup. Then, a bloody suppression would follow.

An 'anti-strike committee' had been formed to implement the scheme, according to the document. Was it really true? Rangoon in August — and increasingly during the first half of September — was a rumour mill where it was almost impossible to verify any reports. This one, however, seemed to make sense despite its devious nature; it was in any case beyond doubt that the military — and especially the DDSI — had not given up, but were watching developments carefully and plotting a come-back.

As the demonstrations escalated, foreign countries became involved in a way which neutral Burma had not experienced for decades. US congressman Stephen J. Solarz flew into Rangoon on 3rd September for a highly publicised two-day visit. He called on the president, Dr. Maung Maung, as well as the main opposition leaders: U Nu, Tin U, Aung San Suu Kyi and Aung Gyi. Deeply moved by the high tide of pro-American sentiments in Burma, Solarz, at a press conference in Bangkok after his return, declared his "moral and political support for the aspirations of the Burmese people in their demand for democracy." Burma could plunge into civil war, Solarz said, if the demands were not met since "most rank-and-file-Burmese soldiers are sympathetic to anti-government protests."

By contrast, the popularity of the Eastern Bloc countries, however, received a severe blow shortly afterwards. The *Working People's Daily* on 6th and 7th September published on its front page "messages of felicitations" to Dr. Maung Maung from his counterparts in Czechoslovakia, Bulgaria and Yugoslavia. A few hundred students immediately demonstrated outside the Czech embassy on Prome Road. Before dispersing, the students stuck hand-written posters on the embassy wall reading : "Czechs get out!", "Mind your own business" and "Make your own people happy."

Probably for the first time in the history of diplomatic relations, the embassies concerned issued statements more or less apologising for the congratulatory messages. "I would like to point out that these felicitations are sent as a matter of courtesy towards the country and the people and do not mean the support or disapproval of this or that personality," the Yugoslav ambassador to Burma, Branko Vuletic, wrote in a letter to the *Working People's Daily* which was published in facsimile on the 10th.

Meanwhile, the general strike committee in Rangoon issued an ultimatum to the government: install an interim government, or face an indefinite strike. On 2nd September, the Bar Council had declared that the 1962 coup d'état had violated the 1947 Constitution and that the present regime, therefore, was illegal. And on the 6th, nine out of eleven survivors of the legendary Thirty Comrades publicly denounced Ne Win and called on the soldiers in the Burmese Army to support the uprising. The only two of the World War Two heroes who did not support the move were Ne Win himself, of course, and ex-brigadier Kyaw Zaw at the CPB's Panghsang headquarters near the Chinese border.

But Dr Maung Maung's government once again ignored the demands for an interim government. Instead, the authorities announced that the BSPP was going to hold a second extraordinary congress on 12th September, to be followed by an emergency session of the *Pyithu Hluttaw*, to discuss the issue of a one-party or a multi-party system. Truckloads of troops entered the city to guard key buildings, including the parliament where the meetings were going to be held. BSPP delegates and *Pyithu Hluttaw* members from upcountry were flown in under tight security by helicopter and military aircraft. Soldiers removed mattresses from the old Strand Hotel and brought them to the heavily guarded parliament building where the country's 'leaders' were being accommodated.

A wave of disappointment swept through Rangoon. "We would like to stop the congress," said Tin U in a telephone interview with *Reuters*. "There will be strong demonstrations...to show that their [the BSPP] activities should be stopped." The newly formed trade union of the Restaurants and Beverages Trade Corporation declared that they would not serve the delegates to the upcoming meetings. And to preempt any decisions made by the congress, U Nu on the 9th announced the formation of an interim government and called for general elections. "I'm still the legitimate prime minister according to the constitution passed in 1947 by the constituent assembly," the 82-year old U Nu claimed at a press conference in Rangoon. U Nu's self-proclaimed 'cabinet' included several former politicians who had once been members of his 'Clean AFPFL' in the 1950s, plus Tin U as 'minister of defence'.

However, U Nu's initiative astounded the other opposition leaders. Aung Gyi branded the move "preposterous". Aung San Suu Kyi convened a press conference at her residence on University Avenue and declared: "I am astonished to hear of the formation of a 'parallel government' led by former prime minister U Nu; the future of the people will be decided by the masses of the people." On the day after this new 'interim government' had been set up, Tin U and his group of former army officers resigned and also declared that they had quit U Nu's League for Democracy and Peace (Provisional). The scheme had clearly backfired; instead of undermining the credibility of the BSPP regime, U Nu now found himself isolated from the rest of the opposition.

The emergency congress was held on the 10th — two days ahead of schedule — behind a wall of bayonets and barbed wire fences. About 100,000 people marched on the Pyithu *Hluttaw* building and were stopped by the troops outside. Monks and children then went to the front of the crowd and bared their chests to the soldiers, telling them to shoot or stand aside. The soldiers backed down and the people surged forward, pleading with the soldiers to join their struggle. That did not materialise but, startlingly, the congress and the following *Pyithu Hluttaw* session agreed to hold "free, fair multi-party general elections", relinquishing the BSPP's official political monopoly and even scrapping the original idea of a referendum on the issue.

The crowd outside cheered the decision when it was announced — but vowed to keep up the pressure until the government had stepped down and handed over power to an interim administration. Public confidence in the incumbent regime's ability and sincerity in organising the elections was virtually zero. The *Pyithu Hluttaw*, however, on the 11th appointed an elections commission to prepare for the polls. It was chaired by Ba Htay, a former treasury commissioner, and included Kyaw Nyunt, a former ambassador to Canada, Kya Doe, the Karen army veteran who had been dismissed in 1949, Saya Chai, an ex-MP, and San Maung, a retired commissioner of savings and insurance.

On the following day, the three main opposition leaders — Aung Gyi, Tin U and Aung San Suu Kyi — countered with their first joint statement. In an open letter to Dr Maung Maung, the trio suggested that an interim government "acceptable to all the people" be installed as soon as possible to solve the crisis. In the streets of Rangoon and elsewhere, the demonstrations were becoming more militant; the defiance was being shouted louder than before and some marchers armed themselves with swords, daggers, clubs and wooden spears. The government's refusal to resign was an ominous sign and rumours of an imminent military coup now circulated every day in Rangoon.

One of the few encouraging signs from the marchers' point of view was that large numbers of troops as well as policemen had begun joining the demonstrations. 16 privates from the 16th Light Infantry Regiment were the first to come over on 7th September. Led by Lance Cpl. Kyaw Win Sein, they marched in their uniforms — but without arms — through Rangoon chanting: "Our military skills are not for killing the people!" Two days later, 150 airmen at the Mingaladon Maintenance Air Base went on strike. Led by Cpl. Tin Kyaing, they set out for downtown Rangoon at 5 am to join the demonstrations. They were followed by other airmen from the 501 and 502 Air Force units in Hmawbi and Mingaladon. Uniformed men and women from the People's Police Force were soon also seen in the streets, chanting slogans with their own drummers and trumpeters marching in front of the well-disciplined columns.

Over the following days, more policemen, airmen, naval personnel and a few regular troops took "refuge in the bosom of the people for the attainment of democracy", to quote the *Working People's Daily*. The BBS, which had become the only remaining outlet for the regime's version of events, confirmed the reports of defectors joining the demonstrations, but described them as "mentally ill due to drunkenness and malaria."

These defections were certainly cause for concern among the top leadership but, astonishingly, the main army remained intact. Any high-ranking army officer who had taken an armed infantry unit into the capital and declared his support for the uprising would have become a national hero immediately, and the tables would have been turned. But it did not happen; only smaller peripheral groups among the armed forces defected. Rangoon was becoming tenser as more people came to realise that nothing was really going to change. Only rumours abounded.

One report said that two regional commanders, brigadier-general Nyan Lin in Moulmein and brigadier-general Tun Kyi in Mandalay, had been arrested for sympathising with the demonstrators. This was never confirmed and most possibly it was an outcome of wishful thinking. Another rumour, fuelled by the moral support expressed by several American politicians, had it that a US aircraft carrier had entered Burmese waters to 'liberate Rangoon]. The report was denied by both the Burmese military and the US embassy in Rangoon.

On 12th September, posters and leaflets appeared all over Rangoon, purportedly issued by navy chief, rear admiral Maung Maung Khin, and the air force leader, major-general Tin Tun. The two officers had threatened to bomb and shell several official buildings if the authorities did not agree to the formation of an interim government "by 1 pm today". The BBS immediately broadcast a denial by Maung Maung Khin and Tin Tun and threatened to shoot the people who spread such rumours. Later, some students from Rangoon actually admitted that the leaflets and the posters had been part of a practical joke to scare the authorities — but the act also reflected the increasing frustrations of the time.

OUTRAGE

Outside the RGH, the City Hall and other places in Rangoon, hundreds of young people staged hunger strikes to press the demands for an interim government. On the 16th, writer Gonthoo Thein Naing was giving a speech near Rangoon's zoo — when a voice came from the opposite ministry of defence over a loudspeaker, ordering him to stop talking or be fired on. Pandemonium broke out, several thousand people gathered at the scene — and eleven truckloads of troops arrived. Young demonstrators, armed with sticks, catapults and daggers, shouted abuse at the soldiers, who withdrew without opening fire. The crowd eventually dispersed on the request of Aung Gyi and the *ba ka tha* chairman, Min Ko Naing, who had both rushed to the scene to defuse the situation.

On the following day, there was another tense confrontation outside the trade ministry on Strand Road. A large group of demonstrators, including many young women, came marching along the road when a platoon of soldiers on the roof of the building began shouting obscenities at the demonstrators. The troopers were obviously drunk and the column came to a sudden halt as the anger of the marchers rose. Kyaw Win, 24, participated in that demonstration on the 17th:

— The soldiers unbuttoned their trousers and called the female demonstrators by dirty names. We went closer to the building and the troops must have been frightened to see the enormous crowd that was closing in on them. They opened fire and one demonstrator was severely wounded. We stormed the building and rushed upstairs to the roof.

The soldiers, 24 of them, surrendered along with their weapons. A demonstrator triumphantly waved one of the captured rifles in the air as the people down in the street applauded. But the taste for revenge had not subsided and the demonstrators literally demanded the soldiers' heads. Aung Gyi and Tin U arrived at the scene and appealed to the crowd to disperse. The situation was getting out of hand; three motor vehicles were destroyed by the angry protesters when they realised that they would not be allowed to decapitate the soldiers. It was not until late in the evening that the commotion subsided.

Simultaneously, other developments were taking place. Since the time of the BSPP's emergency congress, the army had been moving heavy equipment into strategic points all over Rangoon — and hauling food, petrol and other necessities out. Unusual troop movements were also reported in other towns around the country. In his 11th September speech, Dr. Maung Maung had declared: "It will be necessary for the councils, service personnel and police to bring back into motion the public administrative machinery which has been stalled in ruins. The authorities concerned have already issued instructions for the nearest defence-forces units to render assistance as well...run...those of you who resort to force and those of you possessed by the devil, while there is still time!"

On the 16th, the BSPP issued a puzzling proclamation saying that members of the armed forces, the police and civil servants had been "permitted to resign" from the party. On the following day, the defence ministry ordered the armed forces to "fully discharge their original three responsibilities, namely: perpetuation of the union, national unity and safeguarding the sovereignty" of the state. Obviously, a major event was in the offing.

Six SLORC !

On 18th September, a Sunday, there were demonstrations as usual in Rangoon. Some 300,000 people marched in the streets chanting the by now customary anti-government slogans. The hunger strikers were continuing their protests outside the City Hall, the RGH and elsewhere. Many demonstrators were getting impatient, and in some cases also increasingly militant, as Dr. Maung Maung's regime was stubbornly refusing to concede to the demands for the formation of an interim government.

At 4 pm local time, there was an abrupt break in the BBS's afternoon music programme. A male voice came over the air, solemnly proclaiming: "In order to bring a timely halt to the deteriorating conditions on all sides all over the country and in the interests of the people, the defence forces have assumed all power in the state with effect from today." A State Law and Order Restoration Council (SLORC), headed by the chief of staff, Gen. Saw Maung, had been formed to ensure "peace and tranquility" in preparation for "democratic multi-party elections". The brief announcement was followed by strident martial music.

Two hours later, the names of the 19 members of this SLORC were announced. It included all the nine regional commanders of the Burmese Army, including the ones who were rumoured to have been purged, as well as several other high-ranking military officers from the army, navy and the air force. Its vice chairman was the deputy chief of staff, Lt-Gen. Than Shwe, and its secretary the director of the DDSI, Khin Nyunt, who now had been promoted to brigadier-general.

A 8 pm to 4 am curfew was clamped on Rangoon and the SLORC with immediate effect banned "gathering, walking, marching in procession, chanting slogans, delivering speeches, agitating and creating disturbances in the streets by a group of five or more people regardless of whether the act is with the intention of creating disturbances or of committing a crime or not." More martial music blared out of the radio.

"I was visiting some friends in Barr Street when we heard the announcement," recalls Kyaw Thu, the high-school student from Kemmendine who had first participated in the early August demonstrations together with his younger sister. "Our first reaction was one of anger and disappointment.

OUTRAGE

We wanted to fight this new government and immediately contacted other activist groups in North and South Okkalapa and Tingangyun. Some of us armed ourselves with clubs, daggers, swords and crossbows."

It had started drizzling shortly after the brief radio announcement and the late afternoon sky now was heavy with dark rainclouds. Once again, throughout the city, people began felling trees and overturning street-side wooden stalls to make barricades, as they had done in August. Their faces were downcast and the atmosphere electrifyingly tense. The barricades were not only in small streets in residential areas but they also extended along main roads like Prome Road — which leads to the army camps north of the city. Electric wires were cut and street lights destroyed to hamper the movements of the troops everybody was expecting to appear any minute. Some people began banging pots and pans inside their houses in a desperate show of defiance. Others took to the streets with their crossbows, swords and *jinglees*, ready for a fight with the army.

But it was an unusual 'coup' — there was none of the characteristics of a military takeover: tanks and troops seizing strategic points in the capital, the abolition of the constitution, the arrest of state leaders, a new strongman. The only movements in the streets of Rangoon during the first few hours after the radio announcement were bands of thousands of enraged demonstrators who surged down the streets in the eerie evening twilight. Waving banners, flags and crude, home-made weapons, they shouted angrily at the top of their voices:

> *hwe asuya kya hson base! khwe asuya kya hson base!*
> Down with the dog government! Down with the dog government!

But the new, self-proclaimed leaders were conspicuous by their absence. Not even the army appeared until late that evening. But when the army trucks and the Bren-carriers at last rolled into the city this time, it was an entirely different scene from August. The organisation was impeccable and the operation carried out with icy-cold military efficiency. Through loudspeakers, mounted on the military vehicles, the people were ordered to remove the barricades. If the order was not heeded, a machine-gunner sprayed the nearest house with bullets. Cranes moved in and dismantled the flimsy road blocks if the protesters themselves had not complied after the first salvo of machine-gun fire.

Any crowd of people in sight was mowed down methodically as the army trucks and Bren-carriers rumbled down the streets in perfect formations, shooting in all directions. The wounded were carried into the RGH as well as make-shift clinics all over Rangoon. The dead who were left in the streets, were trucked away by the army during lulls in the shooting. Sporadic gunfire could be heard here and there in Rangoon throughout that night.

One of the tensest places that night was the Rangoon University's Convocation Hall where several hundred students had gathered for a meeting. At 6 pm, troops moved in, surrounded the building and commanded the students to come out. Nobody appeared; inside, the students joined each other in prayer — they were all prepared to die. In an almost surreal display of solidarity, various groups of students had class photos taken as if it was the last day before summer vacations. The droning rise and fall of the Buddhist chants continued for several hours. At 10.45 pm, some monks appeared and led the students out through a backdoor. Astoundingly, the troops outside refrained from shooting and nobody was hurt.

The demonstrations continued the following morning. But no one in the large column that marched down past the old meeting-spot near the City Hall and Maha Bandoola Park saw the machine-gun nests on the surrounding rooftops: the City Hall itself, the Union Bank in Merchant Street next to the US embassy, and a six-storey office block further down the same street. As the marchers turned left at the Tourist Burma office opposite the Sule Pagoda, and were entrapped between the three firepoints, the troops at the three roof-top positions opened fire simultaneously. No warning was given. Several demonstrators fell bleeding to the street.

Files of soldiers goose-stepped in perfect formation out from different sidestreets, followed by Bren-carriers. At a barked word of command, the troops assumed the prone firing position, as if they were facing a heavily armed enemy, not young, unarmed demonstrators. They fired into a crowd just outside the US embassy. Two Burmese free-lance cameramen were filming the shooting with a video camera; one concealing it with his body when the soldiers looked in their direction. On the tape that later was smuggled out, a voice could be heard saying in Burmese: "What shall we do? What shall we do?" The other voice replied calmly: "Keep on filming until they shoot at us."

Orders that day were to shoot anyone with a camera to avoid embarrassing international coverage of the 'coup'. A Burmese free-lance cameraman, who was stringing for a Japanese TV company was killed by a sniper; a bullet hit him right through his left eye, which was closed as he held his camera to the other.

Kyaw Thu joined the protesters who were marching towards the Ministers' Office, or the old Secretariat, in the block between Anawratha Street and Maha Bandoola Street. He belonged to a small group of high-school pupils who had set up an organisation which in many ways reflected the romantic idealism of the August-September movement: the Jonathan Liberation Centre. It was named after Jonathan Livingstone Seagull.

"We turned back when we heard that the troops had opened fire into crowds, especially targeting the ones who were carrying peacock flags and portraits of Aung San, or had red head-bands on. The demonstrators tried to flee — and the soldiers ran after them, bayonetting them in the back. The soldiers were very young, in their late teens I guess, and looked rough, as if they just had come out of the woodwork."

Sein Win, the veteran *Associated Press* correspondent in Rangoon, filed to his head office in Bangkok on that fateful Monday: "Army troops under orders to halt all public gatherings today fired into crowds of defiant students, Buddhist monks and largely unarmed demonstrators in downtown Rangoon. Eyewitnesses described casualties as heavy. 'Many students are being mowed down. Can't anything be done?' sobbed a reporter telephoning this correspondent from the scene before breaking down in tears."

Aung Kyaw, a university student, says that the older youths realised the danger and stayed indoors:

"But it was impossible to control the high-school kids. They were angry and militant and just wanted to confront the army. We couldn't stop them. Many, many were mowed down by automatic riflefire and bayonets."

At 10 am that morning, Kyaw Thu heard that his 18-year old sister Win Moe Oo had been shot and wounded. Two of her friends, high-school boys also in their teens, had been killed during the same army fusillade. As she was being carried to a car which was going to take her to hospital, a foreigner took a picture. It later appeared in the 3rd October issue of *Newsweek's* Asian edition. That photograph, however, did not tell what happened a few hours later:

"My father and I arrived at Rangoon General Hospital at 11 am. My sister was bleeding heavily. She asked for a portrait of Aung San, which we placed on her bed. At 1 pm, she died, clasping the portrait."

On the following day, the family took the corpse of the young girl to Kyandaw crematorium. Other corpses had been dumped outside the ovens and people were there looking for their relatives. Kyaw Thu says that several of the corpses he saw had had their faces smashed in to make identification impossible. Some of them, however, were still wearing their green high-school *longyis*. Two days after Kyaw Thu and his family had cremated Win Moe Oo's corpse, the area around Kyandaw was cordoned off by troops and a Bren-carrier was positioned outside. No "outsiders" — relatives and others — were permitted to enter the compound.

Melinda Liu wrote in her cover story for *Newsweek* on 3rd October: "Witnesses at the cemetery said they heard the cries of shooting victims who had been brought to Kyandaw while they were still alive — and were cremated along with the corpses." At Rangoon General Hospital she saw "victims with mangled limbs, chest wounds and legs in blood-stained casts. In the emergency ward, gunshot victims writhed on rusting gurneys, dripping blood onto the grimy floor. Undersupplied in the best of times, the hospital was running desperately low on blood and plasma. It was also running short of morgue space. I saw 30 bodies piled helter-skelter in the refrigerated vault...one man was missing the top of his head; a 10-year old boy had a bullet hole in the middle of his forehead."

A Western ambassador reported that a group of schoolgirl demonstrators, aged around 13 and 14, were attacked and killed by government troops on Monday in Kemmendine. "It's so shameful what's happening, I have no words for it," he said. "It's just a small group of people who want to consolidate their power and are willing to shoot down school children and unarmed demonstrators to do so." The same diplomat added: "It's not a coup — how can you stage a coup if you're running the damn place already?"

The repression followed the same pattern all over the country. In the early hours of the 19th, the army units which had been put on full alert during the week before the 'coup' simultaneously raided strike centres in practically every state and division in Burma. In Mandalay, confrontation was reported between the army and protesters who drove waterbuffaloes in front of them as a shield against bullets. But that hardly provided much protection against machine-guns and automatic rifles. The BBS reported on 22nd September: "The destructive elements, following the animals, attacked the security personnel with slingshots and *jinglees*. Five buffaloes were killed in the return fire."

The unofficial version, related by Mandalay residents, had it that about 150 people were shot when the army broke up the strike centre in their hometown, which had been one of the most efficiently-run in the country. In the oil town of Chauk further down the Irrawaddy, at least 20 people were killed as local army units fired on people who protested against the military takeover.

In Taunggyi, Shan State, a young girl had been killed in the firing on the 18th. The following day, a large crowd gathered outside the Chinese temple on the town's main streets to prepare for the funeral. An army vehicle pulled up — and the troops sprayed automatic riflefire into the crowd. Local residents estimate that about 40 people were killed and that the firing was unprovoked. The official version, however, had it that "about 100 destructive elements made an attack, using slingshots and *jinglees*. When the security units returned fire, one destructive element was killed and one wounded."

In the morning of the 19th the people in the southwestern port town of Tavoy gathered outside their strike centre. Flags and banners fluttered in the wind and the local strike leaders, Chan Hla, a 51-year old high-school teacher, and Pan Kyaw, a school headmaster gave speeches. An army unit arrived at the scene and told the people to disperse. When they did not heed the order, the commanding officer, Lieut-Col. Myint Thein, pulled out his army pistol and killed the old headmaster. Chan Hla and several others were gunned down immediately afterwards.

In the small border town of Tachilek opposite Mae Sai in Thailand, a dozen students were apprehended before dawn on the 19th. An eye-witness said that four nights later, he observed army lorries loaded with both civilians and soldiers drive up in the dark to an army camp on a hill overlooking Tachilek. Shortly afterwards, bursts of machine-gun fire were heard from the camp. The lorries soon returned — empty, save for the troops.

Similar acts of brutality were reported from most townships in Rangoon during the days after SLORC's takeover. In South Okkalapa, local residents claim that two young boys were shot in front of their parents. Elsewhere, private homes were raided by troops looking for student activists, opposition newsletters and pro-democracy leaflets. The *United Press International* on 24th September quoted a Rangoon resident as saying: "In searching for weapons house-to-house they [the soldiers] are [also] picking up any valuables they want and taking them, and the people have no recourse."

In a statement issued on 20th September, Min Ko Naing, who had gone into hiding, had declared that he was prepared "for the last ditch fight...throughout the country. There is no honour greater than the willingness to sacrifice for the freedom of the motherland. We have stopped using our mouths to protest and...warn the group that calls itself the government to seek their last meal."

Small bands of hardline activists tried to fight back, but in vain. The National Liberation Democratic Front, led by Tun Tun Oo, fired rockets — obtained on the black market — on the City Hall on 19th September, without causing much damage. Tun Tun Oo soon left for the Thai border and his replacement as chief of this obscure underground group, Kyaw Than, turned out to be a DDSI plant. Most of the ones who had stayed behind were soon rounded up by the secret police. A number of police stations were burnt down in revenge attacks on Monday and Tuesday and weapons seized. Someone fired a rocket on a microwave antenna in Rangoon, temporarily disrupting the country's telecommunications system.

The impact of these counter-attacks was, however, minimal. But in the midst of all the tragedy, a sardonic sense of humour was displayed by an unknown Burmese who interrupted the official broadcasts over the BBS. Whenever Gen. Saw Maung's recorded speeches were being broadcast, he was on the air also. When the coup-maker spoke of "unscrupulous elements", the gremlin interjected: "You are the unscrupulous ones!" Saw Maung's calm voice continued: "The fact that we formed a government with very few people is evidence that we have absolutely no desire to hold on to state power for a prolonged period." The one-man resistance movement retorted: "Why did you seize it if you had no desire?!?" When Saw Maung paused and said: "I'd like to say a few words," the gremlin fired back: "Don't say anything!" The low signal level of the interference indicated that he was using his own radio transmitter; it could not have come from a broadcasting studio. Nobody was ever able to identify the mysterious heckler, and after a few days, he also fell silent.

By Wednesday, Rangoon was calm. The carnage was over and a weird 'normality' had returned to Rangoon. Doctors and diplomats in Rangoon estimated the death toll at between 500 and 1,000, most of whom were school children and other unarmed demonstrators. Diplomatic observers at the time likened Rangoon to a "city under hostile, foreign occupation." There were armed soldiers everywhere and road blocks had been erected along all major streets leading from the suburbs to the city centre. But there seemed to be no interaction between the troops and the local people except for antagonistic glances.

Brig-Gen. Khin Nyunt of the DDSI claimed in a meeting with foreign defence attachés in Rangoon on 22nd September that 263 people, of whom 238 were civilians and the rest army personnel and policemen, had been killed during the 'coup'. Most of the fatalities were classified as "looters and other unsavoury elements". He went on to say that the army had had to step in order to "restore law and order". "Those bent on violence," Khin Nyunt continued, "had taken advantage of the kindness and benevolence of the *tatmadaw* " and created "a situation of anarchy."

In trying to explain the reason for the military takeover, the intelligence chief mentioned the commotion outside the trade ministry on the 17th. "The army's humiliation was seen all over the world," he said in an apparent reference to the video tapes of the incident which had been smuggled out and shown internationally. But he did not explain why he thought that a massacre of virtually unarmed children would restore the hurt pride of the *tatmadaw* in the eyes of the outside world.

His explanation also lacked a number of other vital points. If it indeed was the trade ministry incident that had prompted the coup, why then had the army already hauled arms and ammunition into the city and sent out troops to all major towns in the country a week before? Most Rangoon residents now also began to realise why the ruling elite on 16th September — also before the commotion outside the trade ministry — had announced that all army people had quit the BSPP. By separating the hitherto inseparable army-cum-party apparatus, the military could always claim that it had intervened to safeguard national interests rather than the interests of "any specific political party."

To reinforce this impression the SLORC on the 19th revoked the 1964

Law to Protect National Unity, which banned all political parties except the BSPP, and a 1974 law designed to protect the ruling party and its organs. The events that followed during the month after the formation of the SLORC also lent credence to the suggestion that it was not a spur of the moment decision, prompted by the trade ministry incident on the 17th, but a carefully masterminded plan. It was put into action almost immediately.

In the early morning of the 18th, Gen. Saw Maung had been summoned to Ne Win's Ady Road residence. The law and order situation had deteriorated sufficiently and a good excuse for a 'coup' could be found. Dr Maung Maung was the next visitor at Ady Road. At 3 pm, he was told that he would be 'ousted'. So that afternoon, the formation of the SLORC was announced. On the following day — while the killings were going on — the new military council dissolved the *Pyithu Hluttaw*, the state council, the council of ministers and all other former organs of power. Only the elections commission was not disbanded.

On the 20th the SLORC set up its own government, consisting of nine ministers, some holding two, three and even more portfolios each. All of them were army officers, except for Dr Pe Thein, the minister of health. All the people who had gone on strike, which was virtually the entire nation, were ordered back to work by 26th September — or "they shall be suspended from their duties".

The official radio soon announced the names of all the strike centres around the country that had been broken up in order to "restore peace and tranquility". A long list of places was made public, presumably in order to make an impression on the public and the international community. Unwittingly, the SLORC at the same time also admitted how widespread the uprising had actually been. Many foreign observers especially had assumed that the movement had been confined to major towns and cities. But now, the BBS proudly announced the smashing of strike centres in small country towns and big villages also, such as Mawchi, Bawlake and Pasawng in Kayah State, Ngaputaw and Thabaung in the Irrawaddy delta, Kyaukpyu and Sandoway in Arakan State, Möng Yawng and Möng Hpayak in Shan State, and Kyaukpadaung, Lewe, and Tatkon in Mandalay Division. Astonishingly, even in the previously tranquil Chin State — long considered one of the most loyal parts of the country — "destructive elements" had been chased from their strike centres in Tiddim, Falam and Haka.

The methodical way in which these raids were carried out reinforced the assumption that the military had never had any plans to relinquish power. By stepping into the background and confining its activities to provoking chaos and anarchy, it not only gave itself a perfect pretext for staging a 'coup'. But more importantly, by keeping a low profile for about a month,

it had lulled the public into feeling confident that change was imminent —
and the opposition that previously had stayed underground and therefore
been impossible to identify had surfaced. The ones who took off their
handkerchiefs in the demonstrations in mid-August now had every reason
to regret that decision.

During raids in Rangoon and elsewhere, army officers were now seen
carrying lists and even photographs of certain student activists and strike
leaders. In Taunggyi, three doctors from the local hospital, Dr Saw Yan
Naing, Dr Tin Win and Dr Nay Lin, who had led the local strike movement
in their hometown were arrested soon after the coup. So was another local
strike leader, Dr Maung Maung Shein, the director of the health service
department in the delta town of Bassein.

On 2nd October, the security forces raided the Sabe-Oo, or Jasmin, video
shop in Barr Street in Rangoon and arrested Zagana, the satirist, along with
three film actors and a film director who had been active during the August-
September demonstrations: Zin Wyne, Moe Win, Nyi Win Sein and Tin Soe.
Dozens of less important activists were also rounded up, or simply disappeared. The general impression was that the army actually left the top
leaders alone, and concentrated on local organisers out in the country,
second-rung leaders in Rangoon and, naturally, the activists who had been
the backbone of the grassroot-organisations.

The defectors from the army, the air force and the police, naturally, were
in an especially difficult situation. The monasteries where they had gone
into hiding after the military takeover were raided by troops; many were
arrested while some managed to flee — and on Sunday evening, dozens of
heads had been shaved and new, yellow robes provided. The number of
monks in Rangoon increased by a few hundred overnight.

But as for the vast majority of soldiers, no report indicated that any of
them had hesitated to open fire on unarmed demonstrators — which
astonished most foreign observers. Instead, it seemed as if the armed forces,
within which cracks had begun to appear in early September, were effi-
ciently pulled together by the move itself. Most army officers probably
realised that the fall of the regime, and a change of *status quo*, could be
detrimental to their vested interests, threatening their privileged position in
Burmese society; when it came to the critical moment, all of them obeyed
orders.

As a consequence of the traditional mixture of little if any education,
strict discipline, blind loyalty and fear of superiors, the rank and file also
appears to have had no qualms about firing into crowds of children. It was
even said that the troops had been told that Rangoon had been taken over
by "communist insurgents" and, therefore, had to be "liberated". "Communists" were identifiable by the red headbands they wore, according to the
same reports. If any soldier had wondered why these "communist insur-

gents" were very young, unarmed and dressed in city clothes, he must have kept that query to himself.

In order to maintain the new 'law and order', the supply of arms and ammunition for the army was a main consideration, and foreigners began to speculate how long the present supplies would last, especially since the state coffers had been almost depleted of foreign exchange. But late in the evening of 6th October, there was a curious black-out along Prome Road in Rangoon, which only affected the three closest rows of houses on either side of the thoroughfare. Meanwhile, heavily laden army trucks rumbled past, from the city's port up to the Mingaladon military area north of the airport. Prome Road residents counted 75 trucks making three trips each; in the port, workers had seen boxes marked 'Allied Ordnance, Singapore' being unloaded from a ship.

The shipment was substantial and reportedly included mortars, ammunition, raw material for making rifle bullets and even 84mm Carl Gustaf rockets which Chartered Industries in Singapore manufacture under licence from the Swedish mother company, Förenade Fabriksverken (FFV). The shipment violated an agreement between the FFV and Singapore, according to which an approval from the Swedish government is needed for re-export to a third country; Chartered Industries never even applied for such a permit.

Singapore's special relationship with Rangoon had been emphasised as late as in January 1986 when Lee Kuan Yew paid a highly publicised visit to Burma. The Singapore prime minster in his banquet speech on 16th January had clearly demonstrated that he knew the rules of the game in Burma. Although his then Burmese counterpart, prime minister Maung Maung Kha, had hosted the banquet, Lee had said: "My first visit to Rangoon was in April 1962, when I got to know general Ne Win. Our friendship has grown these last two-and-a-half decades. Burma-Singapore relations have been close and friendly. No problems have disrupted the even tenor of our relations".

Given Burma's lack of foreign exchange, the 6th October shipment was most probably a barter deal, although it is still uncertain what Singapore got in return. In any event, the firepower of the Burmese Army increased considerably, in Rangoon and especially on the battlefront in the frontier areas and contributed to the military's ability to reassert its power.

The raids against opposition centres in Rangoon continued throughout September and October. Hundreds of civil servants who had participated in the demonstrations were purged or arrested, or both. Among them were a top pilot of the state airline Burma Airways and 18 officials at the BBS. The ones who had returned to work had to fill in elaborate questionnaires, telling "whether you took part in processions or not. Whether you took part in strikes or not. Whether you delivered speeches or not. Whether you wrote, distributed or stuck posters or not", and so on.

On 20th September, the SLORC issued an order, forbidding "stockpiling of illegal weapons" — *jinglees*, slingshots and crossbows. Private homes and monasteries were raided, and most of the firearms that had been captured from police stations were recovered. The BBS even reported the seizure of 11 walkie-talkie sets in North Okkalapa on 22nd September. The raids continued, and on 28th October, the official media claimed that a large supply of arms and ammunition had been seized in the compound of the famous Thayettaw monastery in central Rangoon. "Some rowdy elements seized 23 weapons from members of the security units stationed on the upper floor of the Ministry of Trade on 17th September," the announcement said. "Of the weapons seized by the rowdy elements, 12 were recovered and 11 remained missing". Hidden in the water-closet of the monastery were also 1,400 rounds of 7.62 ammunition, 35 two-inch mortars and other explosives.

Startlingly, the regime was also able to arrest scores of people suspected of "murder", which usually meant that they had been involved in the lynchings of policemen and alleged DDSI informers in August and September. On 22nd October, the official media reported that 38 people had been netted in connection with one such incident. Later, more people were arrested and their pictures displayed publicly. This continued for several months and clearly indicated that the DDSI had collapsed during the August-September demonstrations; more likely, it had observed developments from afar and simply registered the people who had been involved in various acts of violence without either intervening at the time, or attempting to rescue its own agents.

But not all arrests and executions were politically motivated. Just before dawn on 14th October, the residents of Thunada Street in North Okkalapa were awakened by two gunshots, followed by the by now familiar sound of an army truck starting up. When the local people ventured outside, they found the bodies of two young men lying in the street. Each had been shot at close range by a single bullet. A few weeks earlier, the two dead youths had been involved in a brawl with an army sergeant. After the military crackdown, the two youths, seeing the writing on the wall, went into hiding. It took some time, but they were found. Their deaths figured in the state-media as two more "looters" who had been killed.

Myat Han and his wife Ohn Kyi were both shot in a similar manner near the Sinmalaik Jetty in the port. The gunman was an army major, Maung Maung Aung, who had been told to leave a house he had been renting from them some time earlier. The middle-aged couple were shot in full view of the dockworkers at Sinmalaik — and then dumped in the river.

In retrospect, there seemed to be little doubt that the alleged 23rd August meeting at Ne Win's residence actually had taken place, even if the document that circulated at the time may not have been the original minutes of the discussions. The fact remains that events after the purported meeting had followed in almost minute detail the plan the document had outlined. The clearest indication that the "coup" had been planned long in advance was perhaps the very date on which it was staged: the 18th (1+8=9) of the ninth month of the year. If there had been no incident outside the trade ministry on the 17th, the DDSI would most certainly have had to orchestrate one.

The deadline for the people to return to work was extended until 3rd October. On Sunday the 2nd, the SLORC warned over the BBS that "anyone who prevents, obstructs or interferes with workers returning to work...will be dealt with sternly". On the following day, the eight-weeks long general strike collapsed. Facing threats of dismissal and short of cash, civil servants and labourers sullenly trickled back to their offices and factories.

"We have to go back. We need money, our salaries, and the special rations of rice and oil," the *Associated Press* quoted a returning government clerk as saying.

In the beginning, most people showed up at 10 am, had a few cups of tea and left three or four hours later. Little work was done, partly because the people were reluctant to show more cooperation with the new SLORC authorities than merely signing the attendance sheets in order to get their salaries. But most offices and factories were in a total mess after the long strike. When the newly appointed minister of cooperatives, fisheries and livestock breeding, and agriculture and forests, Maj-Gen. Chit Swe, inspected his new offices after the 'coup', the only people in the building were the three heads of government corporations — and the premises smelled of garbage, sewage and weeks of neglect.

Virtually all of Burma's more than 1,000 factories had already faced shortages of raw materials and spare parts before the upheaval. During the general strike, many of them had been ransacked by looters who had taken away or destroyed machinery and whatever they could lay their hands on, including fire extinguishers and corrugated iron sheets which had been stripped off the roofs of the buildings.

One of the first moves the SLORC had taken after assuming power was to regain control of the printmedia. All the free newspapers vanished almost overnight, as did the previously existing official ones — except for the *Working People's Daily* . Henceforth, it became the only daily newspaper in the country, published in a Burmese and an English version. The brief press freedom Burma's newspapers had enjoyed was over; the government organ was now even drearier and less informative than before. Apart from reports praising the army and listing "donations", its columns were filled with reports of people returning to work, factories resuming production, train services and international air links that had been restored. Army lorries also began delivering rice to poorer areas of Rangoon.

At first, many people were reluctant to accept it, believing that they would be shot if they came close to the soldiers, or that the food had been poisoned. Many flatly refused to have anything to do with the army; in North Okkalapa, the memorial which had raised to honour the local people who had been killed in August had been razed by the army shortly after the coup. These victims were "criminals and destructive elements", the army said, so they did not deserve to be remembered. Bitterness against the army ran deep in these suburbs. But some others slowly began accepting the new 'gifts', simply because they were too hungry to be able to afford to refuse them. The government's policy remained unchanged; after the stick came the carrot once more.

The army was soon seen cleaning the capital's shabby streets and painting houses everywhere. The SLORC set a deadline for private buildings as well; all houses had to be painted before the end of the year, or power and water would be cut. People had to use whatever paint they could find — white, green, red blue and pink — and Rangoon soon looked like a patchwork quilt. A joke going the rounds in Rangoon had a man waiting alone at a bus stop who kept pacing back and forth. Asked why, he replied: "If I stand still, someone might paint me".

Step by step, life in Burma seemed to be returning to what it had been before the big uprising. To the SLORC, it was a sign of the success of its efforts to "restore law and order". To the people, it was a sad reminder of the intransigence of their rulers. With trickery, deception, threats, an almost unbelievable brutality — and then a smiling face while distributing food to the poor — the military elite seemed determined to cling to the absolute power they had wielded for 26 years.

They now also decided to drop 'the Socialist Republic' from the official name of the state. Without any special announcement having been made, the country suddenly became 'the Union of Burma'. Any mention of socialism or the use of Marxist rhetoric, which had been part of the official jargon for more than two decades, ceased altogether. On 24th September, even the BSPP changed its name to the National Unity Party (NUP). In the minds of the people, that made little difference, though. The names of the old BSPP leaders — Dr. Maung Maung, Sein Lwin, Aye Ko, Kyaw Htin and Tun Tin — disappeared from official announcements. But the entire central committee of the 'new' NUP, including its chairman Tha Kyaw, consisted of second-rung ex-BSPP leaders with close army connections.

Perhaps more astonishing was the fact that the SLORC had declared that it intended to hold "free and fair, multi-party elections". But in a statement issued on 23rd September, Gen. Saw Maung spelled out three conditions which had to be met first: law and order had to be restored, the living standard of the people uplifted and the country's poor transport network upgraded. The conditions were sufficiently vague to allow for indefinite SLORC-rule, should the military consider it necessary.

Burma's opposition politicians were probably as taken aback by the events as everybody else. However, they all publicly condemned the killings and vowed to continue the struggle for democracy. U Nu reiterated the proclamation of his own interim government — and claimed he was the "legitimate prime minister of the Union of Burma". Aung San Suu Kyi urged that the UN should exert pressure on SLORC to open negotiations with the opposition. She said in an open appeal on 22nd September: "I would like every country in the world to recognise the fact that the people of Burma are being shot down for no reason at all".

On the 24th, the three main opposition leaders set up a political party, the National League for Democracy (NLD). Aung Gyi was elected chairman, Tin U vice chairman and Aung San Suu Kyi general secretary. The trio — who became known as 'Aung-Suu-Tin', said that "the basic objective of this organisation is to achieve a genuinely democratic government". After some hesitation, they also announced that they would be willing to participate in the general elections that the SLORC, after all, had promised. But it was clear that the young organisation was inexperienced and not sure how to deal with this extraordinary situation where a government that had recently been gunning down school children in the streets had now begun talking about 'multi-party democracy' and 'a free market economy'.

The outside world reaction to the military takeover was a mixture of sympathy for the victims of the coup and anger over the arrogance of the military. The United Nations Children's Fund (UNICEF) began airlifting emergency medical supplies to Rangoon to cope with the casualty toll from the crackdown. In the aftermath of the coup, the doctors at the RGH said they had had to treat about 500 people, mostly from army-inflicted gunshot wounds in the chest and back. The International Committee of the Red Cross (ICRC) began sending convoys with medical supplies to upcountry hospitals and the worst medical crisis was averted.

Already in August, the West German government — Burma's second largest donor after Japan — had cut off its DM 68 million a year aid programme to demonstrate its disapproval of the killings. After the 'coup', the US became the first country to officially terminate its aid programmes in Burma. Previously, the US had contributed US$ 7 million in development assistance, US$ 5 million for an anti-narcotics programme in the Burmese sector of the Golden Triangle, and US$ 260,000 for military training.

The British foreign secretary, Sir Geoffrey Howe, in an outspoken address in the UN's general assembly on 28th September, lashed out against the carnage: "In Burma we have been appalled at the killing of unarmed demonstrators, women and children, which has taken place,... The Burmese authorities must recognise that the only way to a lasting solution to the country's internal crisis lies in meeting the desire of the Burmese people for greater freedom and multi-party democracy."

The main donor country, Japan, was slightly more cautious. On 27th September, the Japanese ambassador to Burma, Hiroshi Otaka, met Ohn Gyaw, the director general of the foreign ministry's political department and said that Japan wished to see an end to the bloodshed and the establishment of "a democratic political settlement reflecting the general consensus of the Burmese people" — and he linked this to a resumption of aid from Tokyo which had been suspended but not formally cut during the turmoil.

But the very fact that even Japan, which rarely makes statements about the internal political situation in other countries, had spoken out in favour of democracy in Burma was significant. The most important international outcome of the setting up of the SLORC and the mass killings after more than a month of demonstrations was that the struggle for democracy in the country was no longer considered an internal Burmese affair. Now, it had become an international issue and there could be no way back to the old self-imposed isolation from which the military regime had benefitted for years.

Seven THE BORDER

THE MILITARY TAKEOVER on 18th September immediately triggered a mass exodus to Burma's border areas, where the country's ethnic insurgents operate. Thousands of students and other activists boarded cars and buses, bound for Moulmein and Kawkareik and from there trekked through the jungles and over the hills to the Thai border near Mae Sot or the rugged Three Pagodas Pass northwest of Kanchanaburi; they jumped on fishing boats headed for Kawthaung, or Victoria Point, in the far southeast, and crossed over to the small fishing and smuggling town of Ranong on the Thai side of the wide river estuary that separates the two countries.

From the Shan State capital of Taunggyi, hundreds of people took refuge in the hills east of Inle Lake where Pa-O guerrillas are active, and later trekked through the jungles down to the Thai border opposite Mae Hong Son. From Mandalay and Sagaing, students fled north to the Kachin Hills and eventually reached the Kachin rebel headquarters at Pa Jau, close to the Chinese frontier. Others headed west, towards India, and crossed into Mizoram and Manipur. Many activists from Arakan State filtered into southeastern Bangladesh. An approximately 8,000-10,000 people left the cities, towns and villages of central Burma for the border during the last weeks of September.

"We fled because we realised that this time it was different; not a random massacre as in August. It was meticulously planned and the targets well selected. Because everything had been out in the open during the August-September demonstrations, all the leading activists were known — and the army were looking for us specifically," says Aung Myint, 23, who is now staying in the Thai-Burmese border areas. " And since the military, despite our massive protests, had chosen to seize power, not to give in to our demands for an interim government, we realised that there was nothing more we could do in the urban areas. No more *do-a-ye! do-a-ye!* — our only choice was armed struggle and we arrived at the border, believing that there would be foreign powers interested in helping us."

The first Burmese student who had reached the Thai border was actually Maung Maung Kyaw, one of the leaders of the March and June uprisings. He had trekked to Myawadi on the Moei River and crossed into Mae Sot in

Thailand already on 9th August with the aim of establishing foreign links and seeking aid from the international community. He and his companion Chit Gyi, there were just the two of them, were immediately picked up by Thai intelligence agents and escorted to Bangkok. Major-general Sudsai Hasdin, a controversial Thai officer involved with the ethnic insurgent groups along the border, took them under his protection and promised support.

A rumour spread back to Rangoon that Maung Maung Kyaw and Chit Gyi already had two or three armed battalions of students under their command, and that there were training camps along the border and foreign assistance waiting for the dissidents from Burma. The general feeling that the outside world sympathised with the pro-democracy movement — emphasised by the US Senate resolution of 11th August, the condemnations by the European Community and the fact that even usually apolitical Japan had come out strongly against the Rangoon regime — may also have contributed to the students' belief that it would be an easy matter to organise an armed struggle from the Thai-Burmese border. If the outside world was on their side, surely they now would supply the opposition with arms and ammunition!

The long, hazardous journey up to the border was not always easy for the young people from the towns. Soe Naing, a 19-year old technical high school pupil from Rangoon, left home the same day as the formation of the SLORC was announced:

— Twelve of us fled together. We went by bus and car to Moulmein from where we began our trek towards the Thai border. On the way, as we were resting on a river bank, some government troops in a boat appeared round a bend and shouted out to us not to move. We were frightened and began running away. They opened fire after us. Three of my friends were hit in their backs. They died instantly. Nine of us reached the Thai border a few days later. When other students arrived after us, we heard that one of the villages where the local people had sheltered us and given us food had been burnt down by the army.

Soe Naing belonged to a group of 135 Burmese students who had crossed the Moei river from the small Burmese border town of Myawadi to Mae Sot in Thailand. For a couple of weeks, they stayed at Wat Mae Tao, a Buddhist monastery in Mae Sot where the local monks sheltered and fed them. But on 8th October, the Thai police, at gunpoint, bundled the students at Wat Mae Tao into trucks and took them to a place on the Moei River south of Mae Sot. They were ordered to cross back into Burma at Thay Baw Bo, a border settlement controlled by ethnic Karen guerrillas from the KNU.

Thay Baw Bo camp was actually a trading post on the black market trail from Burma to Thailand, located in a remote border area and surrounded by dense, malaria-infested jungles and rugged mountain ranges. It consisted of more than a hundred ramshackle bamboo shops stacked with contraband goods: textiles, bicycle wheels, tins and bags of Ajinomoto seasoning powder, Thai cigarettes, radios and cheap imitation of Rolex watches, manufactured in backstreet factories in Bangkok's Chinatown for sale to credulous tourists — or destined for the socialist markets across Thailand's porous frontiers.

Usually frequented by black marketeers from Thailand and Burma, KNU guerrillas with Chinese-made assault rifles slung over the shoulders, the camp's security guards, and Karen hill tribesmen from nearby villages, Thay Baw Bo gained another element in its semi-permanent population: hundreds of earnest-looking young men and women, dressed in city clothes and some wearing spectacles. At one stage, nearly 2,000 Burmese students were being sheltered at Thay Baw Bo, all of them waiting for foreign countries to give them arms and ammunition to go back and fight the new SLORC-regime.

Htun Aung Gyaw, a 34-year geology graduate from Rangoon who had participated in the 1974 demonstrations, spent 1975-80 in Insein Jail and later joined the 1988 uprising, headed in another direction: Three Pagodas Pass opposite Thailand's Kanchanaburi province:

— I left Rangoon on 23rd September, leaving my wife and children behind, and reached Moulmein. There, I embarked on a 28-day trek to Three Pagodas Pass. We were about 600 — 200 Burmans from Rangoon and Moulmein and nearly 400 ethnic Mons from Mudon, Kamawek and other places near Moulmein. We marched through the jungle and came to a river. It had rained all night before so the current was swift and it was difficult to cross it. Some of us built a bamboo raft, but it overturned and they fell in the water. But we managed to rescue them. It was cold and some of us had fever. We returned to an abandoned village, walking in the dark with only four torches among all of us. We managed not to get separated by each putting a hand on the shoulder of the one in front of us. So we stumbled along in the dark, like a long procession of blind men. But the next day, the water had receded and we were able to cross the river. We passed a few small villages where the local people gave us rice and vegetables to eat. Some even gave us flowers. They knew who we were and they all hated the government; this was insurgent territory where the army is notorious for its atrocities against ordinary civilians. Three days later, we ran into a patrol from the Mon rebel army and were escorted up to Three Pagodas Pass.

Nai Chan Hteik, a 33-year old ethnic Mon doctor had been one of the local leaders of the pro-democracy movement in Paung township between

Moulmein and Thaton. He had had some previous contact with the rebel New Mon State Party (NMSP) and left Paung together with some friends on 21st September, hid for a day in Moulmein and continued by train down to Lamaing on the trunk line to Ye:

— We were fifteen when we left Lamaing and, as we ran into many other groups of people who had fled the towns after the coup, the column had swelled to several hundred when we eventually reached Three Pagodas Pass eleven days later. The villagers along the way were very generous but there was not enough cooking pots for all of us; we had to use bamboo containers instead to cook rice in. Our group included nine girls and they fell sick in the jungle. We had to carry them on our backs. But we made it and we also managed to avoid any encounter with government troops on the march over the hills.

Sai Myo Win Htun from Taunggyi, Shan State, fled on 19th September, the same day as the army opened fire on demonstrators outside the Chinese temple in his home town. Several hundred people were escaping the crack-down in Taunggyi and heading south, towards the Pa-O inhabited hills southeast of Inle Lake. The massive column of dissidents was chased by government troops and split up into several smaller groups. A contingent of more than a hundred ran into a group of guerrillas from the pro-CPB faction of the Pa-O guerrillas, led by an old rebel chieftain, Tha Kalei, and were escorted to the communist-held areas east of the Salween river, close to the Chinese frontier. But most of the fugitives from Taunggyi eventually gathered at Kyauktalong, the temporary headquarters of Aung Kham Hti's non-communist Pa-O National Organisation (PNO), a member of the NDF.

"Some stayed behind in the PNO's area. Others infiltrated back into Taunggyi to organise the underground movement there. Various other groups, however, trekked south towards the Thai border near Mae Hong Son, where the Karenni rebels maintain their base camp," says Sai Myo Win Htun. "We reached it after twelve days in the jungle. We had heard that some student leaders from Burma were in Bangkok, organising resistance with foreign aid, so we wanted to link up with them."

Others had left Rangoon and other towns well before the coup since they anticipated that the military would step in and seize power. Ko Lin from Yankin township in Rangoon had left the capital already on the 2nd together with three friends from his faculty: "It was obvious that something was being planned. All the prisoners had been released, there was orches-trated looting at night and military intelligence agents were trying to destabilise the situation to give the army a pretext to step in. At first, we really thought that the BSPP regime was going to give way to an interim government. But it soon became evident that the army was planning to take over instead. That was why we left Rangoon; we reached the conclusion that we had to fight the regime."

Ko Lin and his friends went by car down to Moulmein in Mon State and then by boat to Kawthaung, or Victoria Point, in the far south. On 14th September, they crossed over into Thailand and got on a bus bound for Bangkok, where they hoped to link up with other groups of fugitive Burmese students in order to take up arms against the new military government in Rangoon.

Until the student exodus to the frontier areas, the ethnic insurgents had played almost no role in the uprising against the BSPP-regime, although they — and not the urban population — were the ones who had been fighting the Burmese Army for decades. From their isolation in the jungles and hills of the peripheral areas, they had merely watched the birth of the new mass movement in bewilderment, unable to relate to it. The NDF had issued its first statement supporting the uprising already on 30th March and the CPB in a broadcast from its clandestine radio station near the Chinese border on 19th and 21st May had also carried a surprisingly accurate account of the March events — but that was about it.

Despite claims by the SLORC, there was no evidence to support the theory that the CPB had had a hand in the August-September demonstrations in Rangoon. On the contrary, the near absence of any students going to the CPB's area clearly indicated that the communists had had severe difficulties in gaining support from the students. Even the young people were aware of the bloody purges in the Pegu Yoma in the 1960s, when many of the students who had fled after the first coup had been executed.

Soon after the March riots, a KNU guerrilla unit had attacked government positions near the Kyaiktiyo Pagoda in Kyaikto, taking advantage of the withdrawal of units from the 44th LID that had previously been based there. The official media immediately exploited the event and the BBS on 22nd March claimed that KNU guerrillas had killed five pilgrims, stolen valuables and cash from donation boxes and burnt down shops and stalls outside the pagoda. Independent observers, however, noted that the guerrillas in fact had shelled a nearby army camp and not even entered the actual pagoda area. But the KNU failed to present its version of the attack, and many people in Rangoon and elsewhere seemed to believe the official account which severely damaged the reputation of the insurgents.

The weaknesses of the rebels in Burma were probably best demonstrated at the end of July, when the KNU launched a dawn attack on NMSP positions at the Three Pagodas in an attempt to wrest control over the toll gates on the lucrative blackmarket route across the pass. The very purpose of the attack severely discredited the ethnic insurgents in the eyes of the

Burmese public; the timing was even more unfortunate. It was on 23rd July — on the same day as Ne Win announced his resignation from the chairmanship of the BSPP. Heavy fighting raged in the area for weeks with dozens of casualties on both sides, until a peacekeeping team from the NDF managed to negotiate a cease-fire between the Mons and the Karens.

Throughout the entire August-September uprising in Burma, there was almost no fighting between the rebels and the government forces, which was part of the reason why several units were able to be withdrawn from the border areas and be re-posted in Rangoon and other urban centres. But the insurgents were also in a dilemma. Brang Seng, the chairman of the Kachin Independence Organisation (KIO) and probably the most sophisticated ethnic rebel leader in Burma, said in an interview in *Newsweek* which was made before the coup but published in the 26th September issue of the magazine: "Before the present crisis there were preparations for a countrywide coordinated offensive, but we had to put that on hold....we did not want to...appear opportunistic by going on the offensive at this point."

The military takeover, however, changed all that and the rebels did, at last, go on the offensive. The first group to make a major push against government positions was the CPB, the single most powerful insurgent army in the country. The target was the small town of Möng Yang about 25 kms from the Chinese border in eastern Shan State. The CPB unit in that area, the 768 Brigade led by Sai Noom Pan and Michael Davies, is predominantly Shan and enjoys considerable support from the local population who tend to value ethnic affinity higher than ideology. Sai Noom Pan' s own father, for instance, was the local headman of Möng Yang. Michael Davies is a Welsh-Shan insurgent leader who is well known in the mountains north of Kengtung.

Several hundred heavily armed Shan troops from the 768 Brigade launched an all-out attack on the garrison in Möng Yang on 23rd September and the entire town fell to them on the following day. The commanding officer of the Burmese Army's 11th Battalion, major Soe Lwin, was killed in the battle along with about 130 of his men. At least a hundred government troops were wounded and nine captured alive. More than 30 automatic weapons were confiscated by the guerrillas as well as about 15,000 rounds of ammunition.

The government forces immediately launched a counter-offensive and on two consecutive days, aeroplanes strafed and bombed the town, reducing several parts of it to rubble and severely damaging the local monastery. Other units pounded Möng Yang with mortars and artillery. The orders apparently were to recapture the lost positions at any cost; diplomatic observers in Rangoon at the time estimated government losses, dead and wounded, at nearly a full battalion.

After a few days of heavy fighting, Sai Noom Pan's troops withdrew from Möng Yang — and the government took revenge on the local population. Local sources claim that many villagers were shot, their homes robbed and several girls from the town gang-raped by government soldiers. The chief monk at Parliang monastery was reportedly taken away and severely beaten. The headman, Sai Noom Pan's 72-year old father Shan Lan Pang, was made to kneel in front of the Burmese Army officer who subsequently pumped nine bullets into the old man's body before he died.

Surprisingly, the official media in Rangoon reported the loss of Möng Yang and the high government casualties. The *Working People's Daily* on 30 September and the BBS two days later admitted the loss, adding that the government forces had suffered "47 fatalities". However, the government newspaper on 3rd October reported that "due to the valiant and effective counter-offensive of our *tatmadaw*, people's militia and People's Police Force and ground support attacks by the *tatmadaw* (air)", the insurgents were now fleeing into the Chinese border mountains.

Shortly afterwards, the official Burmese media admitted to another defeat; this time on the Karen front near the Thai border. Following heavy fighting in the eastern foothills of the rugged Dawna range, KNU guerrillas on 12th October managed to recapture their old base at Mae Tha Waw, on the western bank of the Moci border river, which had been overrun by the Burmese Army in January 1984. Again, government casualties were reported to be in the hundreds — but even so, the order came to recapture Mae Tha Waw no matter the losses. The Burmese Army's firepower at the battle of Mae Tha Waw was overwhelming. Several hundred rockets — including many Carl Gustafs — were fired into the camp every day, confirming the report of the 6th October shipment from Singapore. Eventually, on 21st December, the Karen guerrillas were forced out.

In the Kachin-inhabited areas of the far north, the KIA, often in cooperation with the CPB and other rebel armies, launched a number of attacks. The official media admitted to an attack on Myothit police station on 18th October and subsequent battles in which about a dozen policemen and soldiers were killed. But the heaviest battle of all went unreported in the *Working People's Daily* as well as the BBS. On 13th December, a combined KIA-CPB force ambushed a 140-men strong Burmese Army unit at Kong Sa near Ta Möng Nge east of Kutkai in northern Shan State. Rebel claims put government losses at 106 dead, 17 wounded and 15 captured alive, including one major Hla Myint. Nearly 100 firearms — including 2" and 81mm mortars — were captured as well as about 190,000 rounds of assorted ammunition, handgrenades and shells. Before long, wounded government soldiers from the various battlefronts filled the military hospitals even in Rangoon.

OUTRAGE

The escalated civil war, however, did not seem to wear the military regime down. If anything, it actually gave it a chance to demonstrate to the public that the Burmese Army was not only slaughtering unarmed civilians in Rangoon and other towns. Analysts viewed the unprecedented official publicity, and admissions to losses and high casualties, in the same perspective. And, again, it was the civilian population that had to suffer for the Burmese Army's humiliation in the battlefield. The message the military seemed to want to convey was that if the insurgents stepped up their activities, it would affect the ordinary people.

Army trucks, mounted with machine-guns and manned by armed soldiers soon began cruising the streets of Rangoon, picking up any young people — or other idlers — they could find. Since all schools, from primary level up to university, were closed, the youths spent most of their time in teashops, talking and waiting for something to happen. Hundreds were rounded up and sent away to work as porters for the army on battlefronts in the border areas. The official version said that the ones who were forced to perform these duties were "law-breakers, looters, criminals, muggers, waifs and strays" who "receive a daily wage".

However, the porters who managed to escape to Karen rebels camps along the Thai border told a different story. Ko Ko, 23, was picked up in a Rangoon teashop along with his brother and other young people:

— We were trucked to an army camp near the Thai border and then forced to carry heavy loads for the troops. There were about 1,500 porters in the area where I was. We got no pay and received food only during the first four days in the jungle. There was water only when it rained. Some died of exhaustion, and the corpses were thrown in streams or off cliffs. Many were killed when they could not stand the hardships, or if they walked too slowly. My brother was one of them; I pretended I was dead also and they just left me by the pathside. When I was sure the column was far away, I got up and walked through the jungle until I met some Karen guerrillas. They escorted me to Klerday camp on the Moei river.

The *Nation*, a Bangkok daily, reported on 28th November that 500 men, aged 18 to 40 and including students, teachers and other professionals, had been rounded up on the 15th and taken to Insein Jail: "They were awakened early the next morning and trucked to Hlaingbwe in Karen State. The army trucks, each carrying 40 people...and the passengers were taken to the army compound of the 28th Light Infantry Regiment."

On the following day, they were assigned to be porters for the army and told to carry heavy loads of ammunition into the jungle. The porters were kept on a starvation diet, if they got anything to eat at all. Several were killed in the crossfire between the government troops and the Karen insurgents, or shot when trying to escape.. On the sixth day in the jungle, one of the porters, 20-year old Maung Tin Htay did manage to get away to a KNU camp near the Thai border, where he related his story.

Other students, according to the *Nation*, say they sighted "decayed corpses at two locations on their way to the Karen camp. At one place they came across 25 bodies covered with flies and maggots and had to circumvent the area because of the smell of rotting flesh. In another place they found 30 more bodies with their faces so deformed that it was impossible to identify them."

Another way of inflicting punishment and humiliation on the civilian population was something that in most other countries would be classified as extortion. When people went to the bank to withdraw money from their savings account, they found that the amount they received did not correspond to what they had requested. The balance, usually 300-400 Kyats, appeared on the following day in a list of "donations to the *tatmadaw* " in the *Working People's Daily* — including the name of the person who supposedly had contributed the funds.

Seamen working for the state-owned Five Star Shipping Line suddenly discovered that 10% had been deducted from their monthly salaries for the same purpose. Some donations which were published in the newspaper were several years old and made at a time when the army had still been popular among the urban population. Curiously, one of the few genuine donations came from James Ross, an American citizen. The *Working People's Daily* on 24th December published a photograph of him, handing over US$100 in travellers' cheques, medicine bottles, 50 plastic ballpens and 100 sheets of carbon paper to a Burmese army officer. His motives for the unusual gesture were not explained.

Among the students along the border, frustrations and disappointment soon became apparent. There was no foreign aid waiting for them at the border. Besides that, the students' basic mistake was that they had also believed the government's propaganda according to which the insurgents were supported by 'foreign interests' — and they had, at least, hoped to get their share of that aid. But instead, the immediate concerns became sickness and malnutrition. Some students died of malaria shortly after their arrival in the border areas. Others suffered from skin diseases and eye infections. Food had been a problem all along since they left the towns, and the remote camps on the Thai-Burmese frontier were hardly havens for gourmets. The rebel groups provided the students with rice but because of the scarcity of meat and vegetables, the urban youths in their new environment soon found themselves eating snakes, lizards, dogs, trunks of banana trees and whatever they could forage in the jungle.

The Thai attitude towards the fugitive students from the very beginning was obscure when not contradictory. The Thai authorities did allow private relief agencies to send rice, medicines, blankets and other humanitarian supplies to the new camps along the border, but they had no desire to let them stay permanently on the Thai side, or even use Thailand as a springboard from which to launch a political campaign against the new regime in Rangoon, let alone organise an armed resistance. Young people who could not stand the hardships in the camps and had crossed into Thailand to seek asylum there were almost invariably pushed back to the camps again, sometimes at gunpoint. Among the students who made it to the Thai side, a few unlucky ones were picked up by the local Thai police, "fined" 1,000 Baht or so and then released, perhaps to be arrested again some time later.

Soon, the students also became aware of the fact that the ethnic insurgents along the border were not receiving any foreign assistance whatsoever, but survived on taxes levied on the cross-border trade in contraband from Thailand to Burma and vice versa. The arms and ammunition they had were bought from private contacts with arms merchants in Thailand, often at exorbitant prices, and the KNU the NMSP and other members of the NDF had hardly enough weapons to arm their own troops, let alone any stocks to share with the thousands of students who had flocked to the border areas.

Some defectors from the 502 Air Force Maintenance Unit, who had participated in the last demonstrations in September, made it to the border and their camps seemed to be better organised and maintained than the others. But not all the airmen made it to the border. Sgt. Hla Soe was arrested along with three of his colleagues at Toungoo, headed for the border, on 1st October. The five were taken to Yay Kyi Aing. Two of them somehow managed to escape; Hla Soe was transferred to Mingaladon Military Hospital on the 22nd, after two weeks of beatings and torture. He was recognised by some of his old comrades, but with difficulty — "he looked like a skeleton and his body was covered in cuts and bruises", they said. His commanding officer made a request to see him, but was refused. Four days later, Soe Hla died from his injuries.

But small numbers of students did receive some basic military training, almost the only thing the ethnic insurgents could provide them with. Even this, however, ran into problems when differences arose among the students as to how closely they should ally themselves with the ethnic insurgents: "We have seen with our own eyes that the insurgents aren't monsters who eat their own babies," says Soe Soe, 25, from Rangoon. "But many people in the towns still believe the propaganda they have been fed by the government for years. It would be a mistake for us if we openly joined forces with the insurgents at this stage; it would inevitably cause misunderstandings and we could lose the popular support we now enjoy."

In some ways, it was easier for the students who themselves came from the ethnic minorities. At Three Pagodas Pass, Nai Chan Hteik and almost 900 Mon students and other intellectuals joined the NMSP. They were trained as guerrilla soldiers — but the drills were carried out with bamboo sticks instead of rifles since the NMSP had no resources to arm all the new recruits.

A few students did join forces with the KNU and participated in fighting. One of them was Moe Kyaw Zan, a 24-year old student from Yankin, Rangoon. He became the first student to die in battle; his unit was ambushed near Wangkha, close to the Thai border in mid-November. When his body was later retrieved, it had been beheaded by the government troops and left behind, probably as a deterrent to other students. The headless corpse was buried at the KNU's Manerplaw headquarters a few days later.

The various groups of Burman students soon came under pressure to, at least, unite under one umbrella so that the ethnic insurgents, relief agencies and others knew exactly who they were dealing with. Then another difficulty became apparent: most of the young people who had fled to the border, often in disarray, were of roughly the same age. Some had led local strike committees in their hometowns — Rangoon, Mandalay, Toungoo, Pyinmana, Taunggyi and so on. Naturally, they expected to become leaders at the border as well. None of the main student leaders from Rangoon made it to the border. Min Zeya tried — but was apprehended in Mergui on 21st November, and subsequently sent back to jail in Rangoon.

On the border, romantic memories of the anti-Japanese struggle of the 1940s lingered; there were many young 'Aung Sans' who dreamt of setting up their own BIAs, BDAs and BNAs. But this 'second struggle for independence' lacked cohesiveness and anything like the Thirty Comrades; stories circulated about 'the Golden Prince' — *Shwe Min Tha* — who was leading a band of armed fighters in northern Burma, and leaflets circulated by underground groups talked about the *Galon-Ni*, or 'Red Garuda' movement, also in the north. If these groups ever existed, they were in any case insignificant and posed no threat to the new SLORC regime.

Before long, rivalries between various student leaders and different factions developed in the camps. The lack of unity, based on personality conflicts rather than ideological differences, and the question of what nature their alliance with the NDF should take remained the major issues that divided the students along the border. There was also another problem which the students slowly became aware of. Not all refugees were genuine; as they began to realise, government agents had infiltrated their ranks.

The situation became even more complicated when a number of Burmese exiles flew into Thailand from abroad to organise the students along the border. Tin Maung Win, the son of U Win, a former Burmese ambassador to the US, arrived in Bangkok in late August together with Ye Kyaw

Thu, another politically active exile. The duo headed the US-based CRDB which also had links in Australia, Britain, West Germany, Thailand and Bangladesh. Together with other exiles, they staged demonstrations outside the Burmese embassy on Sathorn Road in Bangkok — and then headed for the border.

Their arrival was met with mixed feelings among the fugitive students. While many of them certainly welcomed anyone who wanted to support them, others inevitably thought that the CRDB had joined the struggle in order to take advantage of it. From the very beginning until the coup on 18th September, the Burmese uprising had been an exclusively domestic affair; at the border, various foreign interests became involved, which hardly contributed to unity among the students.

Apart from the CRDB, the remnants of U Nu's old border-based resistance re-surfaced in September and October. U Thwin, the only leader of the movement of the 1970s who had not returned to Rangoon during the 1980 amnesty, revived the old PPP/PLA — and travelled from his base in Bangkok to the border areas. The Unites States of Burma, the National Unity Party for Democracy and the People's Liberation Front were some of the other groups of Burmese exiles who moved into the student camps. But none of them had more than a handful of followers — and no arms to offer the students.

However, after many meetings, squabbles and arguments that sometimes nearly resulted in fist-fights, representatives for the dozen or so student camps along the border met at the KNU enclave of Wangkha on the Moei river, north of Mae Sot, in early November. The conference lasted for five days and the establishment of the All-Burma Students' Democratic Front (ABSDF), an organisation that had existed in some camps since September, was formalised. Htun Aung Gyaw, the 'veteran' from the 1974 student uprising, was elected chairman of the new alliance on 5th November. In its manifesto, adopted on the same day, the ABSDF vowed to fight for "genuine democracy in Burma" and to "cease the internal war, to restore peace and national reconciliation...to achieve equality, justice and unity among the nationalities of the Union of Burma."

From the very beginning, the ABSDF was ridden with factional infighting. Htun Aung Gyaw generally favoured close cooperation with the NDF, while others advocated a more independent line. Although many ABSDF activists wanted to maintain a certain tactical distance from the insurgents, two weeks after its formal foundation, the organisation nevertheless signed up as a member of a broader front. On 18th November, at a meeting at Klerday, another KNU camp on the western bank of the Moei river, the Democratic Alliance of Burma (DAB) was formed. The DAB also included the ten ethnic insurgent armies of the NDF, the CRDB, several other, smaller groups of Burmese exiles, two Muslim organisations and, surprisingly, a

Chin group from the Indian border areas. Until the August uprising, there had been no anti-government movement among the Chins and they were about the only ethnic group in Burma which did not have its own rebel army.

Altogether 23 anti-government groups of various descriptions joined the DAB. General Bo Mya, the Karen rebel chieftain was elected chairman and Brang Seng of the KIO, Nai Shwe Kyin of the NMSP and U Thwin of the PPP became vice chairmen. Tin Maung Win, the CRDB's chairman, was nominated general secretary. Of Burma's rebel armies, only two remained outside the DAB. One was the CPB, the inclusion of which would have been unacceptable to several of the non-communist members of the alliance. Nevertheless, the three northern rebel armies of the NDF — the Kachins, the Shans and the Palaungs — had already launched several joint attacks with the communists. The CPB did, however, in a radio message dated 14th November, declare in principle its support for a broader front.

The other group which remained outside was opium warlord Khun Sa's band. Perhaps not surprisingly, a spokesman for Khun Sa said in an interview with the *Bangkok Post* on 18th December that "the students should respond to the Saw Maung regime's call to return to Rangoon." The spokesman also said, cryptically, that Khun Sa "prefers Ne Win or Gen. Saw Maung to rule the country rather than 'foreigners'." Suspicions that Khun Sa indeed had a tacit agreement with the military authorities in Rangoon grew even stronger.

Of the student factions, one group also chose to act independently. When the students first arrived at the border, the main hope had been pinned on Maung Maung Kyaw, the hero of the June uprising. But the rumour that he had already set up an army, as almost everything else the students had heard about the border, turned out to be somewhat exaggerated. He had no armed battalions — but only a handful of followers without guns who sometimes enjoyed the protection of Gen. Sudsai's people, sometimes were locked up in Thai police stations but mostly spent their time worrying about their day-to-day survival. Their group, the Burma National Liberation Party, remained one of the most isolated of all the groups along the border. Its only support, apart from the Sudsai-connection, came from the Sajjatham Party, a local army-backed organisation of Thai students at Ramkhamhaeng University in Bangkok.

The involvement of the Thai students had already begun when Maung Maung Kyaw arrived in Bangkok in August. He was introduced to Prasert Kitsuwanratana, the secretary general of the Student Federation of Thailand (SFT). With Maung Maung Kyaw's defection to the Thai military, the SFT linked up with the ABSDF and the Thai students became some of the few genuine friends the Burmese students won in exile. The SFT helped their Burmese allies contact the foreign press and deal with the Thai authorities. In a strongly worded statement, issued on 10th November, the SFT protested against a proposed visit to Rangoon by Thailand's deputy foreign minister, Prapas Limpabandhu. Surprisingly, the Thai government gave in and the tour was cancelled.

Despite this backing from the SFT, before long, groups of disappointed and disillusioned students began filtering back to their homes in central Burma. In mid-October, the SLORC established 27 reception centres (2+7=9) for students who wanted to return and set 18th November (1+8=9) as the date they had to return — or be "treated as insurgents". The deadline was later extended several times and the Rangoon press became filled with stories of student returnees and the hardships they had faced along the Thai border. The official media invariably described these students as "misled youths who had listened to rumours and been misinformed about the true attitude of the *tatmadaw*"; there was never any attempt to understand the real reason why these young people had fled the towns. Now, the media said they "were back in the legal fold" since they had "understood their misdeeds".

By mid-December, the military authorities announced that 1,500 students had returned. There was no independent confirmation of that claim — but, at the same time, reports were reaching Thailand that several of the returnees had been arrested soon after their homecoming. A Rangoon-based Western diplomat reported in the end of December: "One student leader [in Rangoon] estimates that about 10% of those coming back were re-arrested and then vanished, presumed dead. Some are definitely dead: parents receive letters saying their son has died of malaria. A source who works for the ministry of defence has seen a pile of these form letters being prepared."

Almost forgotten amongst the students who fled the towns were the ones who headed to the north and the northwest. But about 300 Burman students, mainly from Mandalay, along with about 700 Kachin students took refuge in the KIA headquarters area southeast of Myitkyina in north-ernmost Kachin State. There seemed to be fewer frictions between these students and the KIA than was the case in the south with the KNU; the students in the far north were immediately allotted their own camp with its own administration. The Kachin guerrillas provided security for the student camp as well as training and some arms. This group in Kachin State became almost the only student contingent that was properly organised along military lines.

Across the Indian border, the authorities there — unlike the Thais — adopted a clear-cut policy at an early stage. One refugee camp was built at

Leikhul in Chandel district of Manipur, mainly for Burman students who had crossed the frontier near Tamu in Sagaing Division. Two more camps for Chin nationals were set up at Champhai and Saiha in Mizoram. From the very beginning, the Indian authorities made it clear that no one would be forced back to Burma and that the refugees would be granted asylum as long as their lives were in danger.

The number of students who had reached India was not more than a few hundred, but as news about the comparatively fair treatment they received by the Indian authorities reached the towns of Burma, more began to secretly leave for the northwest. Of special interest were the students from Chin State; the Chins are closely related to the Mizos of Mizoram which made it easier for them across the border in India. But unable to secure more than moral support in Mizoram, a few hundred of the more militant Chin activists trekked north to Kachin State, where they set up the Chin National Front (CNF) and received military training from the KIA. Indirectly, the student movement of 1988 thus contributed to the formation of a new ethnic insurgent army among the hitherto quiet Chins.

The Burman students along the Indian border in mid-October had announced the formation of the Freedom Democratic Guerrilla Front (North Burma) and, like their comrades in the ABSDF, vowed to take up arms against Gen. Saw Maung's regime. But like their brethren near the Thai border, they were also unable to secure a supply of arms and ammunition. The armed, student-led uprising from Burma's borders — which many people in the towns had been waiting for since the coup — seemed an impossible dream.

Eight WHITHER BURMA?

TOWARDS THE END OF the stormy year 1988, the situation in Burma seemed utterly depressing. Thousands of lives had been lost in senseless massacres and summary executions. The old regime had reasserted its power under a different name—and it appeared to show no genuine willingness to yield to the demands of the Burmese public at large, or even to take note of the almost total international condemnation. The street demonstrations were over. The armed struggle had never materialised. The brief optimism of August and September soon turned to despair and frustration. Was it back to square one after everything Burma had been through?

Undeniably, the SLORC (could anyone think of a more appropriate-sounding name for the new regime?) had promised "free and fair elections" and that the armed forces would remain "absolutely neutral" in the process. It had also "cleaned up Rangoon" and committed itself to "restoring law and order", because the unity and integrity of the state was being "threatened by insurgents and other destructive elements". But to anyone familiar with Burmese history, this seemed little more than a hollow repetition of old rhetoric from 1951, 1958 and 1962; especially, a much more brutal version of the 1958-60 Caretaker Government. And the Burmese certainly knew what that eventually resulted in, even if there had followed a civil interregnum which had lasted for nearly two years.

It was more than a month before the Burmese public had recovered from the massacre of 18th-20th September. Although more people had been slaughtered during the random, indiscriminate shooting in August, the systematic manner in which the killings had been carried out this time cowed people into submission. And after more than a month of massive, daily street marches, many people undoubtedly were beginning to feel the strain. 'Demonstration fatigue' may not be an ordinary English expression, but after Rangoon in August and September, it had become a new concept.

However, at the beginning of November, the *Yahanpyo* announced that they were going to stage a demonstration in Rangoon only of monks. The SLORC was in an obvious dilemma: if the monks turned out in large numbers, they would feel compelled to shoot, which, in turn, would be an enormous sacrilege and cause further serious disturbances. But in the end the SLORC decided on a use of force even when dealing with monks. Troops entered Rangoon and surrounded all major monasteries — and the soldiers were instructed that if they saw any men in yellow clothes, these were only "robed persons" and not monks. The demonstration never materialised.

The people were off the streets and back to work. Only the schools — from primary level up to universities — remained closed. But within the limits of the new laws that the SLORC had introduced, people continued their political activities. On 27th September 1988, the SLORC promulgated a 'Political Parties Registration Law', which ostensibly aimed at preparing the country for "multi-party democracy elections". Three days earlier three of the four main opposition leaders had finally got together and set up a political organisation, the *National League for Democracy* (NLD). Aung Gyi became its chairman, Tin U its vice chairman and Aung San Suu Kyi the general secretary. U Nu's followers set up two parties: the *League for Democracy and Peace* (LDP), led by Mahn Win Maung and Bohmu Aung, and the *Democracy Party* headed by Thu Wai, a former PDP man who had spent the late 1960s in Thailand.

Before long, new political organisations mushroomed in Burma; the new laws in effect had abolished the old one-party system. By setting up a political party, people could meet legally and discuss politics. Each political party was also entitled to four telephone lines and 70 gallons of petrol a week at the official price of 16 Kyats a gallon — at a time when the black-market price was 100-150 Kyats a gallon and it normally took months to get a telephone installed in a private home. Not surprisingly, more than 100 political parties had registered with the authorities by mid-November. A few of them were genuine, some were mere discussions clubs and a large number were referred to as 'telephone and petrol parties'. A few dozen were considered NUP off-shoots which had been set up solely to confuse the issue.

Predictably, many of the politicians of pre-coup times saw this as an opportunity to build up new political organisations and power bases. The old Red Flag communist, Thakin Soe, on 7th October announced that he had registered the *Unity and Development Party*. A whole series of new AFPFLs — with various additions in brackets after the abbreviation — were also formed. The old labour leader and BWPP veteran, Thakin Lwin, now 73, became the chairman of the *People's Democratic Party* which also included Aung San's elder brother Aung Than. Another BWPP veteran, Thakin Chit Maung, formed the *Democratic Front for National Reconstruction*. There were also an abundance of regional parties in the minority areas and parties that consisted solely of, for example, women or retired diplomats. Some parties bore rather quaint names such as the *New Ideology Improvement Party for Social System*, the *Democracy New Building Social Milieu Party*, the *Ever Green*

Young Men's Association and the *National Peace and Comfort Party* whose chairman, U Kyi, was listed as a "indigenous medical practitioner".

Soon, the number of political parties had passed the 200 mark. Sarcastic Burmese also saw this new political system as a way in which the SLORC wanted to punish and ridicule the public: "When they decided to introduce a multi-party system, the emphasis was clearly on 'multi'. Maybe they hoped that the people now would long for the days when there was only one party — and convey the message to the outside world that Burma was not mature enough to be able to handle a democratic system," a Burmese friend remarked at the time.

With the abundance of parties emerging, the SLORC now also had a new argument which it raised at every opportunity. Law and order could not be said to have been restored because "there's antagonism between all the different parties". An interim government was out of the question since "who shall form it? There are so many parties now".

But this showcase 'democracy' did not convince the international community which had cut off foreign assistance to Burma in the wake of the September bloodbath. Since no aid would be resumed until the new military regime met public demands for democracy, the SLORC had to look elsewhere for foreign exchange, which it badly needed in order to survive. In late November, it was believed that Burma had less than US$ 10 million in foreign exchange reserves. The answer was to introduce a liberal, new foreign investment law on 30th November. It allowed 100% foreign-owned firms to invest in Burma and required at least 35% foreign investment in joint ventures. The law also guaranteed against nationalisation of foreign owned assets and foreign investors would be able to repatriate profits and enjoy tax exemptions for at least three years. Prior to this, the only foreign company that had been allowed to set up a joint venture in Burma was the West German engineering firm Fritz Werner, which made high-grade machinery for manufacturing arms and ammunition for the Burmese Army.

The unprecedented law was announced by Col. David Abel, the new trade minister who is generally considered the most, or probably the only, reasonably competent minister in the present regime. But in view of the still unsettled political situation in Burma, most foreign investors reacted cautiously to the new law. A close association with a regime that had seized power by force, and ruled by methods which were unacceptable to the civilised world, could prove counterproductive in the future, most foreign companies reasoned. The international blockade against the SLORC encouraged many Burmese to think that outside pressure would eventually force the military to give in.

But even that hope faded soon. When no flood of foreign money greeted the new investment law, the SLORC began selling off Burma's vast natural resources to neighbouring countries. The first to respond were the Thais. On 14th December 1988, Gen. Chaovalit Yongchaiyuth, undertook a one day visit to Rangoon. Accompanied by an entourage of 86 people, including army officers, Thai pressmen and staff from the Burmese embassy in Bangkok, he was the first foreign dignitary to visit Burma after the coup — and he did not restrict himself to exchanging diplomatic courtesies in a restrained language. The *Working People's Daily* on 15th December published a full account of the visit on its front page, complete with pictures of Gen. Chaovalit not only saluting, as soldier to soldier, but embracing Gen. Saw Maung at Mingaladon airport.

In his speech at the *Dagon Yeiktha* of the defence ministry in Rangoon Gen. Chaovalit said: "My dear brother, first of all, I don't know how to address you, Sir, I should address you as His Excellency the President, Excellency the Chairman, or Excellency the Prime Minister, or Excellency the the Minister of Defence or Minister of Foreign Affairs. But it is very kind indeed of you, Sir, to address me as a Brother...you yourself and all my Burmese brothers now are working very hard for the peace, stability and prosperity of the Union of Burma. So permit me to thank you yourself and all my brothers for a very very warm welcome and very wonderful hospitality...we are worried very much that you have some students along the Burmese and Thai border. We raise the same subject...you really need all of them to come back and study for the future of Burma. We will do our best, brother...gentlemen, our friends, may I take this opportunity to invite you all to join me in the toast, to my dear brother, His Excellency General Saw Maung, for his happiness, his long life and prosperity" (sic!). Gen. Chaovalit, broke the boycott in a way that upset not only the Burmese public, but even human rights activists in Thailand and elsewhere. Several foreign diplomats were taken aback by this lack of tact and consideration on the part of the Thai army chief.

Hardly by coincidence, some unprecedented business deals were signed between the Burmese authorities and several Thai companies shortly afterwards. By early 1989, a stampede of logging concerns, most of whom had close connections with business-oriented Thai army officers, were entering deals with Rangoon. A document written by the military government's Timber Corporation in February said that 20 concession areas had been contracted along the Thai-Burma border with total exports of 160,000 tonnes of teak logs and 500,000 tonnes of other hardwood logs authorised. The corporation estimated revenues of US$112 million a year from the logging, a bonanza by the scale of Burma's trade. Two Thai fishery companies, the Atlantis Corporation and Mars & Co, received permission to catch 250,000 tons of fish in Burmese waters each. A small firm, the Thip Tharn Thong, on 17th December 1988 signed a contract to barter used cars and machinery in exchange for Burmese gems, jade and pearls. The logging deals especially

were timely for Thai interests; following a mudslide caused by deforesta-
tion in southern Thailand in late November, the government in Bangkok introduced a ban on logging throughout the country.

As part of the deal, a reception centre for students who wanted to return
to Burma "voluntarily" was also set up near the provincial airport at Tak on
21st December and a similar camp was attached to the 11th Infantry
Regiment's camp at Bangkhen, a northern Bangkok suburb. The first batch
of 80 Burmese students from the border areas was repatriated five days
later, followed by several hundred over the weeks that followed. On 5th
January 1989, the US State Department said it had received reports that as
many as 50 Burmese students who had returned via the "reception centres"
set up by the Burmese Army close to the Thai border, had been arrested and
some had been killed in custody. Now, there was also fear for the safety of
the "absconding and misled students" (to use the SLORC's terminology)
who the Thais were sending back by air. But human rights issues had taken
a very definite backseat in Thailand's refugee policy in view of the lucrative
business deals which the Burmese military now were offering their Thai
counterparts.

The forced repatriation proved embarrassing for the Thai as well as the
Burmese authorities. In a feeble attempt to show the increasingly concerned
international community that the students who had been repatriated from
Thailand had not been arrested or maltreated, which several press reports
had claimed, the SLORC in mid-January 1989 made the unexpected move
of contacting the Foreign Correspondents' Club of Thailand. Forty-six
Bangkok-based journalists were invited to visit Burma; it was the first press
tour of its kind since the military takeover in 1962. To maximise the
auspiciousness of the occasion, the SLORC had organised the arrival of the
foreign correspondents for 18th January (1+8=9). The unprecedented press
tour went to Rangoon, Loikaw, Taunggyi, Meiktila and Pagan, but was
strictly guarded by both uniformed military police and plainclothes DDSI
agents — easily distinguishable in their dark sunglasses and with their stern
looks. Helen White, one of the participants of the tour, wrote in the *Asian
Wall Street Journal* on 23rd January: "The military regime's initial public-
relations efforts were far from convincing...the military refused journalists'
requests to visit markets, or to stroll through city streets...however, there
was little the government could do to limit the damage to its image when
several students interrupted a government spokesman in Taunggyi. The
spokesman was explaining that the mass shootings in the city by government troops last September came in response to aggression by demonstrators. The room, which was filled with student returnees and their parents,
erupted in applause as the students shouted that the slaughter — which
they said killed about 74 people — was unprovoked".

The entire repatriation programme came to a halt in late March, following the adverse publicity which the press tour had generated as well as a strongly worded protest from the United Nations High Commissioner for Refugees (UNHCR) in Geneva.

Although the press tour had backfired, the SLORC had managed to earn dollars at a critical moment. The generals in Rangoon were able to make a range of fast-paying deals with no awkward questions or political strings. Burma's foreign exchange reserves soon soared to heights unknown since the first coup in 1962, enabling the SLORC to purchase vast quantities of munitions from abroad. The Thai connection was soon also to yield benefits in direct military operations against the ethnic insurgents that Bangkok previously had quietly promoted as a buffer with its historic enemy. The dissident students along the frontier also suffered since the Burmese and the Thai military together began clearing the border areas to get the timber out. In the past, the Burmese Army had been unable to hold territory along the frontier, the end of tenuous supply lines from the coastal areas. Now, rice and other commodities could be bought from across the border in Thailand. And Burmese forces no longer held back from crossing into Thai territory and attacking the rebel camps from the rear, using their newly acquired heavy mortars, rockets and artillery. With Thai help the SLORC did not merely survive, it actually managed to consolidated its grip on power. And once the Thais had clinched their deals, companies from equally unscrupulous countries such as Singapore and South Korea followed shortly afterwards since they "did not want to be left behind". The SLORC soon became more firmly entrenched than the short-lived regimes that had ruled the country since Ne Win's resignation in July 1988.

Meanwhile, the people of Rangoon were tired and angry, but it would have been a serious mistake to assume that they had given up — despite all the disappointments. Within the limitations of the law, they continued the struggle that had begun months before. The students had held a crisis meeting shortly after the 18th September takeover. In a shrewd manoeuvre, aimed at preserving the movement under the new, extremely difficult conditions, the old *ba ka tha* for tactical purposes was divided into three groups. Min Ko Naing, the almost legendary student leader now in hiding in Rangoon, continued working in the underground. Two of his associates, Win Moe and Aung Naing, had joined the student exodus to the border areas where they hoped to organise armed resistance against the SLORC. Moe Thi Zon established a legal organisation, the *Democratic Party for a New Society* (DPNS), which registered with the Elections Commission on 15th October 1988.

Among the plethora of political parties that had emerged, there were only a few others that were really of any relevance — and among them, the

NLD was by far the strongest. But the popularity of its chairman, Aung Gyi, had been rapidly declining since he had surprised the crowds by praising the army in his speech at Sanchaung on 25th August. In an interview in Asiaweek's 21st October issue, he made the remarkable claim that Ne Win had kicked Sein Lwin out when he heard that children had been gunned down in the streets of Rangoon. He also said that "Sanda Win is like my daughter".

Not surprisingly, Aung Gyi soon became more of a liability than an asset for the NLD, despite the crucial role he had played at the beginning of the 1988 uprising by writing his open letters to Ne Win. In November, Aung Gyi and twelve of his associates demanded that eight alleged 'communists' — mainly lawyers and film actors — be expelled from the league. When asked to substantiate their allegations or resign, Aung Gyi and his colleagues quit the NLD on 3rd December. Two weeks later, they set up their own party, the oddly named *Union Nationals Democracy Party* (UNDP).

Tin U was elected Aung Gyi's successor as NLD chairman. But the focal point of the opposition became its increasingly popular general secretary, Aung San Suu Kyi. When she had first appeared in public outside the Shwe Dagon on 26th August, she had attracted an enormous crowd. But at that time, most people had probably showed up out of curiosity; she was Aung San's daughter and that was why everybody knew her. Over subsequent months — and especially after the military takeover — she matured politically and developed an identity of her own. In a talk at the Asia Society in New York on 29th November 1988, Burton Levin, the US ambassador to Burma, commented:

— Even though she's married to a foreigner, nonetheless she touches a chord among the whole spectrum of Burmese life. The first time she came to my house for lunch, I had every one of my servants just lining up. It was like, in American terms, one of these nutty rock stars appearing at a high school. It was really something. She's got charisma, she's bright, she knows how to speak, she's come to the fore.

On 30th October 1988, Aung San Suu Kyi, along with some NLD workers, left Rangoon and travelled up-country to meet the people in preparation for the general elections which, despite everything that had happened, the SLORC had indeed promised. Over a period of thirteen days, they visited more than 50 towns and villages in Pegu, Magwe, Sagaing and Mandalay Divisons as well as Shan State. The welcome was astounding. Even in relatively small towns such as Monywa and Shwebo, tens of thousands of people turned out in the streets, in effect defying the ban on outdoor gatherings of more than four persons. The army, surprisingly did not interfere; there were even reports of soldiers presenting flowers to the entourage.

In December, Aung San Suu Kyi went to the Moulmein area in the southeast. This time, however, army vehicles mounted with loudspeakers cruised the streets and told the public not to come out and greet her. Thousands of people defied that order, and the welcome she received in Moulmein was as enthusiastic as the one in the north. But after her trip, 13 local NLD workers were arrested — and on 19th December, the SLORC warned the political parties "to behave; this is not the time to incite the people...if [politicians] want democracy, it is necessary for them to abide by rules, orders, laws and regulations".

The criticism was not more specific than that, but it was obvious that the military was getting concerned about the more and more effective organisation of the opposition. By contrast, its own NUP had not managed to re-establish itself after the collapse in August. In Mandalay, when the NUP opened a new office, by the next morning its walls were coated with cow dung. In several towns, landlords even refused to rent out offices to the NUP; it remained as hated as the BSPP despite the name-change.

The next big challenge came soon after. The condition of Daw Khin Kyi, Aung San's widow and Aung San Suu Kyi's mother, was deteriorating. She had been bed-ridden after a series of strokes since April and partly paralysed. On 27th December 1988, she finally died in the family's home on University Avenue. Both the military and the public had been nervously waiting for her death; it was generally believed that her funeral — which would have to be at least a semi-official event — would generate emotion and be the catalyst for some kind of public demonstration.

Huge crowds began to gather outside Aung San Suu Kyi's home — and the military authorities issued a stern warning against "disturbances" during the funeral. The new year 1989 was ushered in and many people began asking what it would bring to crisis-ridden Burma. On 1st January, the three most prominent members of the SLORC — Gen. Saw Maung, the DDSI chief, Brig.-Gen. Khin Nyunt, and the home and religious affairs minister, Maj.-Gen. Phone Myint — called at University Avenue to sign the condolence book. Although Aung San Suu Kyi had had earlier meetings with Phone Myint, this was the first time Saw Maung and Khin Nyunt met her. She invited them in for tea — and their discussions were described by eye-witnesses as "very lively", indicating that she seized the opportunity to remind the military of earlier promises of "free and fair elections" and a return to democracy. The military leaders, however, were as non-committal as usual.

The following day, the funeral took place. More than 100,000 people — some sources say up to a million — marched through the streets of Rangoon, from the house on University Avenue to a special tomb which had been built near U Thant's burial place close to the Shwe Dagon. The marchers carried banners and flags of the NLD as well as student peacock flags. NLD workers ensured discipline and took care of security; the troops who had been ordered out to oversee the event nervously clutched their rifles in the background, probably feeling their isolation as there was actually no need for their presence.

Groups of students sang anti-government songs and chanted in unison: "We won't forget our comrades who fell in the struggle for democracy!" and "We won't kneel to oppression!" But the march, which was the first since the 18th September military takeover, passed peacefully. Min Ko Naing appeared briefly and told the marchers to behave with discipline and dignity. It was a massive display of anti-government sentiment — and the organisation clearly indicated that the opposition had matured considerably since the turbulent months of August and September.

Surprisingly, Aung San Suu Kyi's brother Aung San Oo had been granted a Burmese visa to attend the funeral and paid his first visit to Rangoon in many years. But his presence caused less of a stir than expected; he was seen in the funeral procession, called on Aung Gyi and then returned to California.

Several foreign envoys also participated in the march. Significantly, the ambassadors of Japan, the US, Britain, Italy, France and West Germany flew out that afternoon to Bangkok — to avoid attending another function on 4th January: Burma's Independence Day celebrations, organised by the military. The ambassador of India had left a few days earlier for the same reasons.

In many ways, Daw Khin Kyi's funeral marked a watershed in post-coup Burmese politics; the opposition had demonstrated its strength as well as its ability to control the crowds, the Western democracies had expressed in no uncertain terms where their sympathies lay — and the SLORC found itself isolated and estranged from both its own people and the international, democratic community.

From then onwards, the confrontation between the SLORC and the opposition escalated. The harassment, that began during Aung San Suu Kyi's campaign tour of the Moulmein area in December 1988, intensified during two subsequent trips to the Irrawaddy delta region, and Tavoy and Mergui in Tenasserim Division in January and February 1989. In several towns in the delta, people were told to stay indoors, barbed-wire fences were erected in major streets leading to the places were she was going to deliver her speeches and 34 NLD workers were arrested in the wake of her tour.

But the courage and the determination of the now almost undisputed leader of the opposition encouraged people to take to the streets again. In March, the students and several opposition parties marked the first anniversary of the death of Maung Phone Maw. Troops and armed police patrolled the streets of Rangoon—and on the 16th, scores of demonstrators were arrested. On 24th March, the official media announced that Min Ko Naing had been detained as well. In a much-publicised incident in the delta town of Danubyu on 5th April, Myint Oo, an army captain, ordered his soldiers to load their guns and aim at Aung San Suu Kyi who was walking down the street along with some of her followers. Before the troops could open fire, however, a major intervened. But the fact that Myint Oo shortly afterwards was promoted to major indicated that he had official approval for his action.

The situation had also become even more confrontational since Armed Forces Day on 27th March 1989, when Ne Win had reappeared at a dinner party for foreign envoys, effectively laying to rest all speculation that he was now out of the picture. On the contrary, it soon became clear that precious little actually had changed in the top leadership of the country. 'Number One's' inner circle of cronies still include Sein Lwin and Aye Ko and all the old BSPP people are still enjoying their old perks and privileges: San Yu, Kyaw Htin, Tun Tin and the others. Dr Maung Maung, to whom has been delegated the task of drafting a new constitution, regularly visits Ne Win and his Ady Road residence. Even the hated Thura Kyaw Zwa, the butcher of Sagaing, soon resurfaced as a NUP leader, now in the Pegu area. The remarkable cohesiveness of the armed forces — the main reason why the 1988 uprising was quelled—to a large extent depends on the very existence of Ne Win and how he treats his subordinates, new as well as old. Whether Ne Win takes direct part in the actual decision making process is irrelevant since "what is He going to say?" is the main question asked by the military before anything is ever discussed.

Ne Win's reappearance was ridiculed in a traditional Burmese way by the opposition which staged a slogan competition outside the NLD's University Road headquarters in Rangoon during *thingyan*, or the water festival, on 13th-17th April. Apparently infuriated by this, the authorities detained several students who had taken part in the event — and, at about the same time, arrests began of NLD and DPNS grassroot organisers, especially in Pakokku, Taunggyi, Kyaukpadaung, Monywa, Myinmu and other towns up-country. In Rangoon, the DPNS leader, Moe Thi Zon, went underground in April and soon showed up at the Thai border where he joined the ABSDF. In an interview with an Australian television team shortly before his disappearance from Rangoon, Moe Thi Zon had declared: "The final victory must come through armed struggle. If you see how the military is treating us, we've got no other choice."

But the mainstream opposition continued its peaceful activities, unabated despite the repression. Leaflets, bulletins, unofficial newspapers, audio cassettes and video tapes circulated all over the country and meetings were held in defiance of the SLORC's notorious decree number 2/88 which banned all public gatherings of five or more people. But rather than enforcing this order, the military on 18th June introduced a new printing law aimed at preventing the opposition from issuing "unauthorised publications". Gradually, the SLORC began tightening the noose after a few months of relative political freedom.

In late June, during the first anniversary of the clash in Myenigone market, the army opened fire on demonstrators for the first time since the coup. One man was killed and Aung San Suu Kyi was briefly detained. Responding to these moves — and the worsening repression throughout Burma — she became increasingly outspoken in her criticism of the regime. She also openly attacked Ne Win, accusing him of being responsible for Burma's economic plight and implying that nothing will fundamentally change as long as he is pulling the strings from behind the scenes.

A new movement was taking shape and it was clear that is was of a completely different nature than the joyful, spontaneous uprising of August-September 1988. The opposition now had gained considerable experience. It had competent leaders who began addressing fundamental issues: the absolute power of Ne Win, what democracy means, and the necessity of discipline. The large crowds that gathered around Aung San Suu Kyi did not shout slogans or wave banners; they listened attentively to her speeches and afterwards asked intelligent, relevant questions. The Burmese people had showed that they were indeed politically mature — despite the existence of more than 200 political parties. Perhaps even more importantly, the troops that were sent out to disperse the crowds began to get down from their army lorries — to listen to her message.

From the SLORC's point of view, a new, dangerous situation was emerging. The situation became even more tense in the weeks before Martyrs' Day, the 42nd anniversary of Aung San's assassination on 19th July 1989. Aung San Suu Kyi declared that she would march with thousands of followers to pay respect to Aung San and the other martyrs, and not take part in the SLORC-organised ceremony. However, on 18th July army trucks equipped with loudspeakers criss-crossed Rangoon to announce the newly issued Martial Law Order 2/89, under which anyone defying SLORC decrees would be tried by military tribunal. Those found guilty would receive one of three sentences: three years imprisonment with hard labour, life imprisonment or execution. Early the next morning an estimated 10,000 soldiers, including artillery and armoured car units, moved into Rangoon to reinforce the troops already stationed there.

Roadblocks were erected at strategic points in the city, all major hospitals in the capital were told to expect casualties and all telephone and telex lines between Burma and the outside world were cut. Since the first press tour in January, the SLORC had actually permitted several foreign journalists to visit Burma individually. But that brief honeymoon with the press was over now. David Storey, a Bangkok-based correspondent for *Reuters*, was the last foreign journalist in Rangoon before the crackdown began in earnest: "I was picked up at my hotel late at night on the 18th, after curfew, although I had a valid journalist visa,". David Storey relates. "I was treated firmly but politely and it was clear they did not want any journalist to cover the events that followed. I was taken to the airport in a jeep, guarded by a section of troops, and had to spend the night on a cot on the floor in the departure lounge. The following morning, I was put on the first flight to Bangkok."

In order to avoid a bloodbath, the NLD called off the planned march. On 20th July, both Aung San Suu Kyi and the NLD chairman, Tin U, were placed under house arrest for up to one year, well beyond the promised elections which the SLORC at last had scheduled for 27th May 1990 (2+7=9). In sweeps all over the country, thousands of NLD workers were arrested and party offices closed down by the military. Also targeted was the DPNS. Hundreds of its activists were arrested, especially in Rangoon and Irrawaddy Divisions, and some fled to the Thai border to join Moe Thi Zon and the thousand of other students who had fled to the rebel held areas since the 1988 military takeover.

To make room for the thousands of political activists who were rounded up, Burma's prisons were cleared of criminals. On 10th August 1989, the *Working People's Daily* said that 17,877 prisoners held on criminal charges had been released and the figure rose to more than 18,000 by the end of the month. The witch-hunt on the opposition was in full swing — and the military tribunals got down to work. In summary trials, each lasting only a few minutes, harsh sentences were handed down. Win Tin and Maung Thaw Ka, two prominent NLD leaders, got three years and life imprisonment respectively. Nay Min, a Rangoon lawyer who had been sending news to the BBC during the August-September 1988 uprising, was sentenced to 14 years hard labour. Thousands of other activists also received long prison terms and more than 100 people were sentenced to death. The lid was sealed on 31st August when the hitherto outspoken Bar Council was silenced; the SLORC's own attorney general was appointed its new chairman.

In order to defend these draconian measures, the DDSI chief, Khin Nyunt, gave a lengthy speech on 5th August. He accused the insurgent CPB of manipulating the NLD and plotting to destabilise the government. On 9th September, he spoke out again, this time claiming that his intelligence outfit had unearthed a "rightist conspiracy", involving the foreign media, various American politicians, Amnesty International and some unnamed foreign embassies in Rangoon. But neither of Khin Nyunt's speeches offered much hard evidence. Burmese sources as well as diplomatic observers dismissed the CPB conspiracy claim as an attempt to discredit the NLD in the eyes of the army, whose unity is essential for the survival of the SLORC. Having fought the country's numerous insurgent groups for decades, the military has very strong feelings about the CPB in particular. But Khin Nyunt failed to mention that the CPB in any case had been defunct since suffering a mutiny in March-April. At that time, rebellious ethnic rank-and-file troops captured the party's Panghsang headquarters and drove the ageing leadership into exile in China, thus ending Burma's 41-year-long communist insurgency.

Khin Nyunt's second speech appeared to be meant as a warning to the international community to refrain from "interfering in Burma's internal affairs" and to intimidate local people who were known to have contacts with foreigners in Rangoon. Khin Nyunt's accusations came at a time when several democratic countries—including the US, the 12-member European Community, India and Sweden — expressed concern at human-rights abuses in Burma. A much-publicised, declassified cable from the US Embassy in Rangoon, dated 22nd August, alleged that torture of political prisoners included cigarette burns, electric shocks to the genitals and beatings that caused severe eye and ear injuries, and sometimes death. Hundreds of political prisoners had also been sent up to the battlefront in northern Shan State to act as porters and human mine-detectors for the Burmese Army, the cable alleged. On 7th September, the European Community called on the SLORC to "end political repression and hold free elections." Long before that, the West German Embassy in Rangoon had protested against the army-orchestrated looting of the German-sponsored rodent control project in Gyogon-Insein on 6th September 1988, claiming compensation from the military government. The foreign ministry in Rangoon made a weak attempt to deflect the criticism — only to provoke the West Germans to threaten legal action against the SLORC in a *Note Verbale* dated 8th March 1989.

Shortly after Khin Nyunt had delivered his seemingly contradictory speeches in August and September, the SLORC organised a 'Exhibition on Historical Records of the State', which sought to back up the claim that Burma had been the victim of various conspiracies and that the army had had to step in to uphold "law and order" and to "prevent anarchy" from breaking out. State employees and school children were taken to see the fanciful exhibition. But one night, a daring activist defied the curfew to spray-paint the following message on the wall of the exhibition hall: "Everybody come and see Khin Nyunt's magic show!"

When the SLORC in September 1989 celebrated the first anniversary of its rule, a semblance of normality had returned to Rangoon. Although universities and colleges remained closed since June 1988, Burma's primary schools had reopened on 19th June 1989, followed by the middle schools on 14th August and the high schools on 25th September. Universities and colleges, though, remain closed "indefinitely". The main oppositionists had been detained, the public cowed into submission and Rangoon had become a city virtually under military occupation.

While the SLORC had repeatedly refused to enter into dialogues with the political parties, Khin Nyunt found it expedient to talk to some of them now Aung San Suu Kyi and Tin U had been placed under house arrest — and thousands of their followers had been rounded up all over the country. On 28th November, he held a two-hour long talk with Kyi Han, the secretary general of Aung Gyi's party, the UNDP, as well as with the NUP and a few other like-minded parties. Aung Gyi's role had been intriguing since his release from prison on 25th August 1988, and even more so after he had broken away from the NLD in December that year. His UNDP are emerging as a possible pro-military alternative to the NUP should that party fail to make any headway in the upcoming elections. Significantly, and to the disappointment of many, Aung Gyi's close associate Sein Win, the former AP correspondent in Rangoon who now has joined *Kyodo* of Japan, has become the military's main spokesman in advocating the line that the NLD "is infiltrated by communists". Political opportunism, even among some of the people who played important roles in initiating the uprising of 1988, has also become an important ingredient in the new, SLORC-ruled Burma; to say what pleases the SLORC seemed to the key to advancement and acceptability by the military authorities.

For since its inception, the SLORC had adopted an attitude of paternal despotism; they assumed that they, and only they, knew what was best for the country. At a press conference with local Burmese correspondents in Rangoon on 22nd September 1989, SLORC spokesman Kyaw Sann expressed clear annoyance over the forceful, international response to the military takeover — and he showed no inkling of understanding why foreign countries had condemned the mass killings in Burma. In reference to internal and international criticism of his junta for failing to present even a reasonably well-balanced picture of what had happened in Burma, he declaimed: "Truth is true only within a certain period of time and one is to practice truth taking into consideration time and place. What was truth once may no longer be truth after many months or years. A government that is based on the *tatmadaw* will never lie."

Already in his speech at the Asia Society on 29th November 1988, Burton Levin, the US ambassador, had commented:

— The [Burmese] army is devoid of political instincts and political knowl-edge. I have been in Asia many, many years and I have seen many Asian armies and I assure you that this is an army, of all the armies that I've encountered, that is the least blessed with political instincts. The army comes to power and instead of trying a reconciliation method, instead of saying, "look, we've been through Hell in the last few months, let's work to-gether', instead it comes out, it continues to pursue students, it conducts house-to-house searches, loots while it conducts house-to-house searches, humiliates the Burmese people; it forces people to kneel to them. You hear Burmese saying: "the Japanese occupation was infinitely better than what we have now, the enemy — it is the Burmese Army occupying Burmese towns." The army purges the civil service. The slender body of expertise and technocrats in the Burmese government is now virtually gone...instead of calling for reconciliation and really trying to do something with this economy, the army engages in purges and recriminations".

This 'bunker mentality' has even been reflected in the physical appear-ance of Rangoon. As early as in December 1988, a new double-brick wall was built around the defence ministry on Signal Pagoda Road with loop-holed bunkers, facing the main entrances to the city centre. All the trees along Prome Road, leading to the airport, were cut down and uprooted, making it impossible to build barricades there again. The old, tree-shaded avenue was turned into a four-lane, concrete highway, far wider than needed for the sparse day-to-day traffic to and from Rangoon's sleepy Mingaladon airport—but perfectly suited for quick troop movements from the Rangoon command's military area down to the city centre.

At the same time, thousands of urban residents have been forcibly evicted from their homes in Rangoon and relocated in shanty towns on the outskirts of the city. Politics clearly lay behind the forced evictions. The first victims of the SLORC's city planning strategy lived near the defence min-istry and many of them had participated in the 1988 uprising. In April 1989, 800 households comprising more than 3,000 people were evicted and their houses demolished. These families were resettled in bamboo shacks in Waybagi, a dusty plain north of Rangoon. Ten elderly people died in the move. Since then — and especially in late 1989 and early 1990 — similar 'satellite towns' have been built in Dagon Myothit east of Rangoon, and in Hlaing Thayar and Okpo to the north. Obviously, the SLORC is trying to dilute potential centres of anti-government unrest and to break up opposi-tion strongholds that were active during the demonstrations in 1988.

The Rangoon area has also became the operation zone for a new 11th LID which was raised in December 1988 for the express purpose of providing 'security' in the capital. The total strength of the army is now nearly 200,000. Officially, the minimum age for joining the army is 18, but some of the new recruits in 1989 were as young as 15 or 16. They were given Kyats 350 on joining the army — a considerable sum for a village boy in Burma. The loyalty of these mostly unruly boys from the countryside is being kept strictly in check by the all-pervasive network of brutally efficient DDSI agents, the pillar of Ne Win's power ever since his first coup in 1962.

But on May 24th this year, Ne Win will turn 79 and the 'Sun of Glory' is obviously setting, although his Maha Vizeya Pagoda still remains unfinished in the shadow of the mighty Shwe Dagon. Several of his contemporaries passed away in 1989; the old Red Flag communist leader, Thakin Soe, finally died in Rangoon on 4th May, followed by the former president, Mahn Win Maung, on 4th July. No matter how much the old ruling elite tries to cling the power, the fact remains that during these last days of Ne Win's rule, a time of change has come to Burma. After the turmoil of 1988-89, it is not an exaggeration to claim that the country in 1990 is entering the probably most crucial period of its post-independence history. But the main question is what the future will hold for the strife-torn country: total disintegration or a new era of peace and prosperity?

Economically, there does not seem to be much scope for significant improvements under the present regime. Although the SLORC has vowed to 'uplift the people's living standards' and 'open up the country', the military's record of more than two decades of mismanagement and incompetence hardly inspires optimism and confidence in its ability to revitalise the economy. Sixteen months after the promulgation of the new foreign investment law, nearly all the only deals which have been made are extraction projects aimed at raising badly needed foreign exchange for the regime: logging, fishing, mining and — the most important — oil. In October 1989-January 1990 the military government announced production-sharing contracts with a number of foreign oil companies: Yukong of South Korea, Idemitsu of Japan, Amoco and Unocal of the US, Petro-Canada, Britain's Croft Exploration and Kirkland Resources, Australia's BHP and Dutch Shell. These companies are reported to have paid at least US$5 million each in signing bonuses, providing the SLORC with capital which almost immediately was spent on procuring more arms and ammunition from abroad.

Ironically, Burma's economy in 1990 is even more centralised than it used to be under the previous 'socialist system' despite the new 'open door policy'. In the past when it all was supposedly illegal and conducted in the black market, it worked fairly well in an unofficial way. Now, foreign trade has been institutionalised with the result that many small and middle-scale traders have been squeezed out since they cannot compete with the big, well-connected businessmen who almost invariably are ex-army and ex-BSPP men.

For example, the officially preferred point of first contact for most businessmen, foreign as well as local, is a new Burmese company called the Associated Business Consultancy Services Ltd. This company can arrange deals in an enormous wide range of commercial activities as well as other services — including prostitutes which were unavailable to foreigners in the past. A closer inspection reveals this company to be controlled by Aye Zaw Win, Sanda Win's husband and Ne Win's son-in-law. Many internationally respected hotel chains have been vying for contracts to operate in Burma. However, in October 1989 it was announced that the Austrian investment group IAEG Company had won the contract to build five-star hotels in Rangoon, Taunggyi, Mandalay and Pagan. The IAEG exists only as a shell on the Austrian stock market — but it is owned by a personal friend of Ne Win.

Some foreign companies, understanding the rules of the game, were, however, prepared to play along. The American oil company Amoco employed as its special emissary to Burma a man called Daniel Rosé. He was not an oil expert but happened to be Ne Win's oldest foreign friend. Somboon Prommet, the governor of the Thai province of Tak, sent a personal letter to SLORC chairman Saw Maung on 14th September 1989. After saying that he was delighted to know that Burma was "under Your Excellency's able leadership" the governor went on to mention that his son wanted to get a timber concession in Burma and to set up a sawmill in Myawaddy opposite Tak province. "I understand that my son's intention of setting up business...could only be achieved by Your Excellency's support."

The letter was copied and distributed by enraged office workers at the ministry of defence in Rangoon, reflecting growing anti-Thai sentiments among ordinary Burmese. To outside observers, it was a clear indication that patronage and nepotism, not a free-market economy, still prevailed in Burma.

The fishing and logging deals with Thailand had met with stiff opposition from Burma's new politicians — and anger from the public at large — from the very beginning. Reuters reported from Rangoon already on 7th February 1989: "The army has sold off concessions to foreign timber and fishing companies so quickly and so cheaply that opposition politicians are warning about lasting environmental damage." The dispatch quoted U Nu as saying: "Our forests will disappear. There will be no more fish in our waters."

Local people in the Tavoy-Mergui region of Tenasserim Division — who for generations have depended on fishing for their survival — have now been forbidden to fish there. At the mouth of the Irrawaddy delta, hundreds of Burmese fishing vessels are now idle for the same reasons.

Presumably, any future government of Burma would have to terminate these fishing and logging contracts if it wants to maintain popular support.

This was recognised by a Thai columnist who wrote in the Bangkok daily the Nation on 17th January 1989: "If the Saw Maung regime should fall, the [Western] economic powers will emerge as 'white knights' and be granted the spoils of backing the winning side. Despite the high-flown words of diplomacy, the blatant eagerness of Thai business opportunists to exploit Burma is simply too obvious."

The almost bizarre nature of the present Burmese leadership has also also demonstrated by a number of decisions made during 1989. On 27th May (2+7=9) it was suddenly announced that Burma had changed its name to 'Myanmar'. Most Burmese were puzzled since the name of the country in their own language always had been 'Myanmar'; it was as if Germany had declared that it had changed its name to *Deutschland*, or as if China had decided to become *Zhong Guo*. But it soon became clear that this was just another act of Ne Win's favourite astrological game, *yedaya chay*; in order to protect Burma's indigenous character now when foreign capital and outside influences were entering the country, it was deemed necessary to 'Burmanise' all place names even in English texts. Thus, Rangoon shortly afterwards became *Yangon*, Moulmein was now referred to as *Mawlamyine*, and the Irrawaddy river became the *Ayeyarwady*. The decision to Burmanise even local place names was announced on 18th June (1+8=9).

Ironically, although Burma today is ruled by a clique of superstitious army officers with an appallingly low degree of competence, the country has one of the highest numbers of well-educated people in the Third World. But, hardly surprisingly, none has shown any willingness to cooperate with the present regime. Indeed, most of them have expressed their desire to return and help rebuild Burma only when and of there is a new democratic government. When such a government will take over remains uncertain — and the problems it will inherit are immense. By selling off Burma's natural resources, the SLORC is also undermining Burma's vast development potential and the damage may be irreparable if the military decides to hold on to power for a prolonged period of time.

However, if an able government employing farsighted experts does take over within the medium term, the impending disaster can be averted. Given the sympathy shown for the Burmese people by the international community after the massacres in August and September 1988, it is plausible to assume that foreign aid will start pouring in once the SLORC has stepped aside.

But if the opposition comes to power, what will happen to the military, and especially those officers who were responsible for all the massacres of unarmed civilians during 1988? If they were pardoned, the new government would risk losing its popular support. On the other hand, if there were trials and court martials — which a large segment of the population, especially the ones who have lost their children and relatives are likely to demand — the danger of another military takeover would become a reality. If demands are raised that military officers should be brought to justice, the investigations are also likely focus on graft within the ranks — including rampant narcotics-related corruption — which the army also most certainly would take steps to prevent.

Moreover, a new government would have to adopt a far more tactful approach to Burma's minority problems in order to solve the devastating, decades-long civil war — which is essential to being able to rebuild the country since most of Burma's natural resources are located in the frontier areas. But a truce with the rebels followed by peace talks, which objectively would be the by far most sensible thing to do, could also prompt the military into staging another coup d'etat.

Paradoxically, the very existence of a 200,000-strong army in a country which does not have any external enemies is directly linked to a continuation of the insurgency. With peace and stability, and a federal structure which would be acceptable to the national minorities, the army's strength could be reduced to a 20,000-30,000-strong border security force, which is all that Burma actually needs. But would the army accept such a diminished role? The suggestion has been made that the Burmese Army sooner or later will have to adjust itself to a position similar to that of the armed forces of Thailand or Indonesia: still influential but slowly accepting a greater degree of democracy and civilian participation in the governing of the country. But would it after having been the privileged ruling class in the country for 28 years?

Then there is also the question of Ne Win's wealth. As the case was in the Philippines after the fall of Ferdinand Marcos, many citizens are likely to claim that Ne Win's fortunes rightfully belong to Burma and should be returned. During the August-September demonstrations, this issue was raised by several people who brandished banners saying: "One man's wealth can pay for Burma's foreign debt". Even if Ne Win dies this year, how will his enigmatic daughter Sanda react? How large is her following within the army and the DDSI? And what will happen to the DDSI and all its present agents?

If Dr. Maung Maung's government had resigned in August or September 1988, it would not have been too complicated to answer most of these questions and to find a compromise. But when the army decided to step in, set up the SLORC, stage another massacre and brutally suppress the popular movement for democracy, then it provoked the donor countries into cutting off aid — not to mention totally alienating itself from the people, polarising the nation. Hence, the military now finds itself barricaded in a political *cul-de-sac* from which there is no possible exit apparent.

The official response to this dilemma has so far revealed itself in a variety of clearly hasty improvisations. In December 1988, the official media began to re-write history in earnest by claiming that all the accounts of indiscriminate firing into crowds of demonstrators in August or September were just "rumours and unsubstantiated reports". In an interview published in *Asiaweek's* 27th January 1989 issue, Gen. Saw Maung made the extraordinary claim that only 15 demonstrators were killed in Rangoon after the SLORC's takeover — but added that there were also "over 500 other deaths that occurred during the lootings and the destruction of factories and workshops".

On a government propaganda video tape, distributed to the foreign journalists who visited Burma during the January 1989 press tour, the commentator asserted that only rubber bullets were fired outside the City Hall on the night of 8th August. Military attachés stationed in Burma asserts that the Burmese Army does not even have rubber bullets.To any father or mother whose child was killed while demonstrating peacefully, such statements are bitter insults unlikely to be forgiven or forgotten. History can be re-written but people's memories cannot be erased — and there are thousands of eye-witnesses to numerous mass killings all over Burma, not just in Rangoon. Seen from this perspective, the present, official misrepresentation of events during 1988 is counter-productive since they are likely to provoke anger and bitterness rather than facilitating a badly needed national reconciliation, a prerequisite for a national reconstruction.

However, a development even more disturbing than the presentation of an imaginative but hardly credible official version of events during 1988 has been continuing arrests and persecution of all prominent opposition politicians and activists, despite the promises of "free and fair elections" in May 1990. A severe blow was dealt on 22nd December 1989 when a military tribunal sentenced NLD chairman Tin U to three years imprisonment with hard labour. Ignoring the international condemnation this caused, the SLORC went on to place U Nu and twelve of his associated under house arrest on 29th December. Any remaining hopes of 'fairness' on the part of the SLORC vanished on 16th January 1990 when the elections commission in Rangoon Division barred Aung San Suu Kyi, still under house arrest, from standing in the elections on the grounds of her connection with Britain and her alleged links with insurgent groups, meaning the ABSDF along the Thai border.

The decision to exclude Aung San Suu Kyi from contesting the elections interestingly also revealed internal disagreements within the supposedly independent central elections commission. Its chairman, Ba Htay, and one member, a former brigadier-general, Kya Doe, voted in favour of Aung San Suu Kyi while the remaining three members — all of whom are considered Ne Win appointees — decided "not to interfere with the decision made by the Rangoon elections commission". The decision caused a small stir in Rangoon; a few hundred people took to the streets — but dispersed quickly when heavily armed troops arrived at the scene and threatened to open fire.

But, nonetheless, Burma in 1990 is fundamentally different from two years ago. Today, the socialist system has been discarded. The one-party system has been abolished. The BSPP has collapsed and the NUP cannot expect to make even a minimally decent showing in general elections unless these are rigged. There is a legal opposition, and even if it operates under extremely difficult circumstances, it does still have branches and offices all over the country, a grassroot mass organisation which did not exist two years ago. The pro-democracy movement has bold, courageous and popular leaders although most of them are in jail or under house arrest.

Change has come to stay in Burma, but the question is whether a transfer of power will come through peaceful elections or by violence. The possibility of another popular uprising cannot be ruled out, especially if the promised elections are not "free and fair". Neither can the possibility be discounted that elements within the military itself might shift their allegiance in a last-ditch attempt to restore their vanished prestige and credibility with the public — which could mean the outbreak of civil war. Not without reason, the turbulent events in Romania in December 1989 went completely unreported in the official Burmese media.

Either way, the general consensus in Burma in the spring of 1990 is that the movement towards democracy which began exactly two years ago is irreversible. Clearly, Win Myint, Win Myint and Kyaw San Win could never have imagined the landslide they were about to precipitate when they strolled down to the Sanda Win teashop in Gyogon West Ward to listen to a cassette tape with some songs of Sai Hti Hseng that Saturday night in March 1988.

DRAMATIS PERSONAE

AUNG, Bohmu: Born in 1910 in Kyauktaga near Pegu. One of the Thirty Comrades and a leader of the People's Volunteer Organisation in the late 1940s. Member of the Constituent Assembly and Speaker of the Chamber of Deputies. Minister of Defence and a prominent member of U Nu's *Pyidaungsu* (Union) Party before the 1962 coup. Joined U Nu's Thai-border based resistance in 1972 and later took refuge in Chiang Rai, Thailand. Returned to Burma during the 1980 amnesty. Lived in retirement in Rangoon until the 1988 uprising; appeared at a mass meeting on 25th August together with dissident leader Aung Gyi. Became the patron of the Democracy Party when it registered on 30th September.

AUNG GYI: Born in 1919 in Paungde, Prome district, of a Sino-Burmese family. Participated in the independence movement before World War Two and joined the anti-Japanese struggle in 1945 as one of Ne Win's officers. Later served under Ne Win as an officer in the 4th Burma Rifles. Organiser of the Socialist Party in 1947, key figure in the 1958-60 Caretaker Government and member of the 1962 Revolutionary Council; vice chief of staff and minister of trade and industry. Ousted in 1963 for his pragmatic policies; imprisoned 1965-68 and again 1973-74. Influenced the 1988 uprising by writing and widely distributing a series of open letters to Ne Win, in which he criticised the economic policies and human rights abuses. Arrested on 29th July and released on 25th August after which he participated in the pro-democracy movement. Chairman of the National League for Democracy which registered on 30th September. Resigned from the League on 3rd December and set up his own Union Nationals Democracy Party on 16th December.

AUNG SAN: Born in 1915 in Natmauk, Magwe district. Key leader of the 1936 student strike in Rangoon, secretary general of the *Dohbama Asiayone* as well as the CPB in 1939. Arrested by the British in the same year, left secretly for Japan in 1940 and returned to Burma on a mission to gather recruits for military training in Japan. The group, known as the 'Thirty Comrades', set up the BIA in Bangkok on 26th December 1941 and entered Burma with the Japanese soon afterwards. Minister of Defence in Dr Ba Maw's puppet government in 1943, contacted the British and officially turned against the Japanese on 27th March 1945 . Negotiated Burma's independence with the British on 27th January 1947. Signed the Panglong Agreement with leaders of the Shan, Chin and Kachin minorities on 12th February. Assassinated with six of his ministers and two others on 19th July. Considered the father of Burma's independence and a national hero.

AUNG SAN SUU KYI: Born in 1945 in Rangoon, the daughter of Aung San and his wife Khin Kyi. Educated in Burma and India, where her mother served as ambassador 1960-67. Obtained a B.A. (Hons) in philosophy, politics and economics from Oxford University in 1967. Worked at the UN headquarters in New York and in 1972 married Michael Aris, an Oxford academic and an expert on Tibetan culture and the Himalayan region. Returned to Burma in April 1988 to look after her ailing mother. Her husband and their two sons joined her in July. Emerged as the main opposition leader in August and became the secretary general of the National League for Democracy in September. Placed under house arrest on 20th July 1989.

AYE KO: Born in 1921 in Kyonpaw, Bassein district. Student activist in the 1930s, joined the BIA in 1942 and Ne Win's 4th Burma Rifles in 1946. Fought against the Karen insurgents in the early 1950s. Northeastern commander and based in Lashio, Shan State, 1972-76 and then closely associated with opium warlord Lo Hsing-han. Elected to the BSPP's central committee in 1971, member of the *Pyithu Hluttaw* (Lashio-1 Constituency) in 1974. Vice Chief of Staff (Army) and deputy minister of defence after the purges in 1976. On the BSPP's central executive committee 1977-88; elected joint secretary general at the 4th party congress in 1981 and in the same year appointed secretary general which he remained until September 1988. Still believed to belong to the inner circle of top Burmese leaders.

CHIT MAUNG, Thakin: Born in 1915 in Tharrawaddy District. Participated in the 1936 students' strike and joined the *Dohbama Asiayone* in 1937. Elected MP for the AFPFL in 1947, leader of the All-Burma Peasants' Organisation (ABPO) and founding member of the leftist Burma Workers' and Peasant's' Party (BWPP) in December 1950. Active in the National Unity Front (NUF) in the 1950s. Re-emerged as a leftist leader in September 1988. Now chairman of the Democratic Front for National Reconstruction.

HTUN AUNG GYAW: Born in Rangoon in 1954. Geology graduate who participated in the U Thant 'uprising' in December 1974 and the Shwe Dagon Pagoda demonstrations in June 1975. In Insein Jail 1975-80. Founding member of the Freedom Fighters of Burma (FFB) on 3rd April 1988. Escaped to the Thai border after the 18 September coup and elected chairman of the All-Burma Students Democratic Front (ABSDF) on 5th November. Resigned on 13th October 1989.

KHIN KYI: Born in 1912 in Myaungmya. A nurse by profession; married Aung San in 1942. Leading member of the Women's Freedom League, MP, chairman of the Social Planning Commission in 1953; chairman of the Council of Social Service; Burma's ambassador to India 1960-67. Died in Rangoon on 27th December 1988.

KHIN NYUNT: Born in 1939. Finished the 25th course of the Officers' Training School (OTS) in Hmawbi in May 1960. Commanding officer of the 20th Burma Regiment in Akyab (Sittwe), Arakan State. Tactical operational commander of the 44th LID in 1982. Appointed director of the DDSI in late 1983, secretary of the SLORC and following the 18th September 1988 military takeover and considered its actual strongman; promoted to brigadier-general. Directly controlled by Ne Win and his daughter Sanda Win.

KYAW HTIN: Born in 1924 in Prome. Joined the BDA in 1943 and Ne Win's 4th Burma Rifles in 1945, Attended Ft. Leavenworth staff college in the US in 1962; deputy minister for defence and deputy chief of staff in 1975, Chief of Staff with the rank of general March 1976-Nov 1985. Defence minister March 1976-July 1988. Member of the BSPP's central committee in 1971; on the central executive committee Feb 1977-Sept 1988. Now retired.

MAUNG MAUNG, Dr: Born in 1924 in Mandalay. Joined the BDA during the war and attended an Officers' Training School in Rangoon during the Japanese occupation. Quit the army and became a scholar after the war; earned a B.A. from Rangoon University in 1946 and a B.L. in 1949. Called to the Bar, Lincoln's Inn, in 1950, studied at the University of Utrecht, the Netherlands, and at Yale University, the USA. Started *Guardian* magazine in 1954 and the *Guardian* newspaper in 1956 together with Aung Gyi. Assistant Attorney General under the Caretaker Government 1958-60, Chief Justice after the 1962 coup and the author of Burma's 1974 Constitution. Wrote *Burma and General Ne Win,* a flattering portrayal of the old strongman. Became a member of the BSPP's central executive committee and Chairman of the Council of People's Attorneys in July 1988; president of Burma and BSPP chairman 19th August-18th September 1988. Still believed to belong to the inner circle of top Burmese leaders.

MAUNG MAUNG KHA: Born in 1920 in Rangoon. Studied at Rangoon University and joined the Burmese army in 1944; attached to the Defence Industries after independence and became the director with the rank of colonel after the 1962 coup. Member of the BSPP's central committee in 1973 and the central executive committee in 1977. Prime Minister in 1977, but forced to resign on 26th July 1988.

MAUNG MAUNG KYAW: Born in 1965 in Rangoon; 3rd year mathematics student at Rangoon University and one of the leaders of the March and June movements. Elected general secretary of the RUSU on 17th June. The first student leader to arrive on the Thai border on 9th August. Turned police informer in Thailand. Returned to Burma on 28th June 1989.

MIN KO NAING: At first a name which the students in Rangoon used for signing documents and statements; it means 'Conqueror of Kings' or 'I shall defeat you'. But since 28th August the *nom de guerre* for the most prominent student leader in Rangoon, Baw Oo Tun, a 26 year old 3rd year zoology student. Chairman of the *ba ka tha*, one of the two main student unions in Burma. Went underground in Rangoon after the 18th September coup; arrested on 24th March 1989.

MIN ZEYA: Born in 1958 in Kamawek, Mon State. 5th year law student. Became active in the movement in March and played a prominent role in the June and August-September movements. Chairman of the *ma ka tha,* the other main student union in Burma. Arrested in August 1989.

MOE THI ZON: Born in 1962; also known as Myo Than Htut. Prominent student leader in Rangoon, took part in the June and August-September movements. Patron of the Democratic Party for a New Society which registered on 15th October. Fled to the Thai border in April 1989 and elected chairman of the All-Burma Students Democratic Front (ABSDF) in November.

NE WIN: Born in 1911 in Paungdale, Prome district, of a Sino-Burmese family. Originally called Shu Maung. Educated at Judson College, Rangoon, but left without a degree in 1931. Post office clerk in Rangoon and member of the *Dohbama*

Asiayone in the 1930s. One of the Thirty Comrades and commander of the BNA 1943-45. Commander of the 4th Burma Rifles after the war. Minister of defence and home affairs 1949-50, Commander in Chief 1949-72. Prime minister in the Caretaker Government 1958-60. Seized power in a *coup d'état* on 2nd March 1962 and chairman of the Revolutionary Council 1962-74. President of Burma 1974-81, chairman of the BSPP from its inception till his resignation on 23rd July 1988. Still believed to be the actual ruler of Burma.

NU, U: Born in 1907 in Wakema, Myaungmya district. Educated at Rangoon University and president of the Rangoon University Students' Union 1935-36, treasurer of the *Dohbama Asiayone* 1937. Foreign minister under Dr Ba Maw 1943-45, vice president of the AFPFL 1945-47 and its president after Aung San's assassination on 19th July 1947. Prime minister 1948-56, 1957-58 and 1960-62. Formed the *Pyidaungsu* (Union) Party in 1960. In prison 1962-66, left Burma on 11th April 1969 and organised resistance against Ne Win from Thailand 1969-73; in exile in the US 1973-74 and in India 1974-80, returned to Burma during the 1980 amnesty. Retired in Rangoon but re-emerged as a leading politician in August 1988. Proclaimed his own interim government on 9th September. Placed under house arrest on 29th December 1989.

SAN YU: Born in 1918 in Prome of a Sino-Burmese family. Studied medicine in Rangoon when World War Two broke out and served as a captain in the BDA under the Japanese occupation. Member of the 1962 Revolutionary Council, Vice Chief of Staff (Army) and deputy minister of defence and planning 1963-72; Chief of Staff and defence minister 1972-74, president of Burma 1981-88. General secretary of the BSPP in 1964; vice chairman 1985-88; now retired.

SANDA WIN: Born in 1952 in Rangoon. The daughter of Ne Win and his third wife, Khin May Than (Kitty Ba Than). Studied medicine in Rangoon but failed her English language exam when she wanted to further her studies in Britain in 1979 - after which English education was reinstated in Burmese schools. Army major attached to the Defence Services Hospital, Mingaladon. Considered Ne Win's favourite daughter, she wields considerable influence over the DDSI.

SAW MAUNG: Born in 1928 in Mandalay. Joined the Burmese Army in 1949, commander of the 99th LID 1975-76, Southwest commander (Brigadier-General) 1976-81, adjutant general 1981-83, Vice Chief of Staff 1983-85, Chief of Staff 1985 to present. Deputy minister of defence 1985-88, minister of defence 1988 to present. On the BSPP's central executive committee from 25th July to 16th September 1988, chairman of the SLORC when it seized power on 18th September; minister of defence and foreign minister in the new military government that was announced on 20th September. Considered close to Sein Lwin and a Ne Win-loyalist.

SEIN LWIN: Born in 1924 in Kawkayin village in the Moulmein area where he attended primary school. Joined the BDA in 1943 and Ne Win's 4th Burma Rifles in 1946. Commander of the 3rd Burma Rifles in 1950. Killed Karen rebel leader Saw Ba U Gyi in the Hlaingbwe area near the Thai border in 1950, head of the security unit that massacred students in Rangoon on 7th July 1962, North-West commander, based in Mandalay, 1970-72. Minister of cooperatives, transport and communication, and home and religious affairs in various cabinets until 1981. Member of the Council of State 1981-88, joint secretary general of the BSPP 1983-88. President of Burma and chairman of the BSPP for 18 days, from 26th July to 12th August 1988. Still close to Ne Win and considered one of Burma's top leaders although he no longer hold any official position.

SEIN WIN: Born in 1922 in Bassein in the Irrawaddy delta region. Ran the English-language daily the *Guardian* before the 1962 coup. In 1963 awarded the Golden Pen of Freedom from the International Federation of Journalists for his work in fostering a free press in Burma, for which he was jailed 1965-68. Rangoon correspondent for the *Associated Press* from 1969 to 1989, then with the *Kyodo* News Agency of Japan. Jailed together with Aung Gyi and some of his associates 29th July-25th August 1988. President of the Foreign Corespondents' Club of Burma in April 1989.

SOE, Thakin: Born in 1905 in Moulmein. Employee of the Burmah Oil Company. Joined the *Dohbama Asiayone* and the CPB in the 1930s. Organised anti-Japanese guerrillas in Pyapon district 1943-45, split with the main CPB in August 1946, set up the Communist Party (Red Flag) and went underground in the Irrawaddy delta region. He was captured by the Burmese Army in November 1970 at his Than Chaung camp near the Arakan Yoma. Imprisoned but released during the 1980 amnesty. In retirement until he re-entered politics in August 1988. Patron of the Unity and Development Party in September, died in Rangoon on 4th May 1989.

THAN SHWE: Born in 1933 in Kyaukse. Joined the army in 1953. Commander of the 88th LID with the rank of colonel in 1980. Brigadier-general and southwest commander in 1983. Vice Chief of Staff and Lieut-Gen since November 1985. Member of the SLORC since 18th September 1988.

TIN AUNG HEIN: Born in Mandalay in 1919. Studied law at Rangoon University and an ex-student leader; partly educated in the USA. Joined the BSPP in the 1960s and served for many years as an organiser of the peasants. One of Burma's senior jurists and Chairman of the Council of People's Justices (Chief Justice) until the 18th September 1988 military takeover. Headed an 11-man commission to ascertain "the desires and aspirations of the people" in August and September.

TIN MAUNG WIN: Born in 1938 in Rangoon. The son of U Win, a former Burmese ambassador to the USA. Involved in the 1962 student uprising; in jail 1965-68. Went underground with U Nu along the Thai border in 1969 and joined the rebel Parliamentary Democracy Party in 1970. Set up his own group, the Patriotic Youth Front, some years later. Left for the USA in 1976. A founding member of the Committee for Restoration of Democracy in Burma (CRDB) in 1985 and its chairman since 1987.

TIN U or TIN OO (1): Born in 1927 in Bassein in the Irrawaddy delta. Chief of Staff and minister of defence 1974-76. Accused of involvement in an abortive coup attempt in July 1976 and imprisoned. Released during the 1980 amnesty after which he took a degree in law. Emerged as one of the most prominent opposition leaders in August 1988. Vice chairman of the National League for Democracy on 27th

September 1988 and its chairman since 10th December. Placed under house arrest on 20th July 1989; sentenced to three years imprisonment on 22nd December.

TIN U or TIN OO (2): Born in 1928 in Mudon south of Moulmein. Chief of the Military Intelligence Service 1972-73. Chief military assistant to the then president Ne Win 1974-81; chief of the National Intelligence Bureau 1974-77. Member of the Council of State and joint secretary general of the BSPP from 1981 until his ouster in May 1983. In Insein Jail, but transferred to *Ye Kyi Aing* top security prison during August 1988; then back in Insein Jail. Released on 7th October 1989. Once considered Ne Win's heir apparent.

TUN TIN: Born in 1923 in Myitkyina, now Kachin State. Joined the BIA in 1942 and served under Ne Win in the 4th Burma Rifles in 1946. Fought insurgents in Shan State in the 1950s and later commanding officer of the Burma Military Police. Supported the 1962 coup and served as director general of the labour department, minister of labour and cooperatives 1974-81, deputy prime minister and minister for planning and finance 1981-88. Member of the BSPP's central committee in 1971, on the central executive committee 1974-88. Now retired.

TYN MYINT-U: Born in 1932 in Mandalay. Educated in Mandalay, Rangoon, and the US. Earned a Ph.D. in aeronautical and astronautical engineering in the US. Professor in mathematics in New York; employed by ESCAP in Bangkok 1979. Married Aye Aye Thant, the daughter of the late UN secretary general, U Thant, in 1960. Continues to play an important behind the scenes role in Burmese politics from his base in Bangkok, Thailand.

YE KYAW THU: Born in 1937 in Mandalay. Graduated from Rangoon University in 1958 and active in business and politics. Joined the Thai-border based resistance in 1969 together with Tin Maung Win. Left for the USA in 1975. General secretary of the Committee for Restoration of Democracy in Burma (CRDB).

YE HTUT, Bo: Born in 1918. One of the Thirty Comrades, commander of a battalion in the BNA. Turned communist and went underground with the CPB in 1949. Surrendered in 1963 and went into retirement in Rangoon. Re-entered politics in August 1988 when he and nine of the surviving eleven members of the Thirty Comrades denounced Ne Win and the BSPP.

A Note on Burmese Names

U, *Ko* and *Maung* mean 'mister' of different grades according to rank and age in that descending order. Thus, Aung San would be called *Maung* Aung San by his mother, *Ko* Aung San by his friends and *U* Aung San when addressed formally or by subordinates. *Daw* and *Ma* performs the same functions in regard to women. *Daw* Aung San Suu Kyi is the formal designation while *Ma* Aung San Suu Kyi would be used when she was younger or by her friends. *Bo* and *Bohmu* are military titles for officers which are often carried into civilian life, like *Bogyoke*, which means Supremo or Chief and is more respectful than general, a military designation only. The army itself is usually referred to as the *tatmadaw*, a term which is also common in English texts. *Thakin* is a title used by the young nationalists in the 1930s; it means master and was originally reserved for the British. There are no family names in Burma.

ABBREVIATIONS

ABSDF: the All-Burma Students' Democratic Front. Underground student organisation based on the Thai border. Set up on 5th November 1988. Headed by Htun Aung Gyaw until 13th October 1989, then by Moe Thi Zon.

AFPFL: the Anti-Fascist People's Freedom League. Set up by Aung San at end of World War Two to fight the Japanese and became independent Burma's most powerful political institution. It split in 1958 into two factions, a 'Clean' AFPFL lead by U Nu (later the *Pyidaungsu* Party) and a 'Stable' AFPFL lead by two leftists, Kyaw Nyein and Ba Swe. Kyaw Nyein's daughter , revived the AFPFL during 1988.

BBS: the Burma Broadcasting Service; the state-run Burmese radio. Re-named 'the Voice of Myanmar' in 1989.

BIA: the Burma Independence Army, founded by Aung San in Bangkok, Thailand, on 26th December 1941, under Japanese auspices. It entered Burma with the Japanese forces shortly afterwards.

BDA: the Burma Defence Army succeeded the BIA in July 1942.

BNA: the Burma National Army succeeded the BDA in August 1943 after a Japanese-sponsored 'declaration of independence'.

BSPP: the Burma Socialist Programme Party. Founded by Ne Win and the military in 1962. The only legally permitted party in Burma until 1988. Re-named the National Unity Party (NUP) on 26th September 1988.

CPB: the Communist Party of Burma. Founded on 15th August 1939. Resorted to armed struggle against Rangoon on 28th March 1948, outlawed in 1953. Maintained base areas in northern and northeastern Burma until April 1989, when the rank-and-file mutinied and drove the old party leadership into exile in China.

DAB: the Democratic Alliance of Burma. Umbrella organisation comprising the ABSDF, Burmese exiles and the National Democratic Front (NDF), among them the Karen National Union (KNU), the Kachin Independence Organisation (KIO) and the New Mon State Party (NMSP). Set up on the Thai border on 19th November 1989.

DDSI: the Directorate of the Defence Services Intelligence; Burma's secret police.

DPNS: the Democratic Party for a New Society. Burma's main, legal student organisation after the 18th September 1988 coup. Its first chairman, Moe Thi Zon, fled to the Thai border in April 1989.

LID: Light Infantry Division; the elite units of the Burmese Army. Currently, there are nine LIDs: the 11th, 22nd, 33rd, 44th, 55th, 66th, 77th, 88th and 99th.

NLD: The National League for Democracy; Burma's main opposition party, set up on 24th September 1988. Chairman: Tin U; secretary general: Aung San Suu Kyi.

RUSU: the Rangoon University Students Union; initially founded in 1931, crushed after the 1962 coup and revived in 1988.

SLORC: the State Law and Order Restoration Council; set up by Gen. Saw Maung on 18 September 1988.

UNDP: the United Nationals' Democracy Party. Set up by Aung Gyi on 16th December 1988.

ba ka tha: the Burmese abbreviation for *Bama naingngan longsangya kyaungthamya thamagga* , the All Burma Students Union; ed by Min Ko Naing.

ma ka tha: means the same as *ba ka tha* but it uses *Myanma* for Burma instead of *Bama;.* led by Min Zeya.

CHRONOLOGY OF EVENTS

1987

10 August: Ne Win admits in a nine-and-a-half minute radio and TV speech that mistakes have been made during his 25 years in power, adding that even constitutional changes must be made "in order to keep abreast with the times".

1 September: The government de-controls domestic trade in rice, maize, pulses and beans, ending restrictions that had been in force since 1966.

5 September: In an order signed by Sein Lwin, the secretary of the State Council, the Kyats 25, 35 and 75 banknotes are demonetised without compensation, wiping out 80% of the country's money in circulation. 500-1,000 students go on a rampage in Rangoon.

6 September: The government closes down all universities and colleges. Students in Rangoon who come from upcountry are bused back to their homes.

7 October: A number of tax laws are amended, requiring the farmers to pay in kind rather than in cash, which leads to discontent in rural areas.

9 October: "We have openly declared that any citizen can engage in private enterprise upon registration," Ne Win declares in a speech to a BSPP meeting.

14 October: The *Pyithu Hluttaw*, or the parliament, approves the 5 September demonetisation. New Kyats 45 and 90 banknotes are going to replace the invalidated 25, 35 and 75 ones.

26 October: The educational institutions re-open without incident.

28 October: A bomb explodes in the *Thamada* (President) Cinema at 4.30 am in downtown Rangoon. No one is hurt.

29 October: ECOSOC recommends Least Developed Country Status (LDC) for Burma.

2-3 November: Students at the regional college in Sittwe, Arakan State, demonstrate and shout anti-government slogans.

7 November: Students from the local Ye Zin agricultural college and veterinary students in Pyinmana, Mandalay Division, demonstrate against the government and burn portraits of Ne Win.

11 December: The United Nations general assembly approves LDC status for Burma. IMF figures show that Burma's foreign exchange reserves have fallen to US$ 28 million.

December: Sporadic disturbances are reported from the Rangoon Institute of Technology (RIT) and threatening letters are sent by underground student groups to the police in Mandalay.

1988

2 February: The state run radio announces that co-operatives, and private Burmese citizens, will be allowed to export rice and broken rice.

12 February: "The goal of the socialist economic system is to build a new and peaceful society...the party, the state machinery and the class and mass organisations are to strive to win the co-operation of the indigenous people in carrying out these tasks," president San Yu says in his Union Day speech.

7 March: A bomb explodes outside the Czech embassy on Prome Road at about 9.30 pm. Aung Gyi, a retired brigadier general, writes his first letter to Ne Win, suggesting economic reforms and a new cabinet.

12 March: Some RIT students clash with local people at Sanda Win teashop in Gyogon West Ward, a Rangoon suburb. One RIT student is injured and the culprit arrested.

13 March: The culprit is released and about 200 RIT students march down to the local People's Council office to protest. *Lon Htein* riot policemen clash with the crowds. One student, Maung Phone Maw, is shot dead and estimated 6-7 more students die from gunshot wounds a few days later.

14 March: RIT students distribute leaflets on other campuses in Rangoon, condemning the brutality of the *Lon Htein*— and the demonetisation on 5th September.

15 March: Troops enter the RIT campus and the government issues a communiqué, blaming the students for the unrest. Scores of RIT students are arrested.

16 March: Students from Rangoon University (Main Campus) /RU (Main)/ march down Prome Road towards the Hlaing Campus and RIT. They are blocked by the *Lon Htein* as well as regular army units near Inya Lake. Many students are killed. Troops enter Rangoon University (Main Campus).

17 March: Thousands of people rally outside Kyandaw crematorium for Maung Phone Maw's funeral — just to find out that his body has already been cremated secretly elsewhere. The government announces that it is setting up an Enquiry Commission to look into the cause of his death — but it does not mention the other casualties. The Rangoon University Students' Union is formed at a meeting on the main campus. Approx. 1,000 students are arrested and sent to Insein Jail north of the capital.

18 March: Thousands of students march down to Sule Pagoda in central Rangoon — and are joined or cheered by thousands of others. Army units — the 22nd, 66th and 77th Light Infantry Divisions — are called in. Thousands of protesters are arrested. Scores of people are killed by the *Lon Htein* as well as by the army. The day becomes known as 'Bloody Friday' and Sein Lwin — the commander of the *Lon Htein*— as the Butcher of Rangoon'. Schools and universities are closed down.

27 March: "While constructive tasks are being carried out under BSPP leadership, destructive elements, both above ground and underground, are resorting to all sorts of disruptive acts to hamper the progress of the people," Chief of Staff Gen. Saw Maung says in his speech to the armed forces day parade in Rangoon.

11 April: Ne Win and his entourage leaves for West Germany and Switzerland.

9 May: The government-appointed Enquiry Commission states that three students were killed during the March riots, 625 arrested and 141 are still in custody. Aung Gyi writes a 40-page open letter to Ne Win, reiterating the need for economic reforms.

10 May: Amnesty International publishes a 71-page report saying that the Burmese Army is responsible for summary executions, torture and rape in the frontier areas, and for forcing villagers to act as porters and walk ahead of troops as human mine-detectors during campaigns against ethnic insurgents.

26 May: Ne Win returns to Rangoon from his trip to Europe.

30 May: Schools and universities re-open with an attendance rate of about 30%.

Anti-government leaflets begin appearing on all campuses. The students who have been released from Insein Jail return with tales of torture, beating and electric shock treatment of students. There are also reports of girl students having been raped by *Lon Htein*-men while in custody.

8 June: Aung Gyi writes one more open letter to Ne Win, highlighting the economic and political crisis — and human rights abuses in March.

13 June: A memorial service was planned for those killed in March — but it does not materialise. Some students set a deadline: if not a thorough and accurate report on the March events has not been released before 17th June, "there will be trouble".

15 June: Demonstrations and meetings begin again, mainly at RU (Main).

16 June: More demonstrations on campuses all over Rangoon. Maung Maung Kyaw, Moe Thi Zon and others give speeches.

17 June: The demonstrations on the campus continue. RU (Main) suspends classes. The demonstrations and the meetings move to the Institute of Medicine (1) on Prome Road.

20 June: 5-6,000 students and others stage a peaceful protest in Rangoon. Buddhist monks are seen attending rallies at the RU (Main). Demands: reinstate the dismissed students and punish the guilty for the March killings. The government's economic policies are also criticised. Posters attacking Ne Win appear, mentioning his Swiss bank accounts. Workers at a textile factory near RU (Hlaing Campus) stage a strike in sympathy with the students. The university area is sealed off by police and army units at 6 pm.

21 June: Thousands of students march from the Institute of Medicine (1)'s Prome Road Campus down towards central Rangoon, shouting slogans. The column is stopped at Hanthawaddy intersection where *Lon Htein* units fire teargas and rifles. The crowds fight back with *jinglees* — and the *Lon Htein* flee. Clashes between the police and civilians continue all day. 80 civilians and 20 *Lon Htein* are killed. The authorities declare a 60-day ban on public gatherings, from 21st June to 19th August, and a 6 pm to 6 am curfew is imposed on Rangoon. The Institute of Medicine (1) and the Institute of Dental Medicine in Rangoon also suspend all classes.

22 June: The Institute of Medicine (2) suspends all classes. Many students move to the historic Shwe Dagon Pagoda.

23 June: Students, defying the ban on public gatherings, set up a strike centre at the historic Shwe Dagon Pagoda. The unrest spreads to Pegu, 50 kms north of Rangoon, where at least 70 people are killed. Unrest is also reported from Moulmein and Prome. The Institute of Medicine in Mandalay suspends all classes.

1 July: The curfew is shortened to 8 pm to 4 am. Several curfew violators are shot by police and army units.

3 July: The government warns traders "not to manipulate prices". Because of the curfew — and rumours of another demonetisation — prices skyrocket.

7 July: The BSPP announces that an extraordinary party congress will convene on 23rd July and the state-run radio says that all the students who were arrested in March now are going to be released.

9 July: The authorities lift the curfew in Rangoon, along with similar restrictions in

Pegu, Prome and Moulmein. It is also announced that students who have been dismissed from their universities now can apply for re-admission.

12 July: Emergency measures introduced in Taunggyi, Shan State, following communal clashes between Buddhists and Muslims—which the students claim were instigated by the authorities to divert attention from the main issues.

16 July: Similar communal clashes are reported from Prome where a ban on public gatherings also is imposed on the following day.

18 July: Min Gaung, minister for home and religious affairs, is "permitted to resign" in order to accept responsibility for the admitted deaths of 41 arrested demonstrators who suffocated in a prison van outside Insein Jail in March. This is the first time the authorities admit that more than two people had died in March.

19-20 July: Riots are reported from Ne Win's hometown Paungdale east of Prome.

21 July: The director general of the People's Police Force (PPF) in Rangoon, Thein Aung, is "permitted to retire" and the PPF commander, Pe Kyi, is demoted and transferred.

22 July: A state of emergency is declared in Prome township and the local administration is transferred to the army.

23 July: The BSPP's emergency congress begins. Ne Win makes a speech and says he is going to retire along with BSPP vice chairman San Yu, secretary general Aye Ko, joint secretary general Sein Lwin and central executive committee members Kyaw Htin and Tun Tin. He also proposes economic reforms and the holding of a referendum on the issue of a one-party or multi-party system.

24 July: A number of delegates urge Ne Win to stay on and oppose the idea of a referendum "since this would be detrimental to the economic reform programme".

25 July: Aye Ko proposes sweeping economic reforms and notes that the congress is opposed to the idea of a referendum. The congress concludes; it had "permitted" Ne Win to resign from his post as BSPP chairman decisions obtained on not holding a referendum.

26 July: The BSPP's central committee holds a meeting and elects Sein Lwin as new party chairman after Ne Win. San Yu is also "permitted to resign" but Kyaw Htin, Aye Ko and Tun Tin are re-elected. Prime Minister Maung Maung Kha is removed along with Myint Maung, the chairman of the Council of People's Attorneys (the Attorney General).

27 July: The *Pyithu Hluttaw* convenes. Sein Lwin is elected chairman of the Council of State (president). Kyaw Htin elected secretary to the Council of State, Tun Tin becomes prime minister and Dr Maung Maung chairman of the Council of People's Attorneys.

28 July: A curfew is imposed in Myayde (Allanmyo) 354 kms north of Rangoon following rioting there. It is the Full Moon Day of Waso (the beginning of the Buddhist Lent); students and anti-government protesters gather at the Shwe Dagon Pagoda.

29 July: Students demonstrate outside the Shwe Dagon. Dissident Aung Gyi, *Associated Press* correspondent Sein Win and nine other retired army officers are arrested late that night.

1 August: Leaflets are circulated by the All-Burma Students' Democratic League, calling for a nation-wide general strike on 8th August.

OUTRAGE

2 August: Sein Lwin and other state and party leaders meet to discuss plans for reviving the collapsed economy. Students hold meetings and give speeches outside the Shwe Dagon.

3 August: Martial law is declared in Rangoon at 6 pm. 10,000 demonstrators defy the ban and march through the centre of the city.

5 August: Hundreds of people are arrested for defying martial law — but the demonstrations continue.

6 August: An agreement is signed between the official export-import corporation of Yunnan, China and the Burmese trade ministry to open official cross-border trade between the two countries. Demonstrations continue upcountry; curfews are imposed on Yenangyaung, Thanatpin and Pegu.

8 August: There is a general strike and also massive street demonstrations in Rangoon. Tens of thousands of demonstrators demand democracy, human rights, the resignation of the BSPP government and an end to the socialist economic system. Simultaneously, similar demonstrations are held in all major cities and towns in the country. The army remains in the background until 11.45 pm when heavily armed troops spray automatic riflefire into crowds of unarmed demonstrators outside the City Hall in central Rangoon.

9 August: Mass demonstrations spread to over 40 places all over the country. Army units from the 22nd Light Infantry Division fire on demonstrators in Rangoon. The government say five had been killed — independent sources claim the number of dead is in the hundreds. Thousands of people are arrested. But the demonstrations continue. All schools are closed down. Hundreds of people are killed when police and army units fire on demonstrators in Sagaing.

10 August: Scores of people are killed by troops in the capital as armoured cars equipped with Bren machine-guns fire on demonstrators. The demonstrators fight back with Molotov cocktails, *jinglees*, swords and spears. Troops fire on staff at Rangoon General Hospital. The first policemen — in North Okkalapa — are beheaded by enraged civilians.

11 August: Rangoon remained paralysed by the general strike. Barricades block troops movements. Western diplomats estimate that at least 1,000 demonstrators have been killed in Rangoon alone. Troops and policemen open fire on demonstrators in the northern town of Sagaing, killing at least 100 people. The US senate unanimously approves a resolution condemning the BSPP regime as well as the killings in Burma.

12 August: Sein Lwin resigns after 18 days in power. People dance in the streets of Rangoon. Rangoon General Hospital is full of wounded demonstrators. Despite the joy, an uneasy calm prevails.

15 August: The Rangoon Bar Council issues a statement saying that "the shooting and killing by bayonets of young children, students and the people by the security forces in Rangoon, Sagaing and other towns...since 9.8.88 is acting totally against the Burmese Constitution and international human rights law". Aung San Suu Kyi submits a proposal for a People's Consultative Committee to act as an intermediary between the students and the government. Her statement is endorsed by U Nu, Win Maung and other pre-1962 state leaders.

16 August: The Burma Medical Association protests against the massacre in Rangoon. The authorities say the statement is not authentic. The government announces that tourist hotels are going to be built in Rangoon, Mandalay and Pagan in cooperation with companies from Australia, Japan and Singapore.

17 August: About 3,000 people gather outside Rangoon General Hospital. Armoured cars and troops close in on the demonstrators. Renewed demonstrations are also reported from Mandalay. Doctors and nurses at Rangoon General Hospital reiterate their protests against the killings.

19 August: Dr Maung Maung is appointed new president and BSPP chairman. The Pyithu Hluttaw sets up a commission, headed by the chairman of the Council of People's Justices Tin Aung Hein, to ascertain "the desires and aspirations of the people".

20 August: Flag-waving demonstrators demand the resignation of Dr Maung Maung and the formation of an interim government to prepare for general elections.

22 August: Tens of thousands of people take to the streets in Rangoon. A general strike is proclaimed to force the government to resign. Daily demonstrations are also reported from Mandalay, Henzada, Monywa, Ye-U, Magwe and other towns upcountry.

23 August: An estimated 600,000 people join the demonstrations. A crisis meeting is reportedly held at Ne Win's Ady Road residence and a new strategy for quelling the unrest is drawn up.

24 August: Martial law is lifted. Troops withdraw from Rangoon. Dr Maung Maung promises a referendum on the issue of a one-party or a multi-party system.

25 August: Aung Gyi, Sein Win and others who were arrested on 29th July are released. Aung Gyi gives a speech to a 30,000 strong crowd in Sanchaung, Rangoon. Demonstrations and mass meetings are held daily all over the country. At night, armed soldiers remove Kyats 600 million from the Myanma Foreign Trade Bank in Rangoon. All troops stationed in the capital are given six months' pay in advance. The bank's newly formed trade union protest against the action.

26 August: The general strike cripples Rangoon. All air and rail transport is halted. Aung San Suu Kyi addresses a crowd of several hundred thousand people outside Shwe Dagon pagoda.

26-28 August: A prison riot breaks out in Insein Jail. Almost simultaneously, there are similar prison riots in nine widely dispersed towns throughout the country. Nearly 9,000 inmates escape or are released.

27 August: Tin U, a former Chief of Staff and minister of defence, delivers a speech in front of Rangoon General Hospital.

28 August: The All-Burma Federation of Students' Unions (ABFSU; or *ba ka tha*) is formed in Rangoon. Min Ko Naing is elected acting chairman. U Nu sets up the League for Democracy and Peace (Provisional). Tin U becomes its general secretary.

29 August: Lawyers, writers, film actors and singers join the demonstrations.

30 August: Mass demonstrations of civil servants and others. Thousands of BSPP members quit the party.

31 August: The government permits street demonstrations and meetings. West Germany halts its DM 65 million/year aid programme to show its disapproval of the killings in Rangoon.

2 September: Burmese lawyers call for the abrogation of the 1974 constitution and

197

say the 1962 coup violated the 1947 constitution. The mass demonstrations continue. About 50 cities and towns plus many villages throughout the country are in the hands of protesters. Buddhist monks set up courts and run day-to-day affairs in major towns.

3-4 September: US Congressman Stephen J. Solarz visits Rangoon.

5 September: An ultimatum is given to the government: concede to opposition demands or face an indefinite strike. Many groups of workers and government employees form independent trade unions.

6 September: Nine out of eleven survivors of the Thirty Comrades call on the army to back the uprising. Demonstrators outside the Czech embassy in Rangoon protest against a "message of felicitation" to Dr. Maung Maung's government.

7 September: The government ignores an ultimatum issued by the protesters to resign or face an indefinite strike aimed at toppling the regime.

9 September: U Nu proclaims a parallel government with himself as prime minister and Tin U as minister of defence. About 200 air force men join the mammoth demonstrations in Rangoon in which hundreds of thousands of people participate.

10 September: The BSPP convenes a second emergency congress and proposes to hold general elections under a multi-party system, cancelling the suggested referendum. Three ex-military commanders, Tin U, Aung Shwe and Saw Myint, resign from U Nu's League for Democracy and Peace (Provisional).

11 September: The *Pyithu Hluttaw*'s emergency session decides to hold general elections. Policemen join the demonstrations in Rangoon. Daily mammoth demonstrations with hundreds of thousands of people — including hunger strikers — press demands for democracy and the formation of an interim government to oversee the elections; they reject the government's proposal.

12 September: Aung San Suu Kyi, Tin U and Aung Gyi issue a joint statement supporting the formation of an interim government.

13 September: Japan announces that it will freeze its aid to Burma until the situation calms down. The demonstrations continue.

16 September: The government announces that all 180,000 men of the armed forces are no longer members of the BSPP. A confrontation between demonstrators and police takes place outside the defence ministry. Aung Gyi and others intervene and defuse the situation; the soldiers pull back.

17 September: 24 soldiers surrender to demonstrators after opening fire from the trade ministry. Demonstrations become more militant as the government refuses to resign and install an interim government. Some students begin to leave for the Thai border areas to get arms and military training from the ethnic insurgents there.

18 September: The demonstrations continue. At 4 pm, Gen. Saw Maung announces over the state radio that the military has assumed power and set up a 'State Law and Order Restoration Council' (SLORC). People build barricades at night, cut electric wires, destroy street lights and defy a curfew order. Troops open fire on demonstrators. Gatherings of more than four people are banned.

19 September: Street battles between army units and protesters continue. Hundreds of people are gunned down by the security forces. Urban guerrillas fire rockets at a microwave antenna in central Rangoon. The SLORC dissolves the *Pyithu*

Hluttaw, the Council of State and other former organs of power.

20 September: Saw Maung's SLORC sets up its own government. Saw Maung becomes prime minister, foreign minister and defence minister.

23 September: The US cuts all its aid to Burma to protest the massacres. Some students begin military training in camps controlled by the insurgent Karen National Union near the Thai border.

24 September: Aung Gyi, Tin U and Aung San Suu Kyi form the National League for Democracy (NLD). Mass arrests and summary executions of pro-democracy activists continue throughout the country. Thai International resumes its flights to Rangoon. The rebel Communist Party of Burma captures the town of Möng Yang near the Chinese border and holds it for a few days. Heavy fighting rages in the area for several weeks.

26 September: The BSPP becomes the National Unity Party (NUP). The European Community calls on the Burmese government to stop killings and restore democracy.

27 September: The NLD registers as a political party.

28 September: The British foreign secretary, Sir Geoffrey Howe, gives a strongly worded speech in the UN, expressing his concern at the indiscriminate killings in Burma.

1 October: UNICEF and ICRC begin flying in medical supplies to Burma. About 10,000 students and other pro-democracy activists have fled to the areas bordering Thailand, China, India and Bangladesh.

3 October: The general strike collapses. The government's threats force people to return to work or face dismissal or other punishments are heeded.

6 October: Munitions for the Burmese Army arrive by ship from Singapore. The military begins press-ganging civilians in Rangoon to serve as porters with the army fighting ethnic insurgents. 27 reception centres are set up in the border areas where the students who fled after the coup can give themselves up. If they do not return before 18th November, they will be treated as insurgents, the military says.

7 October: Japan announces that it will provide emergency aid to Burma through UNICEF. Maung Maung Gyi, Burma's representative to the UN, promises free and fair elections. Arrests and summary executions of pro-democracy activists continue. Hundreds of civil servants who took part in the August-September demonstrations are dismissed by the military.

12 October: Rebels from the Karen National Union recapture their old Mae Tha Waw stronghold near the Thai border which was overrun by the Burmese Army in January 1984.

17 October: Banks in Rangoon re-open after having been closed since August.

26 October: Students rally outside Shwe Dagon pagoda and shout anti-government slogans. They disperse when troops arrive at the scene.

30 October: The state-run radio says the security forces have recovered arms and ammunition hidden in Thayettaw monastery in central Rangoon.

30 October-10 November: Aung San Suu Kyi tours more than 50 towns and villages in Pegu, Magwe, Mandalay and Sagaing Divisions, and Shan State, and attracts crowds of tens of thousands.

31 October: Col. Abel, of the military government, announces that Burma has ended the state's 26-year monopoly on foreign trade. He also welcomes foreign investment.

1 November: Purges begin within Burma's foreign service. Diplomats are recalled from abroad.

2 November: 43 registered political parties protest against arrests and harassments of students who have returned to the cities from the border areas.

4 November: Britain freezes its aid to Burma.

5 November: Dissident students form the All-Burma Students' Democratic Front (ABSDF) during a meeting at the Karen rebel camp of Wangkha near the Thai border.

8 November: Three diplomats at the Burmese embassy in Canberra apply for political asylum in Australia. Purges, arrests and summary executions continue.

9 November: An attempt by monks to stage a demonstration in Rangoon is thwarted.

12 November: The Thai government cancels a planned trip to Burma by deputy foreign minister Prapas Limpabandhu because of criticism from Thai students and human rights organisations.

15 November: US congressman-elect Dana Rohrabacher visits the Thay Baw Bo student camp near the Thai border and promises moral and political support.

16 November: The government extends until the end of the year the deadline for students who have fled to the border areas.

19 November: The ten ethnic resistance armies of the National Democratic Front plus twelve underground student groups and Burmese opposition parties form the Democratic Alliance of Burma (DAB) at a meeting at Klerday near the Thai border. Karen rebel leader Bo Mya is elected chairman and Kachin rebel leader Brang Seng its vice chairman.

22 November: The Thai government grants temporary asylum to Burmese students who fled after Saw Maung's takeover.

24 November: Malaysia becomes the first country to have its envoy present credentials to Saw Maung's government.

30 November: The military government promulgates a new foreign investment law designed to attract foreign funds.

3 December: Aung Gyi quits the NLD because it refuses to expel eight alleged communists from the organisation.

10 December: Tin U is elected new NLD president to replace Aung Gyi.

14 December: Thai army commander Gen. Chaovalit Yongchaiyuth visits Burma and returns with generous logging and fishing deals in return for assisting in the repatriation of Burmese dissident students now staying in the Thai-Burmese border areas.

16 December: Aung Gyi sets up the Union Nationals Democracy Party (UNDP).

18 December: Aung San Suu Kyi returns from a trip to southeastern Burma where she also attracted large crowds.

19 December: An editorial in the *Working People's Daily* tells political parties "to abide by the regulations, disciplinary rules, orders, laws and declarations" and says "it is not the time to incite the people". Aung San Suu Kyi replies that "we have to question whether free and fair elections are possible and we are protesting about this".

21 December: As a part of the deal reached between Gen. Chaovalit Yongchaiyuth and Gen. Saw Maung in Rangoon on 14 Dec., a reception centre is set up near Tak airport in Thailand for the repatriation of Burmese dissident students staying in the border areas. The Burmese army recaptures Mae Tha Waw from Karen rebels.

26 December: The first batch of 80 Burmese students are flown back to Rangoon from Tak, Thailand.

27 December: Khin Kyi — Aung San's widow and Aung San Suu Kyi's mother — dies in Rangoon at the age of 76. The Thai government allows Burmese aircraft in Thai airspace to take aerial pictures of border areas until 31 March 1989.

1989

2 January: Hundreds of thousands of people attend Khin Kyi's funeral in the first street march in Rangoon since the coup. The funeral is also attended by several Western diplomats.

4 January: The ambassadors of the US, Britain, India, Italy, France, West Germany and Japan boycott the independence day celebrations in Rangoon, organised by the military authorities.

5 January: US State Department spokesperson Phyllis Oakley accuses the Burmese military of arresting and killing students who have returned from the Thai border areas.

7 January: A group of 26 Burmese students, who had staged a hunger strike at the repatriation centre at Tak to protest their deportation, is flown back to Rangoon.

10 January: Amnesty International alleges that the Thai military is forcing Burmese students to return to Rangoon from Tak. The Thai government declares that the Burmese students along the border have to return before 31st March, or face charges of illegal entry.

13 January: Japan formally suspends all aid to Burma and also the last two outstanding grants totalling 927 million yen (US$ 7.3 million).

18-20 January: 46 Bangkok-based Thai and foreign correspondents are invited to visit Rangoon, Loikaw, Taunggyi, Meiktila and Pagan to meet students who have returned from the Thai border.

19 January: Burmese government troops capture Klerday, the DAB and ABSDF headquarters near the Thai border.

27 January: Aung San Suu Kyi returns from a tour of Irrawaddy Division. Army units are accused of having harassed her, arresting 34 NLD workers and intimidating the people who had come out to welcome her in Bassein, Henzada, Maubin, Labutta and other places in the Irrawaddy delta region.

28 January: Bo Yan Naing, one of the Thirty Comrades, dies in Rangoon at the age of 71.

5 February: Posters begin to appear in several townships in Rangoon urging people to boycott Thai merchandise to protest the logging and fishing deals between Gen. Chaovalit and Gen. Saw Maung as well as the forced repatriation of Burmese students from Tak in Thailand.

7 February: A US State Department report on human rights in Asia accuses the Burmese regime of resorting to indiscriminate killings, arbitrary arrests and torture of political prisoners. Karen rebels along the Thai border declare that they will obstruct any logging operations between Thailand and Burma that do not benefit them economically.

9 February: Visiting Australian senator Christopher Schacht meets Gen. Saw Maung and urges him to set a timetable for the general elections.

12 February: Union Day — but for the first time in independent Burma's history there are no parades in Rangoon and no public meetings.

16 February: The BBS announces that elections will be held in the spring of 1990.

17 February: Japan recognises Gen. Saw Maung's government and says it will partially resume economic assistance.

22 February: Aung San Suu Kyi criticises continuing human rights violations and the resumption of Japanese aid.

28 February: A foreign correspondents club is set up in Rangoon comprising Burmese nationals who work for foreign media organisations plus the correspondents for *Tass* and *Xinhua*. Press officers of the foreign embassies in Rangoon are admitted as non-voting associate members.

2 March: The 27th anniversary of the 1962 military takeover. The SLORC makes public the full text of the new election law.

13 March: Students in Rangoon commemorate the first anniversary of the death of Maung Phone Maw. Opposition politicians declare 13th March Human Rights Day in Burma .

14 March: Wa, Shan, and Kokang Chinese troops of the insurgent CPB break with the main party and discard Marxism-Leninism.

16 March: Army troops prevent students at gunpoint from floating wreaths on the Inya Lake to commemorate the 'White Bridge' massacre a year before. About 1,000 students demonstrate against the military government.

24 March: The official media announces that Min Ko Naing, the country's most prominent underground student leader, has been arrested for leading "about 40 students in an anti-government demonstration" in Rangoon.

26 March: The Burmese Army captures the Karen rebel stronghold of Maw Pokay near the Thai border after fierce fighting.

27 March: Armed Forces Day. Ne Win attends a dinner party in Rangoon making his first public appearance since relinquishing the chairmanship of the BSPP in July 1988. Sporadic gunfire is heard in Rangoon as groups of students demonstrate against the military. Several thousand people demonstrate in Mandalay and shout anti-government slogans.

1 April: the Thai Authorities close down the Tak reception centre for Burmese students.

5 April: Capt. Myint Oo threatens to kill Aung San Suu Kyi in Danubyu during an NLD campaign trip in the Irrawaddy delta region.

11-13 April: Thai deputy foreign minister Prapas Limpabandhu pays a 4-day visit to Rangoon. Gen. Saw Maung offers "priority trade reward" to Thailand.

13 April: The US announces that Burma will lose its present GSP status, which enabled Burmese goods to the enter the US market duty-free.

13-16 April: The Buddhist New Year, *thingyan*, is celebrated in Rangoon with an anti-government slogan competition at the NLD's headquarters on University Avenue. Heavily armed troops cruise the streets of Rangoon.

17 April: Rebellious Wa troops capture the CPB's Panghsang headquarters near the

Chinese border, ending the 41-year-long communist insurgency in Burma. The CPB's ageing leadership flees to Meng Lien in China.

18 April: Aung San Suu Kyi criticises Japan and Australia for maintaining cordial links with the military government.

23 April: Arrests begin of students who participated in the NLD New Year slogan competition. Student leader, Moe Thi Zon, the chairman of the Democratic Party for a New Society, leaves Rangoon for the Thai border.

4 May: Thakin Soe, the veteran Red Flag communist leader, dies in Rangoon at the age of 84.

20 May: 400 Burmese troops cross into Thailand in an attempt to attack the Karen rebel base at Wangkha from the rear and burn town Ban Wang Kaew on the Thai side.

27 May: The SLORC announces that it has changed the formal name of the country from Burma to Myanmar. It also rejects Thai-proposed peace talks with the country's ethnic rebels.

31 May: The SLORC promulgates a new election law for the *Pyithu Hluttaw*, or parliament.

18 June: The SLORC introduces new repressive laws for printing and publishing.

19 June: The primary schools re-open after having been closed since 9th August 1988.

21 June: Thousands of people commemorate the first anniversary of the massacre in Myenigone market. Troops open fire and kill one person. Aung San Suu Kyi is briefly detained.

23 June: *The Working People's Daily* publishes fierce attacks on the NLD and Aung San Suu Kyi who responds by beginning to criticise Ne Win openly at mass meetings in Rangoon.

4 July: Mahn Win Maung, a former president and close associate of U Nu, dies in Rangoon.

7 July: A bomb explodes at the Syriam oil refinery near Rangoon.

10 July: A bomb explodes at Rangoon City Hall.

18 July: The confrontation between the NLD and the SLORC reaches its climax as the former announces its own plans for commemorating Martyrs' Day, the 42nd anniversary of the assassination of Aung San — and the latter responds by sending several battalions of heavily armed troops into Rangoon. *Reuter* correspondent David Storey is expelled from Burma.

19 July: Martyrs' Day. Thousands of soldiers patrol the streets of Rangoon to prevent the NLD's march from taking place. The NLD cancels its plans to hold a separate ceremony.

20 July: The SLORC places Aung San Suu Kyi and Tin U under house arrest for one year. Scores of NLD workers are arrested nation-wide.

23 July: The SLORC announces the formation of three-man military tribunals to "try those who have committed offences". Sentences range from three years' jail with hard labour to death. Arrests of oppositionists continue. At the same time, thousands of criminal prisoners are released.

27 July: Three young NLD organisers are sentenced to death by a military tribunal in Rangoon, charged with having planted the bomb at Syriam oil refinery on 7 July.

OUTRAGE

30 July: 5,000 monks in Mandalay demonstrate against the government.

5 August: Brig-Gen Khin Nyunt holds a six-hour press conference in Rangoon and accuses the NLD of being manipulated by the CPB. He also claims he has unearthed a CPB conspiracy to seize power.

10 August: The *Working People's Daily* says that 17,877 prisoners held on criminal charges have been released.

14 August: The middle schools re-open. Widespread arrests of political activists are reported.

15 August: A spokesman for the insurgent Karen National Union (KNU) says that a Karen rebel carried out the bombing at the Syriam oil refinery on 7th July and not the three people who were sentenced to death.

18 August: Singapore-based SKS Marketing Ltd forms a joint venture with the Burmese government. The Rangoon commander, Brig-Gen Myo Nyunt, accuses merchants of "destabilising the government". Prices of all daily commodities skyrocket in Rangoon.

21 August: Teachers' training institutes re-open.

26 August: The US Embassy in Rangoon says it has credible reports that the government is beating and torturing political prisoners.

29 August: A military tribunal in Shwebo sentences eleven people to death for alleged involvement in an attack on a police station in Taze, Mandalay Division, in September 1988. "So few students were killed during last year's uprising in Burma that it is not even worth mentioning," the Health and Education Minister, Dr Pe Thein, says.

30 August: Munitions arrive in Rangoon by ship from Israel and Belgium via Singapore.

31 August: The SLORC appoints its attorney general new head of the hitherto outspoken Bar Council.

8 September: The 12 European Community governments call on Burma to end political repression and hold free elections.

9 September: Brig-Gen Khin Nyunt gives a seven-hour long speech, claiming he has discovered a rightist conspiracy to seize power, allegedly involving some foreign embassies in Rangoon.

18 September: The first anniversary of the assumption of power by the SLORC passes quietly in Rangoon, amid tight security. Only some middle school children wear red arm bands in defiance of the regime.

23 September: The *Working People's Daily* claims that the Coca-Cola Company has signed an agreement with the government for production, distribution and sale of soft drinks in Burma.

25 September: The high schools re-open. A military tribunal sentences five people to death for beheading three suspected DDSI agents on 8th September 1988.

3 October: Win Tin, a member of the NLD's central executive committee, is sentenced to three years imprisonment with hard labour. Yukong Ltd., a South Korean oil company, becomes the first foreign firm to be allowed to explore for oil onshore in Burma.

5 October: Maung Thaw Ka, a member of the NLD's central committee, is sentenced to 20 years hard labour. Nay Min, a Rangoon lawyer, is sentenced to 14 years hard labour for "sending false news to the BBC."

6 October: A Burmese airliner en route from Mergui to Rangoon is hijacked to Thailand.

7 October: MIS Tin U is released from Insein Jail along with Bo Ni, another former intelligence chief.

18-29 October: A 24-man senior Burmese military delegation, led by Lieut-Gen. Than Shwe, visits China.

27 October: Shell Exploration BV of the Netherlands signs an agreement to explore for oil in Burma

30 October: Idemitsu of Japan signs an agreement to explore for oil in Burma.

6 November: Petro-Canada signs an agreement to explore for oil in Burma.

10 November: Amoco of the USA signs an agreement to explore for oil in Burma.

13 November: Unocal Corp. of the USA signs an agreement to explore for oil in Burma.

15 November: Amnesty International publishes a report, estimating that 6,000 people have been arrested for political reasons since September 1988, 3,000 of them since July 1989. Other estimates put the total higher. Amnesty International also says that 100 people have been sentenced to death by the newly established military tribunals.

16 November-6 December: Secret peace talks are held in Rangoon between the SLORC and insurgent leaders who in March-April led a mutiny against the political leadership of the now defunct CPB.

17 November: Croft Exploration of the UK signs an agreement to explore for oil in Burma.

21 November: Ye Htoon, the supposed leader of the 'Rightist plot', is sentenced to 18 years for his alleged political crimes and for having an 'illegal bank account' in Hawaii.

24 November: BHP (Broken Hill Proprietary) of Australia signs an agreement to explore for oil in Burma.

11 December: About 100 political parties have announced that they are going to participate in the May 1990 elections. Demonstrations continue in Mandalay.

22 December: The NLD chairman, Tin U, is sentenced to three years imprisonment with hard labour by a military tribunal in Rangoon.

29 December: The SLORC places U Nu under house arrest along with 12 of his associates. Government forces, using Thai territory as a springboard, capture the Karen rebel base at Phalu on the Thai border.

1990

3 January: Deadline for names of candidates for elections to be submitted to the Elections Commission. Over 2,000 candidates from 100 parties for 492 constituencies.

8 January: Aung San Suu Kyi's candidature is challenged by a NUP rival on the grounds of her connections with Britain and her alleged links with insurgent groups. The European Community delivers another strong protest to the Burmese authorities. It calls for all candidates, including Aung San Suu Kyi and Tin U, to be allowed to stand in the elections.

16 January: Rangoon's Elections Commission bars Aung San Suu Kyi from contesting the elections. Troops move into Rangoon as hundreds of people protest the decision.

24 January: The Karen rebel base of Thay Baw Bo, which also housed several hundred dissident Burmese students, falls to government forces.

25 January: Kirkland Resources of the UK signs an agreement to explore for oil in Burma.

31 January: Walay, another Karen rebel base on the Thai border, is captured by government forces. 6,000 villagers and dissident students have fled to Thailand since the fighting began at Palu in December.

January-February: Thousands of people in Rangoon and other towns and cities all over Burma are forcibly evicted from their homes and resettled in shantytowns outside the actual urban areas. Arrests of political activists continue all over the country. Several candidates for the elections from the NLD and the Democratic Party for a New Society (DPNS) are among those arrested. Scattered demonstrations are held in Rangoon and Mandalay.

5-11 February: Heavy fighting rages at Three Pagodas Pass on the Thai-Burmese border. Burmese troops cross into Thailand and capture the headquarters of the Mon insurgents on the 11th. 6-10,000 Karen and Mon villagers plus 700 dissident students flee to Thailand.

13 February: The United Nations' Commission on Human Rights decides at its 46th Session in Geneva to appoint a 'special rapporteur' to investigate human-rights abuses in Burma. It also calls on the SLORC to allow "all political parties and personalities...to participate in the electoral process and the elections."

13th March: Thai army chief Gen. Chaovalit Yongchaiyuth pays a 'Goodwill Visit' to Burma. His second since the September 1988 takeover. The second anniversary of the death of Maung Phone Maw and the 1988 'teashop incident'. The students of Burma vow to continue the struggle for democracy.

INDEX